Gender, Dating and Violence in Urban China is a tour de force. With a passionate feminist eye, Xiying Wang lays out the everyday, seemingly "trivial" forms of violence that infuse heterosexual dating relationships in urban China today. Her complex analysis demonstrates how everything from the ongoing rapid socio-economic transformations in China, changing gender and sexual norms and ideals, the often inseparability of love and violence, and gender inequality in China fuel dating violence. A well written, well researched study that will inspire a public conversation.

Lisa Rofel, *Professor, Department of Anthropology, Co-Director, Center for Emerging Worlds, University of California, Santa Cruz, US*

In this courageous and important book, scholar-activist Xiying Wang, a pioneer in the study of dating violence in China, takes us inside the intimate relationships of young Chinese to see the dark underside of the nation's celebrated "romantic revolution." Through first-hand portraits of "sassy girls," "tender boys," and other surprising subjects, she challenges the myths surrounding Chinese sexuality, offering a theory of Chinese intersectionality to explain how individuals navigate their sexual worlds. In charting the human costs of China's unfinished gender and sexual revolutions, Wang delivers what is at once a compelling academic study and a feminist call to action.

Susan Greenhalgh, *Professor, Department of Anthropology, Harvard University, US*

Gender, Dating and Violence in Urban China

This book explores young people's experiences of, and views on, dating, gender, sexuality and violence within dating relationships. Based on interviews and focus groups conducted in Beijing over a long period, and focusing especially on dating violence, the book reveals insights on a wide range of issues of gender and sexuality in contemporary China. It shows how young Chinese people's attitudes and behaviors are changing as urban China develops rapidly, and how their experience of dating violence and meaning-making process are affected by age, gender, location and class.

Xiying Wang is an Associate Professor in the School of Social Development and Public Policy at Beijing Normal University, China.

Routledge Culture, Society, Business in East Asia Series

Editorial Board:
Heung Wah Wong (Executive Editor), The University of Hong Kong, Hong Kong, China
Chris Hutton, The University of Hong Kong, Hong Kong, China
Wayne Cristaudo, The University of Hong Kong, Hong Kong, China
Harumi Befu (Emeritus Professor), Stanford University, USA
Shao-dang Yan, Peking University, China
Andrew Stewart MacNaughton, Reitaku University, Japan
William Kelly, Independent Researcher
Keiji Maegawa, Tsukuba University, Japan
Kiyomitsu Yui, Kobe University, Japan

How and what are we to examine if we wish to understand the commonalities across East Asia without falling into the powerful fictions or homogeneities that dress its many constituencies? By the same measure, can East Asian homogeneities make sense in any way outside the biases of East-West personation?

For anthropologists familiar with the societies of East Asia, there is a rich diversity of work that can potentially be applied to address these questions within a comparative tradition grounded in the region as opposed the singularizing outward encounter. This requires us to broaden our scope of investigation to include all aspects of intra-regional life, trade, ideology, culture, and governance, while at the same time dedicating ourselves to a complete and holistic understanding of the exchange of identities that describe each community under investigation. An original and wide ranging analysis will be the result, one that draws on the methods and theory of anthropology as it deepens our understanding of the interconnections, dependencies, and discordances within and among East Asia.

The book series includes three broad strands within and between which to critically examine the various insides and outsides of the region. The first is about the globalization of Japanese popular culture in East Asia, especially in greater China. The second strand presents comparative studies of major social institutions in Japan and China, such as family, community and other major concepts in Japanese and Chinese societies. The final strand puts forward cross-cultural studies of business in East Asia.

Gender, Dating and Violence in Urban China

Xiying Wang

LONDON AND NEW YORK

First published 2017
by Routledge
2 Park Square, Milton Park, Abingdon, Oxon OX14 4RN

and by Routledge
711 Third Avenue, New York, NY 10017

Routledge is an imprint of the Taylor & Francis Group, an informa business

© 2017 Xiying Wang

The right of Xiying Wang to be identified as author of this work has been asserted by her in accordance with sections 77 and 78 of the Copyright, Designs and Patents Act 1988.

All rights reserved. No part of this book may be reprinted or reproduced or utilised in any form or by any electronic, mechanical, or other means, now known or hereafter invented, including photocopying and recording, or in any information storage or retrieval system, without permission in writing from the publishers.

Trademark notice: Product or corporate names may be trademarks or registered trademarks, and are used only for identification and explanation without intent to infringe.

British Library Cataloguing in Publication Data
A catalogue record for this book is available from the British Library

Library of Congress Cataloging in Publication Data
Names: Wang, Xiying, author.
Title: Gender, dating and violence in urban China / Xiying Wang.
Description: 1 Edition. | New York : Routledge, [2017] | Series: Routledge culture, society, business in East Asia series ; 5 | Includes bibliographical references and index.
Identifiers: LCCN 2016058077| ISBN 9780415810333 (hardback) | ISBN 9781315170350 (ebook)
Subjects: LCSH: Dating violence–China.
Classification: LCC HQ801.83 .W36 2017 | DDC 362.88–dc23
LC record available at https://lccn.loc.gov/2016058077

ISBN: 978-0-415-81033-3 (hbk)
ISBN: 978-1-315-17035-0 (ebk)

Typeset in Times New Roman
by Taylor & Francis Books

Printed and bound by CPI Group (UK) Ltd, Croydon, CR0 4YY

This book is dedicated to my parents, Wang Wenjun and Ji Xiuying, in appreciation of all the values they taught that have made me the woman I am.

Contents

	List of illustrations	x
	Acknowledgements	xi
	Abbreviations	xiv
1	Discovering dating violence in China	1
2	Chinese intersectionality: A critical review of gender-based violence research and gender studies in China	15
3	Dating landscape, power struggles, and love geography	54
4	Sassy girl and tender boy: The transformation of doing gender	94
5	Virginity loss, sexual coercion, and the unfinished sexual revolution	138
6	Remapping the landscape of dating, gender, and violence	172
	Methods: Researching a sensitive topic	184
	Glossary	196
	Bibliography	201
	Index	219

Illustrations

Figure

2.1 Chinese intersectionality 49

Table

A.1 List of participants 192

Acknowledgements

It seems that this book project has taken forever to finish, and I feel extremely happy to write the acknowledgements, close the project and express my gratitude for the many forms and sources of support during the long and sometimes difficult writing process.

I would like to thank all informants who participated in individual interviews or focus groups and shared their experiences, opinions, and stories generously with me. Without their support, this book could not have been produced, although their names must remain anonymous.

Over the decade, certain professors have been my mentors during different periods. I owe a debt of gratitude to my PhD supervisor, Professor Sik Ying Ho, who took over the supervision of my research at the most difficult moment in my PhD journey. Her critical thinking and academic passion have inspired me in becoming a Chinese feminist. Her stimulating teaching and theoretical interrogation have enlightened me to be a good researcher and teacher. I got to know Professor Ada C. Mui at Columbia University in 2006, and ever since then I found that she was always available when I reached out for help and needed emotional support or academic advice. It is my good fortune to have known Professor Joshua Miller, who became my mentor, colleague and dear friend, at Smith College ever since 2008. He helped me recover from 'compassion fatigue,' we co-taught a course together, and he gave me much insightful feedback on all sorts of my written texts, including this book. I met Professor Manfred Henningsen from the University of Hawaii at Manoa at a conference in Hong Kong in 2010 and we became reliable friends. His perspective as a political scientist always gives me different, enlightening approaches to understanding the social phenomenon that I have been studying. In 2014, I was fortunate to be accepted as a CSC–Harvard postdoctoral fellow under the supervision of Professor Susan Greenhalgh at Harvard University. Sitting in her classes on 'Biopolitics' and 'Women and Bodies,' reading her books (*Just One Child* and others), and having numerous conversation with her – all these experiences opened a new door for me to link my current Chinese women's studies to broader areas, including those of medical anthropology and feminist technology studies.

xii *Acknowledgements*

I received generous financial support from many institutions. The University of Hong Kong offered me a four-year studentship and funded a conference trip to Norway in 2005. I received financial support from the Wu Jieh-Yee Research Fund (2006) at the University of Hong Kong to conduct interviews on dating violence among Hong Kong University students. The Ford Foundation China Office generously supported me in attending three international conferences, on 'gender and sexuality' and the 'women's rights movement,' in Buenos Aires, Argentina (2013), in Geneva, Switzerland (2014), and in New York, USA (2015). The Anti-domestic Violence Network financially supported me to attend the 57th Commission on the Status of Women, in New York in 2013. The research fund of the Ministry of Education, China (No. 10YJC840071), and the Fundamental Research Funds for the Central Universities, China (project no. 2012WZD04), have also made the publication of this book possible. I especially want to express my gratitude to the China Scholarship Council and the Graduate School of Arts and Science at Harvard University for providing me with a one-year postdoctoral fellowship in 2014, and to Smith College for offering me an eight-month visiting fellowship in 2015, which gave me time to escape from the teaching load and focus on writing this book.

Over the years numerous professors, friends, and colleagues have read parts of my manuscripts and have given me all kinds of valuable feedback. These include: Professor Yunxiang Yan (UCLA), Professor Kathryn Bernhardt (UCLA), Professor Sven Hessle of the *Journal of Social Welfare*, Dr. Jianhua Xu (HKU), Dr. Xiaoping Xiang (BPU), Dr. Suowei Xiao (BNU), Professor Xiaojiang Hu (BNU), Dr. Lichao Yang (BNU), and many others. The Seminars on Gender and Sexuality organized by Dr. Sik Ying Ho provided a wonderful platform for me to discuss this project deeply with my peers Yuxin Pei, Yu Ding, Yiqian Hu, Yeeshan Yang, Anna Ng and Carmen Ng. I also would like to thank the China Sociology Meetings organized by Professor Martin Whyte and Professor Ezra Vogel at Harvard University for letting me present my work and enjoy stimulating discussions. I would especially like to thank Dr. Daniel Nehring, a long-term research partner and loyal friend. I got to know him in 2010 and began to work on our joint project on transnational dating and marriage, and I have benefited from our discussions and collaborations.

There are many friends who deserve special mention for their friendship and unwavering support: these include Yuxin Pei, Cherry Lau, Helen Goh, Xuesong He, Fucai Cheng, Xiaoya Lu, Bin Fan, Xiaoye Zhang, Shuang Du, Xiaoya Lu, Dong Xu, Yu Liu, Li Teng, and others. I would also like to thank the feminist community in Beijing, including Chinese feminist five, Pin Lü, Yuan Feng, Jinzhao Li, Xiaopei He, Susie Jolly, Bin Xu, Iron, etc., for their courage and solidarity in dealing with the current backlash against the women's movement in China. Special thanks go to Dr. John Thorne for his 'competitive conversation' and English editing.

Earlier and shorter versions of Chapter 3, Chapter 4 and Chapter 5 have been published in peer-reviewed journals, and I thank the publishers Sage and

Acknowledgements xiii

Taylor & Francis for letting me reprint them here (special thanks go to my co-authors Sik Ying Ho and Daniel Nehring):

- Wang, X. & Ho, S.Y. 2007a. My Sassy Girl: A Qualitative Study of Women's Aggression in Dating Relationships in Beijing. *Journal of Interpersonal Violence*, 22: 623–638.
- Wang, X. & Ho, S.Y. 2011. 'Female Virginity Complex' Untied: Young Beijing Women's Experience of Virginity Loss and Sexual Coercion. *Smith College Studies in Social Work*, 81: 184–200.
- Wang, X. & Nehring, D. 2014. Individualization as an Ambition: Mapping the Dating Landscape in Beijing. *Modern China*, 40: 578–604.

My family has lived with this book, always generously and sometimes without knowing it. My parents, Wang Wenjun and Ji Xiuying, have grown older with it but have never complained of their spatial separation from me. I have dedicated this book to them. My sister, Wang Xuhui, and my brother, Wang Binhui, remain to this day my loyal playmates. My husband, Wu Weihua, is present in some way on every page, as this book is a document of our life adventure, in Beijing, Hong Kong, and the USA. My son, Glenn Siyan Wu, did not exist when I first came up with the idea for this book, and now he is an energetic almost-ten-year-old boy. I give them all my love.

Abbreviations

ACWF	All-China Women's Federation
APEC	Asia-Pacific Economic Cooperation
CCP	Chinese Communist Party
CCTV	China Central Television
CTS	Conflict Tactics Scales
DINK	dual income, no kids
DV	domestic violence
ECOSOC	UN Economic and Social Council
GGGR	Global Gender Gap Report
LGBT	lesbian, gay, bisexual, transgender
RMB	renminbi
S&M	sadomasochism
STD	sexually transmitted disease
UN	United Nations

1 Discovering dating violence in China

Two anecdotes

1998 winter: unspeakable secret

In the winter of 1998 I was a master's degree student in a prestigious university in Beijing. One early morning one of my best friends came back to the dormitory in tears. She told me that she had gone out to a disco with a male friend the previous night and had stayed out late, and so could not come back to the dormitory because of the midnight curfew. Her male friend invited her to his place and she agreed, mainly because it was cold outside and she just wanted to find a place to kill time and wait for the dormitory to reopen. To her surprise, as soon as they arrived at his place, her male friend started to make moves on her. At first she remained friendly but she firmly said no, but her male friend just would not listen. He grabbed her, pushed her to the bed and attempted to kiss her and coerce her into sex. She tried her best to fight back and protect herself, during the physical struggle losing a necklace she treasured very much, a gift from her mother. Luckily, she managed to escape and walk all the way back to our dormitory, crying.

I was shocked when I listened to her and was wide awake that very early morning, but I did not know why our discussion quickly shifted to how she might get the necklace back. Maybe because she felt that the discussion was going nowhere, she simply concluded: 'He is such a jerk!' Maybe it was too painful for her to talk about the details and her feeling of being hurt, betrayed, and ashamed. Neither of us was equipped with the concept of 'dating violence,' 'sexual coercion' or 'attempted date rape,' which might define the experience of injustice and violation. It never occurred to us that we should do something, such as call the police, call the counseling center, etc., to seek help and fight for justice. We did not even discuss how we could teach 'the friend' a lesson and prevent him from hurting other women. After that morning, we never discussed the incident again – it seemed that forgetting, ignoring, and remaining silent was the best way to deal with it. It became a secret. This secret bothered me for a long time.

2 Discovering dating violence in China

2014 fall: heroine without satisfaction

In the fall of 2014, Winnie was a female master's degree student in Xi'an. One day during lunch time, in an isolated place on campus, she saw a young couple: a man was furiously roaring at a woman, grabbing and shaking her shoulders violently, and the woman, who was much shorter and smaller than the man, was crying and almost fainting. Winnie wanted to intervene, and she took out her cell phone to video the incident. She asked the woman if she needed help. The man then grabbed Winnie's cell phone, deleted the video and asked her to leave. Reluctant to leave, Winnie accused the man of 'not being human.' Suddenly the man turned back to Winnie, put his hands around her throat and punched her several times in the face. At one moment Winnie felt that she was almost dead. When she came back to her senses, her face was covered with blood.

Winnie immediately called the police but, to her surprise, the couple held hands as they explained the situation to the policemen. The policeman blamed Winnie for interfering in another couple's business, and warned the man he could be arrested for such violent behavior. An ambulance came and took Winnie to the hospital, and the doctors examined her and confirmed that she had fractures of her nose and left cheekbone and that one front tooth was broken and another was loose. She also had a big black left eye.

Winnie felt that the policeman had blamed both sides and then had let the man go too easily, and she was determined to fight for justice. For three months she sought help from relatives and friends, women's rights organizations, legal assistance, etc., and finally she managed to arrange a legal mediation with the man, who apologized to her and paid her 60,000 renminbi (RMB) as compensation. However, Winnie could not feel satisfaction. She still felt uneasy at the results, for two reasons. First, she felt that it was not the abusive man but his parents who had paid the compensation, as the man was also a master's degree student, and she felt that he had not taken full responsibility for his actions. Second, she felt bad for the man's girlfriend who, it seemed, could not fight for justice herself, and was worried about her since she was not sure whether the man had learned any lesson or would stop behaving violently. These remained unsolved problems for her.

***

For Winnie and me, experiencing incidents like this could become life-changing opportunities. I was a volunteer counselor at the Youth Hotline from 1998 to 2002 and received phone calls about the troubles of dating relationships from young people all over China. I became aware of such violent elements as the first incident presented above and as young people expressed their feelings of being trapped in toxic dating relationships. In 2001, I first learned of the concept of 'dating violence' from English-language literature on the subject, and I was thrilled finally to find a name for the violent behaviors and interactions within dating relationships. In 2002 I went to the University of Hong Kong to pursue a PhD and chose to study dating violence among young people in Beijing, from a qualitative feminist perspective. Since then, fighting against gender-based violence has become my life-long project and commitment.

In 1998 the concept of domestic violence had only been introduced into China for a few years, but now it has become a buzzword and almost everyone knows its connotations. In 2003, the Huang Jing case became the first documented date rape case in China. Huang Jing was a 21-year-old primary school teacher, who had been found naked, bruised, and dead in a bed in her dormitory on February 24, 2003, after spending a night with her then 26-year-old boyfriend. Chinese feminists organized all kinds of activities to support Huang Jing's mother in her appeal for justice. It was this case that introduced the concepts of 'dating violence' and 'date rape' in China. Soon scholars started to pay attention to violence in other types of intimate relationships. The concept of gender-based violence has been introduced into China much more recently, and young feminist activists learn the intersectional approach to understand different forms of oppression are linked – both in their structure and also in how they relate to one another – to expand the understanding of violence against women. They have not limited themselves to studying the domain of domestic violence but also have been willing to fight against all kinds and types of such violence, including dating violence, violence in lesbian, gay, bisexual and transgender (LGBT) relationships, gender-based school bullying, sexual harassment and violence, and child (sexual) abuse, etc.

After the 2014 incident presented above, Winnie told me that she had intervened because she had participated in some training about gender awareness raising and gender-based violence, and she felt that it was her responsibility to help victimized women and stop the violence when she saw what was happening. She also told me that once her friend had seen another couple fighting on a street and had called to ask her how to help. Unlike me, who had been a passive listener 16 years previously, Winnie was equipped with the concept of gender-based violence and was more willing to take action to change the situation, though her tactics might need to be further improved. After the incident, Winnie became more actively involved in the women's movement, since she felt that she could not achieve justice without her feminist sisters' help. She participated in a series of activities, such as those against campus sexual harassment,[1] critiques of sexism and gender discrimination on the popular CCTV Spring Festival Gala TV show,[2] performance art for sexuality education,[3] etc.

Like many other young feminist activists, Winnie belongs to a well-educated, courageous, creative, and fearless generation of young women who have grown up in the Reform Era under the one-child policy. 'Instead of pursuing lucrative corporate positions, getting married and having children,' they 'choose to become full-time women's rights campaigners' (Xiao, 2015), deciding not to tolerate sexism and gender discrimination within the current

4 Discovering dating violence in China

system and not to campaign quietly. Performance art is their strategy for pursuing gender equality and opposing all kinds of violence against women and girls in China. This group of young feminist activists is becoming the future and direction of the Chinese feminist movement.

China has experienced earth-shaking changes in the past two decades. In 2010 China took over from Japan as the world's second largest economy.[4] At the same time, the gap between China's rich and poor is now one of the world's highest, surpassing even that in the USA, according to a report by the University of Michigan in 2014.[5] The gender gap and the rural–urban gap are also expanding. As the capital and center of Chinese Communist Party (CCP) political authority, Beijing was chosen as the research site for this present study. Beijing is a significant city with a rapidly developing cosmopolitanism, an important historical background, and significant cultural hybridity. On the one hand, Beijing maintains the comprehensive socialist bureaucracy and strong social institutions, and is politically conservative; on the other hand, Beijing has embraced the irresistible forces of modernization and globalization and has become a cosmopolis.

Idealization and uncertainty, two important characteristics of romantic love (Jankowiak, 1995), are not only fully expressed in young people's dating lives but in other aspects of this city as well. A survey among young professionals in Beijing presented a list of the four most unsatisfactory factors of living in the city: expensive housing, lots of traffic, high living costs, and pollution. In spite of these problems, a lot of young people choose to live in Beijing because they think of it as the political, economic and cultural center of China, with a better professional environment and more resources and opportunities for them to achieve upward mobility (30-Groups, 2011). On a personal level, they have more opportunities to meet interesting ideal dates, and have more exciting dating experiments.

This is a book about young people, their aspirations and ambitions, hopes and dreams, loves and violence, intimacy and sexuality – about their intimate relationships and everyday lives in the city of Beijing, filled as they are with uncertainty, temporality, and instability. This book presents a socio-cultural script of young people's dating lives and describes in detail how they accommodate and resist the hegemony of dating, gender, and sexuality. The objectives of this qualitative feminist study are to explore how young people give meaning to dating violence and do their gender and sexuality through it; and to throw light on the socio-cultural transformation of gender, sexuality, femininity, and masculinity from those of Maoist China (1949–76) to those of post-socialist China (1989–now). This book addresses the following questions:

1 What constitutes dating violence? How do young people in Beijing cope with the contradictions, conflicts, and violence in establishing dating relationships?
2 How do young people in Beijing do their gender and sexuality in dating relationships to negotiate tradition and establish themselves as modern

men and women? How do young people in Beijing accommodate and resist dating, gender, and sexual hegemony?

3 How does the passion to pursue individual agency and desire continue to invigorate socio-cultural transformation in post-socialist China, a country that has been subject to a strong state, a powerful market, and cultural hybridity?

4 What is the intersectional self? How can a theory of Chinese intersectionality be constructed? How can we use Chinese intersectionality to understand young people's everyday lives of love and violence, gender and sexuality?

When love hurts

Dating is a Western word and modern phenomenon, which has no corresponding term in Chinese. Two terms may be used: one is *yuehui*, meaning 'joint activity'; the other is *lian'ai*, applied to romantic relationships, with most *lian'ai* practices still closely relating to mate selection and future marriage, so that the term is similar in meaning to the English word *courtship*.[6] In the process of collecting data, both words were used, often interchangeably but sometimes according to particular situations. Sometimes young people also use casual terms such as *haola* ('to like each other'), *zaiyiqi* ('to be together'), *yuepao* ('hook-up date') and many others to refer to different dating practices. Here 'dating' is defined as a heterosexual relationship involving joint activities, including social activities (such as shopping, going to movies, having dinner together, etc.) and/or physical intimacy (such as holding hands, kissing, bodily touching, sex, etc.), either just for recreation or with an explicit or implicit intention to continue the relationship until break-up or marriage. It can be as casual as a one-night stand or as serious as cohabitation or engagement.

Dating violence is defined as aggressive behavior of intimate dating couples, involving act and/or injury, including attack and self-defense; it includes physical assault, verbal and psychological aggression, and sexual coercion, according to the classification of Straus et al. (1996).[7] This book is focused on heterosexual dating relationships, though I fully acknowledge that violence also exists in homosexual dating relationships, and in some sections in this book I make some reflections on LGBT issues. However, violence within LGBT couples is not the focus of the book. Special attention needs to be paid to it elsewhere.

Dating violence, as an academic term, was formally introduced into Mainland China by Ai Xiaoming in 2003. At the conference of the Anti-Domestic Violence Network (November 25, 2003), held by the Chinese Law Society, Ai Xiaoming raised the concepts of dating violence and date rape (*yuehui qiangjian*), called on the media to pay attention to violence in dating relationships rather than only focusing on domestic violence, and mobilized support for developing education against dating violence among high school

6 Discovering dating violence in China

and college students. I also wrote an article entitled 'Youth is Suffocated by Dating Violence,' published on June 8, 2004 in the *China Youth Daily*, a well-known newspaper for adolescents and young adults all over China (Wang, 2004). On the same day, it appeared on all the biggest Internet commercial domains in China, such as Sina.com, Sohu.com, and Yahoo.com, etc.

This book takes the standpoint of challenging four common myths of dating violence in public discourses. First, I challenge the traditional approach of researching different types of violence separately, and argue that the boundaries of physical, psychological, verbal, and sexual violence are blurred, so that sometimes one violent incident may include elements of different types of violence.

Second, I challenge the idea that only severe violence counts as violence. I argue for the importance of researching the spectrum of violence, including both 'minor,' 'trivial' violence and long-term, severe violence. In fact, 'minor' and 'trivial' violence extensively exist in young people's daily lives and has been ignored. The most common depiction of dating violence in China is 'failed dating and murder,' which appears everywhere in the media. Such bloody, violent descriptions in the media resemble horror stories or movies more than reflections on the overall social phenomenon. They usually attribute murders to failures of love and the abnormal personalities of the criminals, and regard these as rare and isolated incidents, with no relation to the conflicts and violence that occur in regular dating lives. This stereotypical depiction of violence makes it difficult to raise people's awareness about the spectrum of violence and to prevent 'minor' violence from escalating into 'severe' violence.

Third, I challenge the dichotomy of 'abusive men and abused women,' and the idea that women are the only victims of dating violence. I have studied the violent behaviors of both men and women, and argue that the roles of perpetrators and victims sometimes are fluid and interchangeable, especially in the situation of mutual violence and 'trivial' and 'minor' violence.

Last but not least, I challenge the dichotomy of romantic love and violence, and argue that romantic love and violence sometimes co-exist in violent dating relationships. In past studies, romantic love and violence have been dichotomized, just as they are in the general public's perception. However, many studies (Borochowitz and Eriskovits, 2002; Chavez, 2002; Fraser, 2003; Jackson, 2001) reveal that romantic love is co-existent with violence in intimate relationships and that love is even often used to justify violence. On the one hand, it is argued that the discourse of romantic love legitimates the jealousy of 'people in love,' their desire to possess the other, and their attempts to control their partners' lives in order to feel more secure and loved. On the other hand, it is argued that perfect-love discourses may bind women in relationships with abusive men, normalize dominance and superiority for men and deference and dependence for women, regulate women in a variety of ways to remain in the relationship, keep women silent about men's violence, and lead the women to attempt to change the men. These studies imply that love and violence can be mutually functional, which means that violence results from love and violence even becomes a means of preserving love.

This book starts with dating violence, but attempts to work far beyond the violence. Through discussing dating violence, I attempt to explore how young people navigate and negotiate dating relationships, what their romantic expectations, desires, and behaviors are, and how they construct gender, sexuality, and a new dating culture. Dating violence is a perfect site for researching the relationship between youth and society, and between individual subjectivity and social structure as well. It paints a complex picture of the problems and difficulties that young people face in their lives, such as communication and coping strategies, interpersonal relationships with parents and peers, identity development and crisis, dating practices and sexual behavior, virginity loss and abortion, education, career ambitions, etc. How do young people develop their agency and subjectivity in coping with all the problems and difficulties? How do they negotiate with tradition and modernity and gain better positions within a society in transition? Dating violence has become a site contested by competing and multilayered discourses regarding gender, love, and sexuality in contemporary China, and this provides a good entry point for reflecting on the transformation in the dating and sexual culture of contemporary Chinese cosmopolitan cities and for capturing the flavor of the future of China in a very concrete and private matter.

APEC Blue and Beijing Smog: imagined paradise

In November 2014, the period of the Asia-Pacific Economic Cooperation (APEC) Summit, the Central and Beijing governments adopted all kinds of means to clear the Beijing skies of pollution,[8] including granting special holidays to students, government officers and workers, and shutting down hundreds of construction sites. The sky did live up to the expectation of a beautiful blue during this period. Some 'naughty' netizens ('online citizens') spontaneously linked the intimate relationship of the APEC Summit with the Beijing sky and created two terms – 'APEC Blue' and 'Beijing Smog.' The former means something beautiful and ephemeral, symbolizing an unreal beautiful relationship quickly gone; the latter means a long-term persistent and exclusive relationship that just cannot be gotten rid of. In order to help others to understand their creations, they even made up two example sentences: one is, 'He is not really into you, it's an APEC Blue!'; the other is, 'He is so into you. He is all over you like a Beijing Smog.' Intimacy and politics were thus woven together within the two metaphors to link love and violence, and to construct an imagined paradise of dating, gender and sexuality.

Through the site of dating violence, I attempt to articulate three different types of stories – dating stories, gender stories, and sexuality stories. Above all, I want to tell individual personal stories intertwined within the bigger script of dating, gender and sexuality. In doing this, I depict how young people establish individuality, subjectivity, and agency through dating and

8 Discovering dating violence in China

sexual practices, and how the intersectional self rises in dealing with competing social discourses.

The glory of the achievement of 'gender equality' in Maoist China seems long gone, especially as the country marches into hyper-capitalism, and women's status and gender situation has been worse in recent years. Measuring countries' achievements in attaining gender equality and empowering women in economic life, education, health, and politics, the World Economic Forum has annually published the *Global Gender Gap Report* (GGGR) since 2006, and the ranking of China has been decreasing almost every year, from 63rd (2006) to 87th (2014).[9] In the 2014 GGGR, China was among the nine countries that were below average on the Health and Survival subindex. China was also among the five lowest-performing countries on the sex ratio at birth[10] indicator. The scores for women's economic and political participation lagged notably behind those of the most highly ranked countries.

The gender gap for education years narrowed to 0.3 year in 2010 (ACWF and NBS, 2011). According to statistics from the Ministry of Education, the colleges and universities nationwide recruited 51.35% female students[11] in 2012. Female students generally do better academically but have much more difficulty in finding a job after graduation (Tong and Su, 2010). Women work harder but are paid less than men: the average annual income of women laborers is equal to 67.3% of that of men in urban areas and 56.0% of that of men in rural areas, although on working days the average number of working minutes per person is 574 for women and 537 for men (ACWF and NBS, 2011). At home, women are still the primary caregivers, and their average leisure time is much lower than that of men (ACWF and NBS, 2011). The GGGR for 2014 shows that China ranks 48th on the professional and technical workers indicator (with a higher percentage of women than men), but 101st on the legislators, senior officials and managers indicator. This result shows clearly that a glass ceiling has been formulated firmly to prevent women's development on career paths. According to corporate records examined by *The New York Times*, fewer than one in ten board members of China's top 300 companies are women.[12] Women held two out of 25 positions on the Politburo,[13] and women have never held positions on the Politburo Standing Committee throughout the history of the CCP (Li, 2013).

The women's movement is facing an unprecedented backlash at different levels. President Xi Jinping, in several speeches, has emphasized women's 'unique role' in the family, and that women should consciously shoulder the responsibility of respecting the elderly and educating their children to become useful to the country. The president of the All-China Women's Federation (ACWF), Shen Yueyue, gave a speech on International Women's Day, 2015, and basically implemented the guidance of President Xi: pay attention to family, pay attention to family education, and pay attention to family values (*zhuzhong jiating, zhuzhong jiajiao, zhuzhong jiafeng*). Only emphasizing women's family role as mothers, wives, and daughters is a countermarch to the idea that 'women hold up half the sky' of the socialist era. Most male elites do not care about gender issues and pay no attention to feminism and gender studies, and the 'let women go home' proposal was initiated by two male professors in the 1980s and since then it has repeatedly reappeared, with some sexist congressmen openly declaring that 'women'd better not to pursue Ph.D.'[14]

The neo-liberal market force not only objectifies women's bodies, but marginalizes women in the social, political, and cultural arenas, and re-asserts the hegemony of ruling elites. The mass media depict feminists as some of the most undesirable women in the world, and most established female celebrities, writers, and even gender studies scholars, have distanced themselves from the label of feminist. According to a study by *Ms. Magazine*, the number of American women calling themselves feminists increased from 50 percent in 2006 to 68 percent in 2012.[15] While no corresponding study can be found in China, I am sure that the percentage would be much lower. The feminist movement in China cannot obtain worldwide women's support and endorsement, and this will be a huge barrier to future development. The political discourse echoes with the revival of Confucian traditional gender roles – 'men work outside, women work inside,' and 'husband leads and wife follows' – and establish a powerful 'guideline' for gender roles that represent a strong backlash. At the same time, across the world, there has been a very direct conservative backlash against the values and achievements of feminism – for instance, Christian nationalism in the USA, public debates about the rollback of women's rights in the USA, and the widespread Islamic fundamentalism in certain areas.

Hu and Scott (2014) compare gender values in China from generational and geographic perspectives, and they have found similar results to those of Western research in that, among recent generations, higher education, women's employment, and smaller family size all reduce support for traditional gender roles. Their findings are also consistent with suggestions that the one-child policy might help endorse more egalitarian gender role beliefs (Deutsch, 2006). They find that people who have received higher education hold significantly fewer traditional attitudes toward gender roles. This study helps us to understand that, although under the current strong backlash and gradually worsening gender situation, the younger generation of women have grown up with liberal, modern ideas of gender roles because of their parents' educational investments which have allowed them to obtain higher education and the tremendous expansion of educational facilities in China. Many of them do well at school and transition smoothly to college or university, but when they graduate and try to find jobs, suddenly they find themselves entering a world they do not understand, a world filled with discrimination and exclusion, with a glass ceiling, a world filled with the pressure to define their values by marriage. A small number of them cannot accept this and decide to become young activists to fight for change, while the majority learn to accommodate to the situation and try hard to put themselves in advantageous positions. For them, dating and sexuality usually become one of their biggest battlefields.

10   *Discovering dating violence in China*

As the China scholars Frank Dikötter (1995), Gail Hershatter (2007, 2012), Harriet Evans (2008, 2010) and Judith Farquhar (2002) have shown, over the course of the twentieth century in China, romance, sex, and marriage became prime sites of social contestation where positive and negative aspects of tradition and modernity were defined and assessed, and the promise of 'liberation' from 'feudal traditions' or 'feudal superstitions' was offered. Lisa Rofel (1999) also raised an enticing connection in showing how young people's practice in their intimate relationships turns into an allegory for post-socialism:

> It holds out hope and excitement; it celebrates national strength and private pleasures; it appears to move beyond the regulatory politics of Maoist socialism; it seems to carve out a space separate from the state.
>
> (p. 255)

Dating and sexuality, on the one hand, are a private matter; on the other hand, they always embody invisible contestation between individual and society, tradition and modernity. 'Romantic love and free dating (*ziyou lian'ai*)' is one of the most prominent themes associated with the May Fourth Movement[16] in the Chinese cultural imagination. During the May Fourth Movement, this theme became an embodiment of people's individuality, revolutionary spirit and national modernity in response to Western imperialism and colonialism. However, after the establishment of the People's Republic of China in 1949, dating was for a long time deeply repressed by the state discourse and became highly politically oriented. Since China entered the Opening-up and Reform Era in the late 1970s and early 1980s, the transition of the society has changed family structures radically – the decline of patrilocalism (multigenerational co-residence), nuclear family residence (Ma et al., 2011), love matches, rocketing divorce rates and hence single motherhood (Wang and Zhou, 2010), and the rise of dual-earner and dual income, no kids ('DINK') families (Hu and Scott, 2014). Personally oriented dating, for the first time in Chinese history, has become dominant, but is increasingly filled with diversity, complication, and uncertainty. People finally feel that they are entitled to 'choices' and 'opportunities' in the dating market, and therefore they have different preferences and criteria for selecting their ideal dates – including romantic love, feelings, shared interests, physical appearance, personality, communication skills, money, power, education, family background and social status, to name a few.

As Yan (2003) argues, rural girls develop 'girl power and youth autonomy' in the process of mate selection, which had produced a 'romantic revolution of courtship' by the end of the 1990s (pp. 64–85), which was characterized by three major developments. The first was an increase of intimacy in courtship and post-engagement interactions, including the increasing popularity of premarital sex. Second, contemporary young women began to pay more attention to their future spouse's individual characteristics, such as physical appearance, respect and caring, emotional expression, and communication skills. Third, young women tended to be more open and vocal in expressing their emotions. The same, or a more radical 'revolution,' was sure to happen in urban China, and cosmopolitan Beijing in the new millennium has become a hugely chaotic place filled with all kinds of opportunities to pursue love and dating experiments.

Some young people may still link dating with engagement and marriage, but many others regard dating as an important experience of establishing identity, finding companionship, engaging in sexual intimacy, etc., none of which may necessarily be related to future marriage. Young people's dating lives thus have become complicated and diverse: the age of first dating and first sex is decreasing; experience of dating is increasing; and besides, monogamous heterosexual dating relationships, homosexual relationships, triangular relationships, multiple relationships, extra-marital affairs, and one-night stands and other different kinds of dating practices have become more and more popular in urban areas (Farrer, 1997, 2002; Li, 2002a, 2002b). Pop culture and mass media seem to be the most obvious and direct influence on the development of the language of love and intimacy, which both enriches and alters the discourse on an ideal mate and the practice of mate choice (Yan, 2009, p. 137–138), and reflects socio-cultural change in attitudes and practices concerning dating and mate choice.

With the development of LGBT activism and nongovernmental organizations that organize all kinds of events and activities including lectures on campus, movie festivals, self-discovery support groups, etc., the younger LGBT generation more actively embraces their sexual orientation and promotes their dating culture.[17]

The concept of 'leftover women' has been created to discriminate against well-educated women in their late twenties who have not married (Fincher, 2014), though more and more young people enjoy their single status and delay marriage as long as they can. However, their parents just cannot respect adult children's choices and so organize blind dates, putting their pictures in parks in all the big cities while, in most cases, unmarried adult children are hidden in the dark (Sun, 2012). Spring Festival traditionally is a holiday for family reunion, but it becomes the most challenging time for singles to face pressure from parents. In these situations, lesbians and gays have to come up with strategic solutions, and help each other to forge formative marriages, while for other singles, renting a girlfriend/boyfriend becomes a rational and timely but costly choice[18] – since single women face extremely high stress, renting a boyfriend is especially popular.

While dating has become a common practice in high schools and universities, most educational institutions still adopt an approach of 'don't ask, don't tell,' remain reluctant to provide comprehensive sex education, and stick to abstinence moral education for love, dating, and sex (Wang and Wang, 2012). As premarital sex becomes a rather common practice among young couples, many young men still hold on to the 'female virginity complex' attitude (Wang and Ho, 2011), and a few billionaires are still determined to find

12   Discovering dating violence in China

'pure virgin' brides through advertisements.[19] More and more young people accept the Internet as just another way to expand their daily friends circles and find desirable dates, and match-making websites like jiayuan.com (*shijijiayuan*) and baihe.com (*baihe*) make fortunes from this (Osnos, 2014). The match-making television show 'If You Are the One' successfully created an image of a female 'gold-digger' in the free dating age, who claimed that 'I would rather cry in a BMW than smile on a bicycle.'[20] Discos, bars, movie theatres, restaurants, shopping malls have all become popular places for dating. The development of social media apps – WeChat, momo, papa, tataUFO and many others – makes online hook-up dating (*yuepao*) more convenient and accessible, apparently becoming part of the emerging youth subculture. Though some scholars preach that the sexual revolution is already finished in China (Pan, 2006), based on the active existence of all kinds of sexual practices, sexual capital has been unequally distributed and the sexual double standard has been intensified. Illouz (2012) argues that:

> To perform gender identity and gender struggles is to perform the institutional and cultural core dilemmas and ambivalence of modernity, dilemmas that are organized around the key cultural and institutional motives of authenticity, autonomy, equality, freedom, commitment, and self-realization. To study love is not peripheral but central to the study of the core and foundation of modernity.
>
> (p. 9)

Based on feminist intersectionality theory, I raise the concept of the 'intersectional self' in order to capture how individual choices are made and how individual agency and subjectivity are exercised through negotiating within the dating, gender, and sexuality hegemony and its broader social structural context, in order to construct personal stories in unexpected ways.

Structure of the book

This book has six chapters in total. Chapter 1, 'Discovering dating violence in China,' explains the background, definitions and objectives of this study. Chapter 2, 'Chinese intersectionality,' establishes a theoretical framework of Chinese intersectionality based on a critical review of research on the women's movement, violence against women, state, and market; on the interaction between Western and Chinese feminism; and on the dislocation of Confucianism in current violence studies. Chapter 3, 'Dating landscape, power struggles, and love geography,' charts the dating landscape and love geography in Beijing and discusses the power struggles in dating relationships. The distinction between Beijingers and *waidiren* (lit., outsiders) serves as a framework to examine the cultural and socio-economic differentiation of dating practices. Chapter 4, 'Sassy girl and tender boy: the transformation of doing gender,' focuses on the verbal, physical and psychological violence in

Discovering dating violence in China 13

dating relationships, with a particular emphasis on women's aggression. It describes how young people do their gender, challenge the gender hegemony, and justify women's aggression as socially acceptable. It illustrates the social transformation of femininity and masculinity from the Maoist Era to the Post-socialist Era. Chapter 5, 'Virginity loss, sexual coercion, and the unfinished sexual revolution,' focuses on sexual violence in dating relationships; interprets how young people do sexuality and challenge sexual hegemony, contributing to a new understanding of virginity loss and sexual coercion; and sheds light on the social transformation of sexuality from the Maoist Era to post-socialism. Chapter 6, 'Remapping the landscape of dating, gender, and violence,' concludes the major arguments of the book and highlights the contributions and implications of this study. I deliberately put the methodology separately as an appendix in order to keep the readers engaging with the story.

Notes

1 A sexual harassment case reported in Xiamen University in June 2014 drew great attention throughout China. On September 10, 2014 (National Teachers' Holiday), groups of young feminists dressed as Little Red Riding Hood appeared in Beijing Foreign Studies University, Fudan University, Zhejiang University, Wuhan University and other famous universities in nine cities to appeal for the establishment of standardized prevention measures against sexual harassment on campus as soon as possible. www.womenofchina.cn/womenofchina/html1/news/china/17/5831-1.htm.
2 A group of feminists posted an open letter online which criticized a sketch on China Central Television's (CCTV) Spring Festival Gala in 2015, for being sexist. Please see: www.washingtonpost.com/blogs/worldviews/wp/2015/02/25/chinas-feminists-stand-up -against-misogynistic-tv-gala/, www.globaltimes.cn/content/912071.shtml.
3 At 2:00 pm on July 28, 2014, at the south gate of Beijing Normal University, a couple of young feminists presented a piece of performance art for sex education, some holding books, some wearing bath towels. They carried slogans including, 'Porn does not equal Sex Education' and 'College Students Demand Comprehensive Sex Education.' Please see: www.youtube.com/watch?v=7120LU6ObKk.
4 www.theguardian.com/business/2011/feb/14/china-second-largest-economy.
5 ns.umich.edu/new/releases/22156-income-inequality-now-greater-in-china-than-in-us.
6 *Courtship* is the period in a couple's relationship that precedes their engagement and marriage, or establishment of an agreed relationship of a more enduring kind. During courtship, a couple gets to know each other and decides if there will be an engagement or other such agreement. Please see: en.wikipedia.org/wiki/Courtship.
7 In detail, different types of violence include the following concrete behaviors. Verbal aggression includes insulting or swearing at the partner, sulking or refusing to talk about an issue with the partner, stomping out of a room or house, and doing or saying something to spite the partner. Sometimes verbal violence and psychological aggression are cross-linked with each other (Straus et al., 1996). Physical assault includes 'minor' and 'severe' violence. The former is defined as throwing something that could hurt, twisting, pushing or shoving, grabbing and slapping, while the latter includes using a knife or gun, punching or hitting, choking, slamming, beating up, burning or scalding, and kicking (Straus et al., 1996). Psychological aggression: insulting, saying things to upset, saying mean things, criticizing, calling names, making the other person feel guilty, making the

14 *Discovering dating violence in China*

other person feel inferior, giving the other person the cold shoulder, degrading, and hurting feelings (Stets, 1991). Sexual coercion typically ranges from verbal manipulation (insistent arguing, false pretense, threats to terminate a relationship, or threats of physical force), to forced physical aggression and rape.

8 www.bloomberg.com/bw/articles/2014-11-18/beijings-blue-sky-act-for-apec.

9 The ranking of China from 2006 to 2014: 63 (2006); 73 (2007); 57 (2008); 60 (2009); 61 (2010/11); 69 (2012/13); 87 (2014). Please see *Global Gender Gap Report* (2013, 2014): www3.weforum.org/docs/WEF_GenderGap_Report_2013.pdf; www3.weforum.org/docs/GGGR14/GGGR_CompleteReport_2014.pdf.

10 Normal sex ratio at birth is in general between 103 to 107 male live births per 100 female live births, but the sex ratio at birth in China peaked at 120.5:100 for 2005 (Li, 2007), 117.8:100 for 2011 (UNFPA, 2012), and 115.88:100 for 2014. Data from www.stats.gov.cn/tjsj/zxfb/201502/t20150211_682459.html (accessed June 28, 2015).

11 gaokao.xdf.cn/201311/9718770.html.

12 Didi Kirsten Tatlow and Michael Forsythe, February 20, 2015, 'In China Modern Economy, Retro Push,' www.nytimes.com/2015/02/21/world/asia/china-women-lag-in-work-force-especially-in-top-jobs.html.

13 Benjamin Kang Lim and Michael Martina, 'China's Politburo has More Women, is Younger – but Barely,' Reuters, November 15, 2012. www.reuters.com/article/2012/11/15/china-congress-politburo-idUSL3E8MF1VR20121115.

14 phtv.ifeng.com/program/zbjsj/detail_2014_01/22/33234523_0.shtml.

15 www.nytimes.com/2014/05/22/fashion/who-is-a-feminist-now.html.

16 The *May Fourth Movement* was an anti-imperialist, cultural, and political movement growing out of student demonstrations in Beijing on May 4, 1919, protesting the Chinese government's weak response to the Treaty of Versailles, especially allowing Japan to receive territories in Shandong which had been surrendered by Germany after the Siege of Tsingtao. The term 'May Fourth Movement' in a broader sense often refers to the period of 1915–21, more often called the New Culture Movement.

17 www.cnn.com/2014/11/26/world/asia/china-rainbow-flag/.

18 www.foreignaffairs.com/articles/china/2015-02-20/chinas-boyfriends-hire.

19 www.nytimes.com/2006/01/24/international/asia/24china.html?pagewanted=all&_r=0.

20 www.nytimes.com/2010/07/19/world/asia/19chinatv.html.

2 Chinese intersectionality

A critical review of gender-based violence research and gender studies in China

Locating dating violence in the context of development of gender-based violence over the past two decades, this chapter starts with a critical review of violence research on, and feminist practices in relation to, violence against women. A victimized-woman image has emerged predominantly from gender-based violence research. This image is shared in contemporary Chinese sociological women's studies, which covers a huge disparity of state-sanctioned programs and policies to liberate women, beginning with the Maoist Era. The contrast between images from different historical periods provides an entry point to discuss the interconnection of gender, state and market, the interaction between Western feminism and Chinese feminism, and the dislocation of Confucian ideas within feminist scholarship. This chapter proposes to establish a new theoretical framework of Chinese intersectionality, to include state, market and cultural discourses in the gender analysis matrix both for gender-based violence research and Chinese feminism. The following questions are posed to explore the possibilities of establishing a Chinese intersectionality theory within current feminist scholarship:

1   How can we understand Chinese women, initially represented since 1949 as having been liberated by state sanction, and now as victims of patriarchal oppression in the post-Maoist discourse of violence against women? How does this gendered turn echo the dichotomy of state discourses concerning New China-emancipated women, whose condition has moved 'from oppression to liberation'?

2   How can we understand the role of the market in producing the images of both victimized and liberated women?

3   How can we understand the interaction between gender, state, and market?

4   How does Chinese feminism interact with Western feminism? Is the image of victimized women influenced by the radical feminism in the West, which has portrayed women as victims and men as perpetrators of oppression?

5   How can we understand Chinese feminists' attempts to establish indigenous feminism? How should we perceive the part played by Confucian ideas within existing violence studies and in the tensions between Chinese feminism, Western feminism and state discourse?

16   *Chinese intersectionality*

The proposed new framework of Chinese intersectionality gives special attention to: 1 the micro-politics of self and desire, resistance and accommodation, subjectivity and agency; 2 the meso-politics of multiple oppression and interlocking systems of oppression – the matrix of gender, class, race, ethnicity and age; and 3 the macro-politics of state, market, and cultural hybridity. This theoretical position offers a new perspective and vision for gender-based violence studies, and therefore for gender studies in China.

Gender-based violence: the past and present

The emergence of studies of gender-based violence did not occur in isolation, but in close association with the evolution of women's studies (*funüxue/ funüyanjiu*) and the feminist movement in the Reform Era in China:

> As the central hub of women's organizing against gender violence in China, the DV (domestic violence) project not only signals the formation of a local women's movement, it also represents an intricate outcome of increasingly transnationalized feminist organizing around the world in the era of globalization.
>
> (Zhang, 2009, p. 67)

Many scholars (e.g. Chow et al., 2004; Wang, 1998; Wesoky, 2002) argue that there have been two waves of women's studies in Chinese history. Chinese-language writing on women's issues started in the 1890s, during the last gasp of the Qing Dynasty, when male reformist intellectuals began to depict Chinese women as weak, victimized and sexually oppressed within a semi-feudal, semi-colonial social context. The New Cultural Movement of the May Fourth Era (1915–25) is commonly regarded as having included the first wave of women's studies, marking the formation of ethnographic representation of Chinese 'modern women' and formulating frameworks within which to project images of suffering, victimized women within the contexts of Confucian thought and a colonized China. The focal goals for women's liberation within the May Fourth Movement were to change 'female chastity codes and the inhumanity of arranged marriage' and forced foot-binding to promote women's education, financial independence, and independent personalities (Zhou, 2003). The connection between violence and women is significantly related as a metaphor for the struggle for Chinese modernity – liberating women therefore meant saving the country from the turmoil of semi-feudalism and semi-colonialism; but such violence was also presented as an everyday 'reality' affecting Chinese women's subjectivity. Elite males acted as leaders and educated women took active part in challenging the trapped situation of women.

The current wave of women's studies emerged in 1980s Reform-era China, promoted by an urban Chinese feminist scholars' movement, with academics as chief participants and academic exploration as the main goal (Li and Zhang, 1994; Min, 2005; Xu, 2009). Min Dongchao's (2005) article on

Chinese intersectionality 17

'travelling feminism' emphasizes 'how the ideas and knowledge of feminism travel from the West to China, and in what form they were received, understood, and localized during the 1980s' (p. 276). She argues that Chinese women's studies and feminism in the 1980s was quite different from what they were in the 1990s:

> If the trend of Chinese Women's Studies in the 1980s was dominated by Chinese scholars and activists, there has been a shift to what was occurring in a global context since the beginning of the 1990s – the trend of asserting the 'global' and transnational feminist ideas has become a new wave in academic Women's Studies circles and Women's Federation.
>
> (Min, 2005, p. 286)

The phenomenon of gender-based violence arose as one of the most important domains of Chinese feminist concern and was worked on in the 1990s under the impact of transnational feminist ideas and United Nations (UN)-based international feminism. Two UN conferences, the International Conference on Population and Development in Cairo in 1994, and the Fourth World Conference on Women in 1995 in Beijing (hereafter the '1995 Beijing Conference'), boosted the feminist movement and advanced women's rights in China. Especially, the 1995 Beijing Conference made a huge impact on gender-based violence research and activities, and domestic violence in particular has been a hot topic ever since (Hester, 2000, 2004; Kaufman, 2012; Milwertz, 2003; Milwertz and Bu, 2005, 2009; Wesoky, 2002, 2007; Zhang, 2009). Joan Kaufman was a project official in the Ford Foundation China Office during the 1995 Beijing Conference period, and recalls how the women's movement rose through and after the conference:

> Through preparations for the Beijing Women's Conference an independent Chinese women's NGO [nongovernmental organization] sector was born – The connections made at Beijing helped to launch social movements in China on women's rights issues such as domestic violence, divorce, women's labor rights, and sexual discrimination, and women's land tenure and property rights.
>
> (Kaufman, 2012, p. 594)

In her paper on women's writing in post-Cultural Revolution China, Larson (2000) concludes that the second-wave women's movement in China had worked in four ways since the beginning of the Reform and Opening-up Era (1979/80–2000):

> The first way is in the practice of advocacy, engagement, and change characterized by the socialist approach to gender problems under Mao. Second, academic feminism has thrived and resulted in the establishment of a number of feminist university programs. Third, a strong interest in

18   *Chinese intersectionality*

women has emerged in popular culture books. The fourth area of feminism activity is the creative involvement of elite artists, filmmakers, and writers with gender concepts.

(Larson, 2000, pp. 202–203)

This second wave, as Larson suggests, had been one of socio-cultural mapping, with cultural and academic elites as leaders, rather than politically oriented activity from grassroots women, and this is perhaps accurate for 2000, but it needs to be updated for current China. First, gender has become a much more popular concept than feminism, since the latter still has some negative connotations in mainstream Chinese discourse. Feminists in public discourse are always stereotypically portrayed as women who are 'men-haters,' are 'ugly,' 'strong,' and 'not feminine,' and are brainwashed by Western viewpoints. In contrast, gender is a less provocative term for exploring women-related issues, and therefore gender analysis is widely used in current scholarship, and gender mainstreaming is a strategy widely used within NGO activities and events, and in policymaking processes. 'Gender is everywhere in the scholarship' (Hershatter, 2012, p. 877), and gender studies becomes a 'fractured, unpredictable, and expansive terrain' (Hershatter, 2012) that interacts with the different disciplines of sociology, anthropology, psychology, political science, literature, history, etc. Gender has become a powerful analytical concept in the study of women's lives and experiences. The discussion of issues is not only limited to reflecting on the gender issues of the Maoist Era, but has expanded to include the study of all kinds of gender-related social issues.

Second, the women's movement now goes beyond the limits of socio-cultural remapping and attempts to be more involved in the political domain. 'Gender mainstreaming' has become a feminist strategy for assessing and improving local legislation, policies, or programs, to fulfill the long-term mission. On most occasions, 'gender mainstreaming' faces institutional barriers, in all areas and at all levels, but has international NGOs' support.

Third, cultural and academic elites are no longer the only leaders of feminist activities, and grassroots feminist movements led by young activists have bloomed everywhere, especially in cities like Beijing, Shanghai and Guangzhou, where they formulate collaborative relationships with LGBT, civil society and labor rights movements that give voice to extensive marginalized groups.

The shift of gender-based violence mapping

The development of the second wave has also witnessed a change of terminology in the field of violence research. In the late 1980s and early 1990s discussion of domestic violence was more on a case-by-case basis rather than a systematic effort to understand the problem and its roots in patriarchal value systems (Honig and Hershatter, 1988; Wesoky, 2002). At that time, even the term 'domestic violence' (*jiating baoli*) had not been imported to China – scholars had simply appropriated *dalaopo/aida* (wife-battering) to describe the phenomenon. It was not until 1993 or 1994[1] that the concept of domestic violence was formally introduced as an academic term describing a social problem. It was not until the revised Marriage Law was adopted in 2001 that actual 'domestic violence' wording became included as a legal matter at the national level (Milwertz and Bu, 2009). According to Zhang (2009, p. 68), the term 'violence against women' was introduced, through the 1995 Beijing Conference, into the 'Chinese state's policy discourse, forcing the state to recognize the topic as a legitimate "woman question" and to introduce the issue into public discourse.' Milwertz and Bu (2009) outline the four stages of new knowledge production concerning gender-based violence by Chinese feminists during the 1980s and 1990s:

> They more or less 'accidentally' discovered wife-beating (*da laopo*) in the course of addressing other gender inequality issues. They then started investigating the characteristics and extent of wife-beating. This in turn led to their re-interpretation of wife-beating as a women's movement issue and the re-naming of the phenomenon as domestic violence (*jiating baoli*). Finally, some activists defined domestic violence as an issue involving gender relations and as a human rights issue.
>
> (p. 136)

For quite a long time, domestic violence has been used interchangeably with 'violence against women' to emphasize men's perpetration and women's victimization within violent marital relationships. The term 'intimate partner violence' has been much less used than 'violence against women' since it seems to take a rather neutral stance about both men's and women's aggressive behavior and regards such behavior as a result of unhealthy interaction and mutual conflict. The concept of domestic violence has been used to emphasize violence between married partners, ignoring different forms of violence within the family, and violence in other intimate relationships, including dating and cohabitation.

Compared to domestic violence, 'gender-based violence' is a broader concept that encompasses a wide variety of attitudes, values, and practices. The UN Economic and Social Council (ECOSOC) defines gender-based violence as:

> Any harmful act that is perpetrated against a person's will and that is based on socially associated differences between males and females. As such violence is based on socially ascribed differences, gender-based violence includes, but it is not limited to sexual violence. While women and girls of all ages make up the majority of the victims, men and boys are also both direct and indirect victims. It is clear that the effects of such violence are both physical and psychological, and have long-term detrimental consequences for both the survivors and their communities.
>
> (ECOSOC, 2006)

20 Chinese intersectionality

From this perspective, gender-based violence covers a wide range of behaviors that are based in systematic and pervasive inequalities of power between individuals and social groups within the gender order of a particular society (O'Toole et al., 2007). It is often perpetrated by men against women and children, at the same time violence against men, against LGBT individuals, and within homosexual relationships must be equally considered. Relevant forms of violence are equally wide-ranging. They include, but are not limited to, domestic violence, dating violence, school bullying, intimate partner violence, sexual violence/rape, child sexual abuse, homophobic hate crimes, sexual harassment in the workplace and public life, and sex trafficking, etc. Moreover, it is important to consider physical violence as well as verbal violence, psychological violence, sexual violence and systematic gender-based discrimination. It is a broader concept emphasizing violence based on gender inequality, but in this study I am particularly focused on dating violence.

Dating violence, as well as domestic violence, is one form of gender-based violence. I define dating violence as the aggressive behavior of intimate dating couples, and as act and/or injury, including attack and self-defense; it includes physical assault, verbal and psychological aggression, and sexual coercion, according to the classification of Straus et al. (1996).[2] This book also attempts to extend 'violence occurring within dating couples' to include 'violence associated with dating.' The reason for this redefinition has to do with two disruptive phenomena I have noticed within dating violence: one is violence associated with triangular relationships – there are at least five male informants who reported they had the experience of physically fighting with other men to compete for a girl, and a few female informants also mentioned that they were beaten up by a boyfriend's other girlfriend; the other is that of family members or relatives who interfere in a dating couple's intimate life with abusive behavior. The focus of this book is mainly on 'violence occurring within dating couples,' but with some expansion to include 'violence associated with dating,' which may in some way fill a gap in the existing literature on dating violence.

In this study, I argue that different types of violence do not have clear boundaries, as many quantitative studies demonstrate, and a single violent incident may include all types of violence. In most cases, there is a spectrum of violence, which may run from something as trivial as name-calling to acts as severe as homicide and date rape. Furthermore, even one type of violence includes a wide variety of behaviors. This study emphasizes violence that is regarded as 'minor,' 'trivial,' 'subtle' or 'unimportant,' and therefore ignored by existing studies, because it is much more common in young people's dating lives and tells us a lot about the way they manage their intimacies and everyday lives in a fast-changing society. At the same time, I have to admit the different degree of seriousness of the consequences and trauma brought on by 'minor' violence and 'severe' violence, acknowledging other feminists' contributions in studying severe violence and reminding myself not to 'lose sight of the general patterns in intimate partner violence that need to guide antiviolence work' (Worcester, 2002, p. 1391).

The frontier and cutting-edge feminist activism

Under the influence of the current direction of women's studies, gender-based violence, especially domestic violence, has had greater attention all over China, resulting in many achievements and a rising awareness of the issue among the general public. First, a lot of studies of domestic violence have been carried out and published as journal articles and books on theoretical, educational, and advocacy levels. In addition, research on school bullying, child sexual abuse, dating violence, violence among LGBT couples, and sexual harassment began to emerge in the past decade.

Second, a series of feminist organizations have been established, with 'anti-gender-based violence' listed as their major working task – for example, the Sex/Gender Education Forum at Sun Yat-sen University (Ai Xiaoming, founder), Maple Women's Psychological Counseling Center Hotline (Wang Xingjuan, founder and director), Media Monitor for Women's Network (Lü Pin, director), Center for Women's Law & Legal Services of Peking University (Guo Jianmei, founder; name changed to Zhongze Women Legal Aid Center in 2010), Chinese Anti-domestic Violence Network (Chen Mingxia, Feng Yuan, directors in different periods, ended in 2014), Shannxi Women, Marriage, and Family Research Association (Gao Xiaoxian, founder), etc. (Milwertz, 2003; Milwertz and Bu, 2005, 2009; Wesoky, 2002, 2007; Wang and Zhang, 2010). Some organizations, such as Tongyu (Common Language, Xu Bin, founder), Ai Bai (Keinng, Kevin, founders), and Rural Women Knowing All (Xie Lihua, founder), have been involved in researching violence in lesbian relationships, as well as school bullying and child sexual abuse, and their endeavors are extending the focus of domestic violence to involve broader gender issues including sexual and reproductive rights, LGBT rights, etc.

Third, feminists have done tremendous work and utilized all kinds of methods, including information sharing and knowledge building through media, new media and social media (websites, brochures, information sheets, email groups, QQ group newsletters, weibo, WeChat); the training of professionals; campaigns, lectures, seminars and conferences; performance arts, drama and documentaries; reading groups, etc., to raise the general public's awareness of gender-based violence and expose the general public to the idea that certain forms of behavior previously not considered as violence actually should be considered forms of gender-based violence – for example, dating violence, sexual harassment, violence in homosexual relationships, and child sexual abuse.

Nowadays domestic violence has become a household concept in urban China, and most ordinary women are well informed about the concept and have learned to use it to define their own experiences. In contrast, the concept of gender-based violence is still mostly used by scholars and activists, but not by the general public. A new generation of young feminist activists (*Qingnian Nuquan Xingdong Pai*) emerged because of the development of women's NGOs and the extensive usage of new media and social media. According to

22 *Chinese intersectionality*

Li Sipan (2014a) and Lü Pin,[3] the year 2012 was regarded as a turning point in the Chinese feminist movement since young grassroots feminist activists took action and spoke out by implementing a series of 'performance art style' activities – occupying men's toilets in order to create women-friendly environments by drawing attention to the needs of women that are daily ignored; having three young women wearing wedding gowns with fake blood as 'wounded brides' on Valentine's Day in Qianmen Street, a popular tourist location in Beijing, to remind the public of the seriousness of gender-based violence on a particular day that promotes romantic love; and supporting the domestic violence case of Kim Lee, the abused American wife of successful businessman Li Yang, the founder of the Crazy English Company. On the day when their divorce case was on trial, young feminists danced in front of the courthouse with large Chinese characters about anti-domestic violence on their backs, and distributed flyers about anti-domestic violence to the bystanders. Chinese feminists also started to fight against sexual harassment in subways, gender discrimination of girls during admission to college and other public domains. Most of these young women in their twenties or early thirties are urban daughters who have benefited from the one-child policy; they are well-educated, single, they are fans of the *Women's Voice* newsletter,[4] many of them are openly lesbian and bisexual, many of them work in NGOs for women's rights and human rights or are active volunteers for these NGOs, and some of them are performers of *The Vagina Monologues*. They are willing to fight against all kinds of gender stereotypes, discrimination, and inequality by using creative methods – weibo, performance arts, drama performances, and peaceful demonstrations.

On the academic level, Chinese studies of gender-based violence can be categorized into five types. The first type is that of the survey to explore the prevalence and risk factors of domestic violence, carried out in Chinese communities, mostly in specific sectors, and a few with a national representative sample. Here I list some representative studies:

1   According to the ACWF's survey in 2004, among the 0.27 billion families in China, 30% experience domestic violence to different degrees (He and Zuo, 2004). According to the third-wave survey on Chinese women's social status by the ACWF and the National Bureau of Statistics of China (ACWF and NBS, 2011), conducted through 125,978 questionnaires, 24.7% women were reported to suffer different kinds of domestic violence, including physical, psychological, economic, and sexual abuse.
2   The Chinese Law Society Domestic Violence Network's random sampling survey on domestic violence carried out from 2000 to 2003, which received 3,543 filled questionnaires distributed in Zhejiang, Hunan and Gansu provinces, showed that 34.7% of families encounter domestic violence.[5]
3   Using a nationally representative sample from the 1999–2000 Chinese Health and Family Life Survey, Parish et al. (2004) found that 34% of

women and 18% of men between 20 and 64 years of age had been hit during their current relationships.

4   Wang, Fang and Li (2013a) conducted a quantitative study on men's perpetration and women's experiences of gender-based violence in China with 1,103 women and 1,017 men aged 18 to 49. Among female respondents who were in intimate relationships, 39% reported experiencing physical and/or sexual intimate partner violence. Men's reporting was higher, with 52% of men reporting their own abusive physical and/or sexually violent behavior towards their intimate partners. Different types of intimate partner violence overlapped, as 27% of the men who reported they had perpetrated physical intimate partner violence also reported having perpetrated sexual violence against a partner.

The reported figures consistently suggest that domestic violence continues to be a serious and widespread issue in China. Extant research offers a snapshot of different factors associated with gender-based domestic violence in China, and gender norms associated with hegemonic patriarchal masculinities were found to lie at the root of the problem (Chan, 2012; Tang et al., 2002; Xu et al., 2001). The patriarchal organization of Chinese families and society, which affirms men's dominance over women, is a key issue cited by various authors (Chan, 2012; Tang et al., 2002; Xu et al., 2001). Within prevalent cultural narratives, men are represented as subject to violent impulses, while women are represented as liable to provoke men through nagging and disobedient conduct, or even simply by being too beautiful.

The second type of study is that using case studies to explore why women have been abused and still stay in abusive relationships. The *Cases by Women's Hotline on Domestic Violence Research Report* (The Maple Women's Psychological Counseling Center, 2001) is a representative example of this. Based on the perception that women are abused due to the patriarchal nature of society, this type of study is deeply influenced by Western feminists' concepts of 'learned helplessness' and 'battered women's syndrome' to understand women's suffering and negative impacts. They focus on 'why' rather than 'how,' and are inclined to use psychological explanations of this social phenomenon, wherein women are turned into miserable abject victims rather than survivors with agency. Based on focus group discussions conducted in Mainland China, Hong Kong, and Taiwan (Tang et al., 2002), the authors point to the existence of certain cultural scripts in Chinese societies that legitimize violence against women. They argue that, 'Chinese tend to adopt victimological shared responsibility explanations that blame women for provoking men to violence' (p. 992). In fact, little has been done to explore the experiences of women, their aspirations and expectations of intimate relationships, and how they cope with, and make meaning of, different kinds of violence involved in intimate relationships.

The third type of study on gender-based violence is that conducted through legal discussion of how to protect abused women through law, with the view

24 *Chinese intersectionality*

to enacting a special law against domestic violence. For example, Guo Jianmei's (2003) book, entitled *Domestic Violence and Legal Assistance*, and Lü and Zhu's (2011) *Report on Anti-Domestic Violence Action in China* are important examples of such studies. Stipulations against domestic violence remain spread across various laws, while an anti-domestic violence law has so far not been passed (Lü and Zhu, 2011, p. 20). However, in 2001, the marriage law included domestic violence as grounds for divorce for the first time (Guo, 2003; Hester, 2004) in Chinese history. Though the criminalization of domestic violence represents a major step forward in curbing gender-based violence, however, the criminal law only defines 'long-term,' 'repetitive,' 'serious,' and 'injurious' violence as domestic violence. Lobbying for and pushing domestic violence legislation at the provincial and national levels has been the long-term mission of many feminist NGOs. The Anti-Domestic Violence Network used to be one of the leading organizations.

Fourth, the multi-level and multi-sectoral approach has been proved globally to be the most effective method to prevent and intervene in gender-based violence, and has been introduced into China and promoted by NGOs and various levels of the Chinese government. There are numerous studies focusing on introducing the best Western practices of the approach and discussing how to establish effective multi-level and multi-sectoral approaches in the Chinese local setting. In general, compared to women's issues in the area of family planning and reproductive health, domestic violence is regarded as a less politically sensitive issue, and therefore the government engages in less surveillance and NGOs have more space to exercise their influence. The central government is more willing to turn what was formerly regarded as a private issue (*jiawu shi*) into a public matter based on the universal understanding that hitting others, especially intimate others, is terribly wrong and intolerable. In July 2008, seven central governmental bodies – including the Publicity Department, Supreme People's Procuratorate, Ministry of Public Security, Ministry of Civil Affairs, Ministry of Justice, Ministry of Public Health, and the ACWF – jointly published *Opinions on Preventing and Deterring Domestic Violence*, to regulate the responsibilities of each institution. This was regarded as a breakthrough in implementing the multi-sectoral approach to fight gender-based violence in China. However, this 'regulation' remains a matter of opinion, as there are no concrete mechanisms to institute collaboration, the responsibilities of each institution are not clear, and failure to fulfill expected responsibilities has no corresponding consequences.

Zhang Liu's (2012) case study was on Dong Shanshan, a young Beijing woman who had suffered long-term serious abuse from her husband and died due to it. She tried to escape many times, but she could not find any safe shelter available. Every time her husband managed to find her, and the violence escalated to the unbearable extreme level. In August 2009, she was found, kidnapped by her husband and taken to a remote place in Hebei Province, where she was physically and sexually abused for two months. She miscarried, and was bruised all over her body. In October 2009 she finally found a way to

Chinese intersectionality 25

escape to her grandmother's house and then was sent to the hospital. Two days later she died from multiple organ failure. This case vividly demonstrates how the dysfunctional muti-sectoral system in Beijing failed an abused woman who actively cried out for help; who had called, or whose family members had called, the police station eight times; who had gone to hospital, a psychological counseling center, a legal aid center, etc., and had done whatever could be done, but in the end could not escape from her tragic fate of being abused to death.

Finally, as part of the UN multi-country Study on Men and Violence in Asia and the Pacific, both quantitative and qualitative studies on masculinity and gender-based violence have been recently conducted in China (Wang et al., 2013a; Wang et al., 2013b). Since the majority of gender-based violence involves abusive men, it is important to examine the notion of masculinity, as well as visions of femininity. Both studies show that gender norms associated with hegemonic patriarchal masculinity were found to lie at the root of the problem of gender-based violence, which affirms men's dominance over women. Gender-based violence is strongly associated with unequal gender power relations and beliefs, and with personal exposure, and witness to or experience of violence, starting from childhood, in the home or at school. Both studies explore the possibilities of changing gender norms and preventing gender-based violence through the socialization of boys and men and the influence of media and films, especially in relation to how they relate to girls and women, and of promoting multiple non-violent masculinities by opposing hegemonic masculinity. Both studies confirm that adolescence is a critical and unique period for fostering respectful relationships and endorsing cultural norms supportive of gender equality.

When dating is struggling with violence

Dating violence is under-researched in China, either compared to studies on dating violence in the West or domestic violence studies in China. In the USA, Makepeace (1981) conducted the pioneering investigation of dating violence and found that one in five college students had experienced at least one incident of physical abuse in dating relationships. Later, dating violence has been examined in thousands of research articles and books across multiple disciplines in the USA. Straus (2004) presents the prevalence of dating violence slightly more globally – that by students at 31 universities in 16 countries (16 in North America, five in Asia or the Middle East including one in Hong Kong, one in Australia and one in New Zealand, six in Europe, and two in Latin America). At the median university, 29% of the students had physically assaulted a dating partner in the previous 12 months (range = 17% to 45%) and 7% had physically injured a partner (range = 2% to 20%). This result is consistent with the findings offered by Sugarman and Hotaling (1989) in the USA, which were that between one in three and one in two college students reported that they had experienced or been the initiator of

26 Chinese intersectionality

violence in a dating relationship. The above three studies only concern physical violence, but if verbal and psychological aggression were counted, the prevalence rate of dating violence would escalate to 64.9% (Laner, 1983), 82% (Shook et al., 2000) and 95% (Ryan, 1998).

Most of the aforementioned studies emanate from the discipline of psychology, employing a traditional positivist epistemology and using quantitative methods and CTS (Conflict Tactics Scales) to measure the prevalence of dating violence and test hypotheses of risk factors, thus acknowledging that violence in intimate relationships is a significant problem not just among married heterosexual couples but also among both heterosexual and homosexual cohabitating and dating couples (Rhatigan et al., 2005). These studies suggest that it is worthwhile to explore the social phenomenon of dating violence in a Chinese context. However, these studies also have some drawbacks: except for a few nationwide surveys (Koss, 1989; Tjaden and Thoennes, 2000) in the USA, most studies involve a small, convenient sampling, the participants being predominantly white female college and high school students. Most importantly, CTS do not offer the context of violent behavior and cannot compare to the descriptions of torture and abuse detailed in narratives (Dobash and Dobash, 2004; McHugh et al., 2005). As McHugh et al. (2005) argue:

> Reliance on a single measure that oversimplifies, reduces, or reifies our construction of violence can clearly interfere with our full understanding of these issues. From the postmodern perspective, different conceptualizations of violence and abuse can contribute to a pluralistic, complex, and multilayered conception of intimate partner abuse.
>
> (p. 323)

In order to establish a pluralistic, complex, and multilayered picture of young people's dating lives in contemporary China, this book fills a gap by systematically researching dating violence. Unlike the aforementioned studies, which use quantitative research methods and focus on prevalence rates, this study uses qualitative research methods and focuses on young people's lived experiences of violence. Unlike most studies, which use high school and college students as their sample populations, this study is not limited to students but includes all kinds of young people of different family backgrounds, education, classes, household registrations and jobs. Physical assault is overemphasized in the above studies; this study will regard violence as a continuum process and also pay attention to verbal, psychological, and sexual violence.

Many incidents of violent behavior in dating relationships are reported in newspapers, magazines and TV every day, and are discussed extensively on the Internet, which shows that people have begun to pay attention to the social phenomenon, but in a very gossipy way – violence is ignored, but romance, jealousy, and triangular relationships are emphasized. Until now, no nationwide survey of dating violence has been carried out in Mainland China, and only a few quantitative studies can provide limited information on this topic in the country. Tang Can (2005), in her study of sexual harassment in China, found that 6.51% of her sample of 169 women had experienced being forced to have sex in dating relationships. Wang Xiangxian (2009) conducted a survey with a convenient sampling of 1,015 college students in Tianjin to understand the prevalence of dating violence. She found that 58.1% participants reported that they had experienced psychological violence, 25.6% reported experiencing physical violence, among whom 12.3% reported serious physical violence and 3% reported sexual violence. Chan (2012) conducted a survey among 3,388 university students in Beijing, Shanghai and Hong Kong, and found that psychological aggression was the most common type of violence perpetrated (71.6%), more than physical violence (47.7%) or sexual violence (17.5%). Shen et al. (2012) conducted a questionnaire survey among 976 Chinese adolescents in Taiwan, Hong Kong and Shanghai, and found a perpetration rate of 27.3% and victimization rate of 39%. In 2010, one of China's leading LGBT rights organizations, Tongyu (Common Language, 2010), collected 419 questionnaires from lesbians in eight cities including Beijing, Shanghai, Anshan, Chengdu, Kunming, Nanning, Zhuhai and Guangzhou. They found that 42.2% of participants reported that they had experienced violence and abuse from their girlfriends, and that 10% of them had suffered serious violence. Yu et al. (2013) collected questionnaires from 418 gay men and 330 heterosexual men, and found that 32.8% of gay men had suffered at least one kind of dating violence and 12.4% of gay men had been threatened with outing by a partner. Among those experiencing abuse, 83.9% of gay men had never told anyone about it; this proportion was far higher than that for heterosexuals who had experienced violence. The listed information is evidence that dating violence is also a social problem in China, sharing similar prevalence rates with those in the USA, and that it exists in different age groups and in both heterosexual and homosexual intimate relationships.

Though the prevalence of dating violence (including sexual coercion) is offered in some studies of some Chinese communities, these studies fail to offer further explorations of young people's lived experiences from their own perspectives. Details on the specific events of violence, backgrounds, and the contexts of relationships are usually withheld. Since 2007, I have adopted qualitative research methods and started to publish a series of journal articles on dating violence in contemporary China, (Wang and Ho, 2007a, 2007b, 2011; Wang and Nehring, 2014). Focusing on young people's violent experiences, their practices of doing gender and sexuality, and their meaning-making process, these articles look at dating violence as an important area of study in its own right, rather than as a topic subsumed under the larger topic of domestic violence, and thus fill a gap in Chinese academic research.

28 *Chinese intersectionality*

Gender, state, and market

In this area of violence research, most studies focus on domestic violence within marital relationships, and violence in other intimate relationships, such as dating, courtship, cohabitation, and homosexual intimacy, is neglected. Even in the field of domestic violence, studies mainly focus on wife battering (Hester, 2000; Wang, 1999; Xu et al., 2001), leaving out other types of violence such as child abuse, elderly abuse, etc., and tending to focus on serious events that last a long time and even involve physical harm. Thus in China, violence always refers to, or is only reduced to, severe wife battering involving abusive husbands and abused wives. One of the most distinguishing characteristics of these studies is that they have created an exclusively victimized woman image.

This victimized image not only exists in Chinese violence research, but is shared in contemporary Chinese sociological women's studies as well, and became one of the major motivations of the second-wave feminist movement. Here the emergence of the market marks a clear-cut boundary between the lack of women's studies in the Maoist Era and the sprouting of the second-wave women's studies in the Post-Mao Era, and also makes a divide between two different images of women: those of liberated women in the Maoist Era, and victimized women in the Post-Mao Era. The images of liberated women as propaganda for the advantages of socialist New China were promoted by the political ideology; at the same time, the disruption of social science research made it extremely difficult to provide solid empirical data to explore women's victimization.

To what extent can the two images reflect the reality and shed light on the real situation for women in different periods? How were the images produced and reproduced? Who was applauding and who was discounting the images, and for what purposes? The contrasting two images and representations of liberated and victimized women in different eras lead us into a theoretical adventure: to explore the interconnection between women, the state, and the market.

Victimization of women and their representation

Hester (2000) presented a landmark argument on the emergence of the studies of violence against women in Reform-era China:

> It is argued that the reappearance of these exploitations and violations of women are both a result of 'feudal' leftovers (especially in rural areas), and the tensions created by the economic reforms (especially in cities).
>
> (p. 157)

Hester also situates domestic violence as one of the 'women problems' that re-emerged in the Post-Mao Era, together with issues of gender discrimination

Chinese intersectionality 29

in job recruiting, the difficulties of mate selection for 'left-over,' well-educated single women, women returning home, prostitution, rape, infanticide, trafficking of women, etc. (Li, 1994a; Lin, 1997; Tan, 1995; Fincher, 2014). Among Hester's (2000) arguments, two points need to be especially noted in referring to the situation in the cities: one is 'reappearance,' and the other is the suggestion that the 'reforms appear to be increasing the degree of violence against women' (p. 157).

The word 'reappearance' simply takes a binary position to imply the 'purity' of the social environment in the Maoist Era and the 'polluted' situation in the Reform Era, acknowledging that violence against women and other 'women's problems' did exist in imperial China but that in the Maoist Era they somehow disappeared, while the reform and opening up brought them out again. This conclusion echoes Milwertz's (2003) observation from the state's standpoint: 'In the 1930s, the problem of domestic violence was addressed by communist party revolutionaries. However, efforts to stem violence against women waned after the early 1950s. Only in the 1980s did ACWF and media again begin to focus public attention on violence against women' (pp. 630–631). Similarly, Fincher's (2014) book, *Leftover Women: The Resurgence of Gender Inequality in China*, makes similar mistakes. By using 'resurgence,' the title implies gender equality past and gender inequality present, which is never true since gender inequality and sexism have long been deeply embedded in the socio-cultural and political fabric of China. The claim of 'reappearance' and 'resurgence' ignores all the goals that the second-wave Chinese feminists have achieved concerning critical reflection on gender politics in the Maoist Era. The conclusion of 'reappearance' of gender-based violence is drawn mostly from feelings and is not based on empirical data, since no baseline data on domestic violence are available for the Maoist Era for the purpose of scientific comparison. Using a retrospective approach, Xu (1997) conducted questionnaire survey among 586 married women, whose ages ranged from 20 to 70, in Chengdu, Sichuan Province, and she found that the post-Mao Reform period trends in wife abuse tended to decrease or level off. However, this is only a faint voice among all the other papers in the area of violence against women, which argue that it is 'increasing' (Hester, 2000, 2004) in the Reform Era.

Hester's (2000) conclusion that the reforms appeared to be increasing the degree of violence against women in China displays an interconnection between reform and 'increasing violence.' Other arguments, such as 'violence against women is a by-product of the reform,' more directly blame the reform and the opening up of the market as the reason for the 'reappearance' of violence against women and other 'women's problems.' For a long time, the relations between gender and market have been controversial, and different feminists and sociologists have different views.

Li Xiaojiang is a representative feminist who argues that in different historical periods during the Reform Era, the market functioned differently and played different roles. According to Lu Hsiao-peng (1997), 'reform China' needs to be further classified into two periods:

30 *Chinese intersectionality*

Evidently, 1989 is here taken as a turning point in China's cultural and intellectual history. In a more euphemistic expression, Chinese historians and critics have drawn a dividing line between what they call the 'New Era' and the 'Post-New Era.' The New Era is the Post-Mao period that begins with the Reform in the late 70s. It came to a sudden end in 1989 as a result of the Tiananmen Incident.

(p. 112)

Li Xiaojiang (1994a; Rai, 1999) argues that the economic reform and 'Four Modernizations' (agriculture, industry, national defense, and science and technology) that Deng Xiaoping introduced in 1978, at the beginning of the New Era, discarded or abandoned women, and that the incompatibility of women's development and social development was pushing women to the margins of society, while in the Post-New Era the market has been represented by market economy and globalization, so that the Post-New Era 'witnesses the rise of consumerism, the commercialization of cultural production, and the expansion of the mass media and popular culture' (Lu, 1997, p. 113), thus offering chances and opportunities for women. For the Post-New Era, Li (2001) re-evaluates the impact of the market, expresses her optimistic attitude towards the World Trade Organization and globalization, and even claims that globalization is the salvation of Chinese women from those 'women's problems' created by modernization. Both the Chinese state and feminists perceive 'globalization' as pathbreaking (*jiegui*), which means that China is 'heading for the world' (*zou xiang shijie*) (Li, 2001).

The optimism was shared by the ACWF (*fulian*), which started a program called 'two studies, two competitions' (*shuangxue shuangbi*) as 'adult women's basic education' in the 1990s, which included *xue wenhua*, or 'the study of culture,' and *xue jishu*, or 'the study of technology,' to get practical technical training. These 'two studies' fed into the 'two competitions' for 'achieving economic success' and 'making social contributions' (Judd, 2011; Wesoky, 2007). This program particularly emphasizes an increase in women's *suzhi* (quality) and in market participation, reinforcing rather than overturning the gender division of labor. In this way, women's liberation is connected to 'the heart of current political culture and its discourse of modernity' (Judd, 2011; Wesoky, 2007). Thus, accepting and even embracing the market has been integral to the Chinese party-state's version of 'women's liberation,' which is also intimately tied to notions of a Chinese modernity (Wesoky, 2007, p. 343). Wesoky (2007) further argues that:

Fulian's discourses have reinforced hegemonic conceptions derived from within the party-state, including the idea that the chief salvation for women lies in their participation in the market and the particular vision of 'modernity' it promises.

(p. 344)

Chinese intersectionality 31

Therefore, in the Maoist Era, urban women began to participate in all kinds of public jobs and the workplace was the most important site for demonstrating gender equality and women's liberation. Meanwhile, in the Reform Era, the messages became ambiguous: on the one hand, the discourse of 'let women go home' emerged in the early Reform Era by the male elites' attempt to destroy the limited gender equality achievement of the Maoist Era and lure urban women to go back home to be 'virtuous wives and good mothers'; on the other hand, the ACWF encouraged women to improve their *sushi* by learning practical skills and fully participating in the employment army. Millions of rural women left their homes, many of them leaving their children behind, to migrate to the big cities and become working laborers in factories and all kinds of industry. Such women may feel liberated and vulnerable at the same time. The other group of feminists have taken a more consistently cautious position and perceive the impacts that the opening up of the market has brought to women, questioning the manner in which it has promoted gendered structures rather than transforming these structures (Wesoky, 2007). It is necessary to take a rather neutral standpoint to reflect the relationship between women and the market: some impacts of the market on women are positive, others may be rather negative; different women from different family backgrounds, and with different education levels, ethnicity, and class, may have different experiences in relation to the same market forces.

Women, nation and modernity in question

In China's long imperial history, women were long regarded more as the embodiment of the country rather than its subjects. They are traditionally credited as being symbols of the saving (such as Hua Mulan)[6] or destruction (Daji, Baoshi)[7] of the country, and constituted the gendered tropes of social morality and social immorality, respectively (chaste widows/dangerous whores). Male Confucian intellectuals established a clear teleology (good women = good nation), and then devoted much time to lecturing on women's chastity and disciplining women to be good in the name of the nation (Edwards, 2000).

In modern history from the late nineteenth century until the May Fourth/New Cultural Movement (1915–21), the deployment of modern women again became an embodied icon for China's modernity and international position relative to the West. As Edwards (2000) argues in a paper on policing Chinese modern women in Republican China,

> The Kang-Liang reform of the last years of the nineteenth century argued that the reform of the China's women was fundamental to China's modernization. The weakness of China's women represented China's national vulnerability. The logic was that China's women were letting the nation down – while China's women remained weak and crippled by foot

32 *Chinese intersectionality*

binding and ignorant, unproductive, dependent and isolated in the domestic sphere, there was no hope for the nation.

(p. 126)

Both Kang Youwei and Liang Qichao were ardent Chinese nationalists and internationalists, and their reform movement in the late nineteenth and early twentieth centuries advocated the establishment of a constitutional monarchy to save China from its predicament. They made a connection between weak women and a vulnerable country, and thus liberating women was one of the most important approaches that motivated and was practiced by intellectual reformers to make the country stronger. As many scholars (Barlow, 2004; Edwards, 2000; Greenhalgh, 2001; Rofel, 1999) argue, a narrative of salvation of oppressed women has preoccupied Chinese intellectuals and the CCP throughout the twentieth century. In the process of creating modern nationalism, both intellectual reformers and the CCP constitute 'new patriarchal elites who gain the power to produce the generic "we" of the nation' (Grewal and Kaplan, 2000, para. 6); hence the emancipation of women naturally becomes a part of the national revolution and the slogan of 'equality between men and women' becomes a signifier of Chinese modernity and 'an integral part of nationalist and class campaigns' (Zuo, 2013, p. 98). As Zhong Xueping (2006) argued, women's issues have always constituted a major part of the Chinese modern experience – as part of Chinese desire for change and questions of different modernization projects and their consequences. In Greenhalgh's (2001) paper analyzing the one-child policy and Chinese women's lives, she elucidates the relations between women and the Maoist state:

The party, – emerged as the hero that saved women from the oppressive bonds of the traditional patriarchal family. Women's liberation was inextricably linked to national liberation: in emancipating women, the party was also liberating the nation from a semicolonial, semifeudal past, transforming it into a modern, powerful nation able to reclaim its rightful place in the world.

(p. 853)

One of current Chinese feminists' most important theoretical achievements is their critique of the gender equality policy in the Maoist Era, in which 'nation' and 'class' were always situated as priorities before 'gender.' They (such as Ferguson, 1997; Li, 1994b; Liu, 1993; Meng, 1993; Ming, 1997; Tao, 1996) argue that the CCP's official position, at least since 1942, has been that Chinese women and men are equal, and this standpoint did improve women's status in a general sense. Equality between women and men became the official state policy and a representation of the success of Marxism/Maoism, the superiority of the new communist China and the march to modernization. The state enacted laws to discard oppressive marital practices and legalize divorce. Women were encouraged to participate in wage labor. However,

Chinese intersectionality 33

women in the workplace became the major (almost the only) solution to gender inequality and the embodiment of gender equality, implying that males and females were substantially the same. This non-differentiation of the two sexes produces a distorted notion of equality and brings the 'double burden'[8] to Chinese women (Li, 1994a, 1994b, 2004). Thus the images of the liberated daughter and the strong female party leader are created for the purpose of abolishing the patriarchal discriminatory construction of gender, but end up denying difference between women and men. Zuo Jiping (2013) interviewed 80 elderly women and men to explore their personal experiences of work and family in 1950s urban China, arguing that equality in the 1950s meant 'obligation equality' to the state, as both genders were molded into state persons to suppress family autonomy and individual freedom, while in the home traditional gendered roles remained rather intact. Meanwhile, Gao Xiaoxian and Ma Yanyi (2006) focused on the 'silver flower contest,' a competition for the 'high-yield cotton plot,' in rural Shaanxi Province in 1950s China, and argued that the socialist state's development policy became intertwined with policies for women's emancipation, with rural women empowered to challenge gender and class hierarchies while they simultaneously remained constrained by existing gender norms and practices of gender inequality.

During the Maoist Era, some new metaphors, images and characters, such as 'Iron Girls' (*tie guniang*), 'holding up half the sky' (*banbiantian*), and 'daughter of the party' (*dang de nüer*) – strong, robust, muscular women who boldly performed physically demanding jobs traditionally done by men – were celebrated in newspapers, pamphlets, and posters (Honig, 2002), and become socialist clichés, embodying the myth of class struggle and liberation and advancing the state's ideological control over every corner of intellectual and social life. Jin Yihong et al.'s (2006) article on rethinking the 'iron girls' campaign in the Cultural Revolution clearly shows that the women's labor force functions as a 'cistern' – backup resource – to boost socialist economic development, and the image of the 'iron girl' and the discourse of 'men and women are the same' were just created to make the political mobilization passionate and efficient.

Since women's liberation is only in the public and not in the private spheres, the powerful liberated women images were portrayed in political and social campaigns, but we know much less about what was happening behind closed doors at home. The workplace was the only location to display women's empowerment, which may explain why, though there are so many strong women characters and images in socialist literature, none of them ever speaks a word about their gender and sexuality (Meng, 1993). Thus these women again were turned into an 'empty signifier' (Meng and Dai, 2004) of the socialist liberation, and their gender identities, bodies and sexualities remained invisible. Such is Xier, in the revolutionary model drama (*yangbanxi*), *The White-Haired Girl* (*baimaonü*),[9] who, to use contemporary language, experienced acquaintance rape by the evil landlord Huang Shiren. However, in the public discourse of that time, Xier's body and sexuality have

34 *Chinese intersectionality*

completely faded from the story, the empty conceptual space being marked by the term 'class conflict' between farmers and landowners, and the political code entirely displaces the sexual code as a functioning part of the story (Meng, 1993, p. 121). In the Maoist Era, women were situated in circumstances filled with extreme socialist optimism and strong ideology of 'regarding country as family' (*yiguoweijia*), which made intimate partner violence invisible since romantic relationships were devalued as not significant on an ideological level. Meanwhile, violence on the platform of class struggle was much displayed publicly, either by the Red Guards' (*hongweibin*, both men and women) ruthless abuse of 'class enemies,' including their teachers and principals; and the public shaming, humiliation and criticism of 'loose women' – unfaithful women always paid a higher price than men in the age of abstinence of sex outside marriage, as only sex within marriage was legitimate in Maoist China, and a lot of women were accused of being 'loose' just because they paid attention to their appearance. When scholars claim that the gender-based violence 'reappears' in the Reform Era, they ignore the extensive existence of all kinds of violence against citizens during the turmoil of the Cultural Revolution. How does the public deployment of violence make society regard violence as socially acceptable behavior and tolerate violence within intimate relationships? This is an unsolved question to be answered.

Women's images in neo-liberal China

Although Chinese feminists criticize furiously the gender policy of the Maoist Era, some of them also inconsistently attribute 'women's problems' in the Post-socialist Era to 'their lacking of state protection' (Liu et al., 1998). Actually, protection is always the other side of survcillance, and the state's protection of women in the Maoist Era was just an expression of ideological benevolence under the gaze of national power, which asked women to be strong and thus become symbols of their collective liberation and therefore of the nation's emancipation. Also, state protection has, in its implicit epistemological foundation, contained prejudice against the particularities of the female sex and been verbally formulated in this way in post-revolutionary China. The laws or regulations, although intended to be pro women, are nonetheless primarily based on the assumption of a 'weaker' female sex in terms of its inborn disadvantage, physiologically and psychologically (Lin, 1996).

While others take a different standpoint and propose a new concept of 'gender equality' to replace the official gender discourse of 'equality between men and women,' since they believe that the latter 'connotes the control of women by an authoritarian socialist patriarchy' (Wang and Zhang, 2010, p. 48), Wang Zheng and Zhang Ying (2010) argue that:

> Their aim is not simply to replace an obsolete concept with a new concept that has more analytical power. Rather, they mean to put into play a

feminist challenge to the continuing power of the party-state and a feminist demand for a new notion of citizenship that acknowledges women's agency and autonomy.

(p. 48)

The powerful market in the neo-liberal era has challenged and disrupted the unitary state gender discourse of the Maoist Era and has created more spaces for multiple discourses, among which women attempt to shake off the idea of ideological benevolence and place themselves in the context of having comparatively more freedom and autonomy. In this situation, researching violence against women and other women's issues becomes possible and multiple images of women emerge.

In the 1920s and 1930s, there were two types of images of modern women: one was women students and revolutionaries conceived of as politically aware, patriotic, independent, and educated; and the other was that of glamorous, fashionable, desirable, and available women, which was emerging in the commercial context of Shanghai (Edwards, 2000), and which served as a referent for Western cosmopolitanism (Ko and Wang, 2006). Intellectual reformers appreciated the first image and refuted the second one as being the same as that of the fake modern women of the May Fourth Movement. The Maoist Era inherited this discourse, denouncing the latter image and advocating the former. As Ko and Wang (2006) put it, 'new women' in 'New China' break with the West and the portrayals of Soviet working-class heroines. The images of 'liberated women' were the formulations of the state discourse and party mobilization, though women were also actively involved in, practiced and enhanced their identity as new modern women. Women who paid attention to their looks were regarded as worshiping the Western degenerate lifestyle and were even degraded as 'loose women' in the Cultural Revolution. Wang Anyi's novel, *The Song of Everlasting Sorrow* (*Chang Hen Ge*), which traces the life story of a young Shanghainese girl from the 1940s all the way till her death after the Cultural Revolution, is a great example that shows the historical transformations of images of women. History somehow 'repeats' itself, and the open market since the end of the 1970s has witnessed the second women's image in the 1920s and 1930s bloom and flush all over neo-liberal China. Fashion models, actresses, singers, flight attendants (*kongjie*), Miss China/Global, etc., turn into symbols of beauty and success that every woman dreams of, and this time the state no longer opposes the rising 'Westernized bourgeoisie women images,' even promoting it for the purpose of economic development. Focusing on the full bloom of beauty pageants, Xu and Feiner (2007) argue that China's neo-liberal policies divert attention to the personal, promote 'Beauty Economics' (*meinü jingji*) and consumerism, and reinforce and symbolize commodification. Emphasis on femininity becomes a strong characteristic among the aforementioned desirable-women images. Some feminists argue that it is an advancement for Chinese women to re-emphasize gender difference and femininity in the neo-liberal era rather

36   *Chinese intersectionality*

than to promote the gender sameness of the Maoist Era. This argument may be valid to some extent, considering the peculiar gender politics of Maoist China; however, it has the potential risk of being exploited according to two canons to justify the purposes of those who employ them: on the one hand, femininity is traditionally associated with the image of 'virtuous wife and good mother' under the patriarchal system, and of weak women in 'old China,' a collective icon that embodies internalized Confucian ideas; on the other hand, 'bourgeois feminine imaginary' and 'female essence' (*nüxing qizhi*) (Zhong, 2006) is strongly promoted by consumerism, thus serving as the backdrop for the market, in which women's bodies, sexuality, and femininity are commercialized, turning women into objects under the male gaze.

The neo-liberal era becomes a big stage on which images of both victimized and liberated women negotiate with one another and generate diverse images of women. Pei and Ho (2006) illustrate four images of women from the 1960s until now: 'iron girls' (*tie guniang*, the 'iron girl campaign,' occurred in 1966–76, with the claim that 'what men can do women also can do' in order to break gender boundaries in employment opportunities); 'strong women' (*nü qiangren* – the term emerged in the Reform Era and especially refers to those women who achieve career and economic success); 'beautiful women writers' (*meinü zuojia*, referring to young women writers, mostly born in the 1970s and 1980s, whose writing is directly related to their gender and sexuality); and 'Super Girls' (*chaoji nüsheng*, a Chinese singing talent show similar to *American Idol*, which was launched by Hunan Satellite Television in 2004, on which the participants demonstrated different types of femininity).

The first image, that of 'iron girls,' belongs to the Maoist Era, and the latter three images emerged during the Reform Era. Pei and Ho (2006) discussed how young women born in the 1970s in Shanghai construct their femininity and perform their gender through negotiation with different images which have virtuous, masculinized, commercialized and androgynous qualities. Based on the textual analysis of four different women's magazines, Chang Yuliang (2009) presents three different images of women – 'iron girl,' 'better half' (*xian neizhu*, women who sacrifice their own career ambitions to be their husbands' strong domestic supporters and family caregivers), and 'fashion girl,' to describe the transformation and representation of images of women within women's magazines in different historical periods, the diversity of these images in the Reform Era, and the negotiation of images of women with state capitalism and consumerism. The aforementioned studies pay attention to the existence of multiple images of women and symbolize women's situations and their tactics for dealing with them. From these studies, we can say clearly that images of women are always changing and contest each other; there are always multiple truths about how women want to be or what women can be; and in different historical stages, certain political investments always favor certain narratives and images over others.

As for the dominant image of victimized women in the current sociological women's studies, Dorothy Ko's (1994) retrospective of the origin and development of victimized women images shows that both images are essentialist and twisted together, and cannot be separated:

> The identification of women with backwardness and dependency has been associated with China's modernization movements; this image of Chinese women as victims was intensified during and by the May Fourth New Cultural Movement, re-enforced by the Chinese Communist Party's need to claim credit for the 'liberation' of women, and readily accepted [and one might add, stereotyped] among Western readers.
>
> (p. 10)

Under strong political and ideological surveillance, women in the urban setting enter the multiple-discourse territory enforced by the reform and opening up, migration, urbanization, and global capitalism. They may represent individual vulnerability, weakness and helplessness, and at the same time may demonstrate their autonomy, resistance and agency. The broad social, political, and economic consequences of the transition in contemporary China from a planned socialist to a free market economy constitute a significant area of sociological research, in which gender studies cannot ignore the matrix of state and market, the 'gradually neoliberalizing market that coexists with a still strong state' (Greenhalgh, 2010, p. 38), and particularly migration, urbanization, consumerism, cosmopolitanism and global exposure, all elements that are playing out within the matrix. However, different scholars have different viewpoints on the relations between gender, state and market.

Many current Chinese gender and sexuality studies and cultural studies, such as those by Farrer (1997, 2002) and other scholars (Ferry, 2003a, 2003b; Pei, 2013; Knight, 2003; Weber, 2002), emphasize the individual agency and subjectivity that has arisen during the retreat of the state and the growth of the market, based on personal narratives and cultural creations, and the fact that young urban adults are regarded as capable of establishing their unruly sex and dating culture. Therefore, individualism, professionalism, opportunities and choices have become embodied symbols of the progressive open market and the retreat of the state. Other studies, however, pay more attention to the interactive conspiracy between the state and market to set women in a rather disadvantaged position. Fincher's (2014) study shows how the state media create and promote the 'leftover women' phenomenon, and how Chinese women have been shut out of the biggest accumulation of real-estate wealth in history, in their desperation to get married before becoming 'left over.' Friedman's (2006) book, *Intimate Politics: Marriage, the Market, and State Power in Southeastern China*, paints a vivid portrait of 'Hui'an Women' – a group of women officially classified as ethnic Han, but having unique marital customs and fashion style, who display their ambivalence to tradition and modernity. At the beginning of the Reform Era, they began to abandon their traditional customs and dress style while the local government

38   *Chinese intersectionality*

has started to promote the traditional dress as 'natural beauty,' and therefore a 'tourist attraction.'

In the area of gender, labor and China studies, discussing the gender issue in the intersection of state and market becomes popular for analyzing gender dynamics and the marginalization of women. Adopting Foucault's concepts of subjectivity and governmentality, Pun Ngai (2005) inherits the post-colonialism feminists' view of globalization as a process of recolonization which reproduces the exploitation of Third World women (Alarcon et al., 1999; Grewal and Kaplan, 1994, 2000; Mohanty, 2002, 2003). Her book, *Made in China: Women Factory Workers in a Global Workplace*, situates women's exploitation within the matrix of state oppression and global capitalism. She argues that the term *dagongmei* (female working laborer) embodies a specific ethics of self, construed at the particular moment when private and transnational capital engulfed contemporary China. As a new social identity, it reveals the story of how a state socialist system is giving way to the capitalist global economy and how capitalist practices depend entirely on a complex web of regulations, and on class, rural-urban differences, and sexual relations. Liu Jieyu's (2007) study shows how working women, especially older, less educated women from the Cultural Revolution generation, lost out in the process of China's economic restructuring. Hanser's (2008) book, *Service Encounters: Class, Gender and the Market for Social Distinction in Urban China*, compares service interactions in three different retail fields, including fancy shopping malls, state-owned department stores, and marketplaces; she argues that 'gender and generation are set within a broader imagery of transition and become the raw material for the production of class and status distinctions' (p. 18) in contemporary China.

The aforementioned books share some qualities that are useful, particularly for this study of dating violence. First, they arc more or less influenced by Foucault's concept of 'governmentality,' regarding the state discourse as 'a combination of governing and political rationality – the particular regime of modern government that takes population, its size, health, welfare, security, and prosperity, as its primary end' (Greenhalgh, 2008, p. 7). Second, they experimentally embrace the intersection of gender dynamics and class analysis in the contemporary context of Post-Mao China, either based on different gender (e.g. urban middle-aged female workers were the first to be laid off in the Reform Era), citizenship (e.g. urban or rural household registration – *dagongmei* as 'half peasant and half proletariat' (p. 193), age (e.g. young, sexualized, and overtly feminine workers in a fancy shopping mall or old, sturdy, gender-neutral female workers in a state-owned department store), etc. Most importantly, these studies point out a new conspiracy relation between state and market in dealing with gender issues. As Greenhalgh (2010) argues in her book, *Cultivating Global Citizens*:

> With the rise of a more confident China in recent years, however, growing numbers of analysts are seeing not state retreat or retrenchment, but

Chinese intersectionality 39

rather successful adaptation to a complex domestic and international environment ...

(p. 79)

Market logics affect state practice, while state logics deeply influence market choices ... The state is strategically using market dynamics and neoliberal-type principles and policy instruments to its own advantages.

(pp. 39–40)

The study of gender issues in contemporary China should not ignore the complex relations between the state and market, their benefits and drawbacks, their continuities, disruptions, contingencies, and influence on each other, as well as their mutual repulsion. Wang Zheng[10] recently argued that, in historical perspective, it is right now that women in China are facing their most serious predicaments. Schaffer and Song (2007) came to the following conclusion concerning all the challenges that women are facing today:

Women in China have had to confront a powerful array of patriarchal traditions, ancient and modern, that include the enduring Confucian belief systems and more recent Communist ideologies, compounded by the demands of a new market economy and the influx of Western knowledge systems – a profusion of 'isms.'

(p. 18)

In the next section, I will focus on the discussion of the interaction between Western feminism and Chinese feminism, especially on how the interaction impacts gender-based violence research. In the way they develop indigenous studies, Chinese violence research scholars adopt Confucian ideas to demonstrate their theoretical construction of the uniqueness of Chinese women's situation today. How can we combine the discussion of the intersection between gender, state and market, the interaction of Chinese and Western feminism, the theoretical development of Western feminism, and the dislocation of Confucian ideas, and establish a new theoretical framework to study gender-based violence and other gender issues in China?

Feminist interaction between local and global

The development of Chinese feminism in terms of its interaction with Western feminism can be concluded by introducing Western concepts and theory, presenting how they have correspondence to or conflict with each other, and attempting to develop indigenous studies. Spakowski (2011) has a good illustration of the process:

40   *Chinese intersectionality*

Feminism in China over the past ten to fifteen years has been marked by three related characteristics. The first is the introduction of 'Western' feminism, with 'gender,' as a core theory import. The second is the articulation of the 'trouble' this import of Western theory has caused. Chinese feminist texts abound with terms such as trouble (*mafan*), difficulty (*kunjing, kunnan*), predicament (*kunjing*), deficiency (*quexian*), and clash (*chongtu*) which are used to express worries about the consequences of this new orientation of feminism in China. They prove that the import of Western theory and the transition to 'gender' as the basic category of analysis is not the logical development some authors claim it to be. A third characteristic is the search for an identity for Chinese feminism in a global context. Differing from an earlier preoccupation with defining the feminism of the reform period vis-à-vis the Maoist approach to women's liberation, Chinese scholars, under the impact of Western theory, rather turn to spatial definitions of Chinese feminism vis-à-vis international feminism and adopt the notion of the 'local' to define their place in the world.

(p. 31)

Within the development of Chinese violence research, the above description seems valid. However, we can see quite clearly that the connotation of 'Western feminism' here mostly refers to feminism in North America, Europe, and maybe Australia and New Zealand, while Chinese feminism mostly refers to the Han context. Therefore this kind of dialogue originally has some limitations: 1) it ignores the dialogue between Chinese feminism with feminists in other developing areas, including India and South America; 2) it ignores the inner dialogue within 'greater China,' especially that among the Mainland, Hong Kong and Taiwan; 3) it ignores the interaction between Chinese feminism and feminism of Japan, South Korea, and other Asia countries; and 4) it pays rather little attention to feminist issues in minority areas.

Bearing all these limitations in mind, it is important to acknowledge that Chinese violence research has been deeply influenced by Western feminism, especially in the following ways. First, cross-cultural encounters and international exchange, including international conferences and events, seminars, academic exchanges (Chinese scholars/feminists were trained in the West, Chinese scholars/feminists go to the West for one- or two-year fellowships, Western scholars visit China and give talks), and training workshops before and especially after the 1995 Beijing Conference (Hester, 2000, 2004; Milwertz, 2003; Milwertz and Bu, 2005, 2009; Wesoky, 2002; Wang and Zhang, 2010). Second, translations of Western feminist theory have introduced and adopted Western concepts, such as domestic violence and dating violence, violence against women, intimate partner violence and gender-based violence, within Chinese academia, and these have helped Chinese feminists name these phenomena. Naming per se is a powerful strategy for dragging social phenomena from private life to become public issues and for bringing them from invisibility to visibility. As Ko and Wang (2006) argue, feminism is always already a global discourse, and the history of its local reception is a history of the politics of translation. Sometimes, however, translations are misinterpretations and may miss unique cultural distinctions. Third, Chinese feminists have adopted some global feminist campaign strategies, for example, the annual '16 days of violence against women activism' (starting on November 25 with the UN International Day to End Violence Against Women and ending on December 10 with UN Human Rights Day) has become an annual activity on many college and university campuses, with performances of the 'Vagina Monologues' a part of it. All these activities raise consciousness among the general public and help women to speak out. Fourth, many big gender-based violence research and advocacy projects have been financially supported by international organizations (UNWomen, UN Population Fund) and Western foundations (Ford Foundation) (Kaufman, 2012). The research methods, theoretical approaches, and research findings are mainly influenced by the standpoints of Western donors and foundations.

In the USA, in order to fight 'violence against women,' second-wave radical feminists have organized consciousness-raising groups to help women to 'speak out' since the 1970s (Alcoff and Gray, 1993; Mardorossian, 2002; Naples, 2003), and to analyze violence against women (DeKeseredy, 1989; DeKeseredy and Kelly, 1995) as an abuse of male power that occurs as a result of sexism, patriarchal society, and phallocentrism. Within this theoretical framework, the almost exclusive focus is on the suffering of the 'victims' and the application of the trauma paradigm to explore such consequences as depression, anxiety, low self-esteem, feelings of isolation and stigmatization, re-victimization, substance abuse, and sexual difficulties (Armsworth and Stronck, 1999; Denov, 2004; Gilfus, 1999; Lubell and Peterson, 1998; Rachman, 2000). These feminists focus on the psychological injury that women have suffered as a result of being abused, and on empowering women politically and educating society at large about the dimensions of violence against women. However, they have also created a dominant, stereotypical, expert institutional dichotomy of 'abusive husband/boyfriend and abused wife/girlfriend' and, more generally, of 'men exercising power over women' (Lamb, 1999, p. 4).

This is exactly what Chinese feminists have done in the field of gender-based violence in the last decade. They have almost fully adopted the Western radical feminist theoretical framework for understanding gender-based violence in the Chinese context, so that even the research foci are similar to those of existing Western studies, such as that of pathologizing individual battered women 'who don't leave' particularly through the adopted concepts of 'learned helplessness,' the 'cycle of violence,' and 'battered women's syndrome,' focusing on the suffering of the victims and the application of a trauma paradigm to explore such consequences as depression, anxiety, low self-esteem, etc., that result from the experience of violence. They have achieved a lot, as mentioned, but they have failed to jump out of the theoretical framework of Western second-wave feminism, trapped in the binary

42 *Chinese intersectionality*

feminist victim discourse and so in creating a victimized women image in the New Era. They have failed to realize that this discourse tends to deprive the 'victims' of 'authority regarding the complexity of their own experience and may inadvertently reinforce viewing audience presuppositions that violence is an event that women cannot prevent, recover from, or explain without expert advocacy' (Hengehold, 2000, p. 194). They have also failed to recognize the strengths that 'victims' often exhibit in the face of extreme injury and develop in the process of surviving (Gilfus, 1999). While Chinese feminists still stick to the Western second-wave feminists' standpoint, Western feminism had already developed into the third wave in the mid-1990s (Heywood and Drake, 1997) and established intersectionality theory to deal with gender-based violence.

Third-wave feminism in the West contains elements of the second-wave critique of violence against women and power structures while it also acknowledges and makes use of the concepts of desire, pleasure, danger, agency and subjectivity to redefine the power of those structures. The new wave of violence research (Alcoff and Gray, 1993; Bass and Davis, 1994; Dunn, 2005; Gilfus, 1999; Hengehold, 2000; Heywood and Drake, 1997; Naples, 2003) has involved a change from victim feminism to power feminism, and has tended to use the term 'survivor,' in place of 'victim,' of the abuse situation, because 'victims are often presented as trapped, and survivors, conversely, are shown as making choices, they are constructed in ways that place them at opposite poles of an agency continuum' (Dunn, 2005, p. 2). Compared to the word 'victim,' the term 'survivor' makes visible the two sides of lives: one a passive picture of victimization, the other an active and positive script for resistance, coping, and surviving. There are two exemplary books that clearly symbolize the transition of violence research from victim feminism to power feminism: one is Nicola Gavey's (2005) book, *Just Sex? The Scaffolding of Rape*, and the other is Sharon Lamb's (1999) edited book *New Version of Victims: Feminists Struggle with the Concept*. The main focus of the former book is rape and sexual coercion: the author sees that 'rape on a continuum with other forms of sexual victimization, however, opens up a new vista for considering the specifically gendered nature of sexual coercion' (p. 12). The latter book deals with the issue of violence against women and victimization of all kinds of violence. Both books 'proceed to a more nuanced approach toward victimization while retaining feminist politics and sensitivity to those who have suffered' (Lamb, 1999, p. 5), highlight women's agency and resistance to cope with their experience of being abused, and shift the scholarship emphasis from attending to the pathology of abused women in the 'victim' camp, to theorizing the complicated 'women-centered' experiences that are embedded and constructed socially and historically.

The rise of intersectionality

During the transition of new violence research, intersectionality theory has been rising to become a 'buzzword' (Davis, 2011), 'fast-travelling concept'

(Knapp, 2005) and predominant method (MacKinnon, 2013), and an approach for tackling violence in intimacy. The term 'intersectionality' was introduced by Kimberlé Crenshaw (1993), when she discussed issues of black women's employment in the USA. Collins (1990) renamed black feminist thought as intersectionality theory, which describes race, class and gender as a 'matrix of domination,' 'interlocking system of oppression,' 'multiple axes of inequality,' 'simultaneous oppression,' and 'multiple jeopardies,' etc., thus challenging the second-wave radical feminism for its alleged essentialism, white solipsism, and failure to address adequately the simultaneous and multiple oppressions that women experience (Andersen, 2005; Andersen and Collins, 1994; Collins, 1998; Eriksson, 2013; MacKinnon, 2013; Mann and Huffman, 2005). For Collins and her associates, the key phrase of intersectionality theory is the race-class-gender matrix, by which they emphasize the race discrimination, class stratification, and gender inequality in the USA.

Later, postcolonial third-wave feminism (Alarcon et al., 1999; Grewal and Kaplan, 1994, 2000; Mohanty, 2002, 2003) inherited and developed the intersectionality theory by embracing a macro-structural and relational analysis of oppression, with 'state-nation' as a keyword joining in the former matrix of race, class, and gender. Intersectionality thus set itself within a dialogue with 'local' and 'global' within the context of globalization.

The intersectionality theory also provoked some critiques: first, that gender, sex and race may be more like static 'categories' or 'locations,' and fail to illustrate the uniqueness of everything, every person, every event, every context, and every intersection (MacKinnon, 2013; Nash, 2013); second, Erel et al. (2010) critique that 'through the angle of intersectionality, we might grasp how a subject position is constituted by gender, race, sexuality, and class, but how this subject position is related to other subjective positions in a specific field of power and domination is not necessarily addressed' (p. 64); and third, other scholars critique that intersectionality deals with local rather than translocal situations (Anthias, 2013).

In response to these critiques, Prins (2006) proposes 'constructive intersectionality,' Ferree (2011) promotes 'interactive intersectionality,' and Walby (2007) creates 'complexity theory' to further this idea of intersectionality to emphasize 'social reality as multidimensional, lived identities as intertwined, and systems of oppression as meshed and mutually constitutive' (May, 2014, p. 96). Walby (2007) argues that intersectionality is an active system with both positive and negative feedback effects, non-linearity of relations, and non-hierarchical overlaps among institutions. Intersectionality cannot be located at any one level of analysis, whether individual or institutional, which links the agency and structure, lived body and social location, power and knowledge, particular and universal, the micro-political and the macro-political within historical, cultural, material, and political dimensions.

Intersectionality as a concept, theory and method has seldom been introduced into Mainland China. Most mainstream Chinese feminism (for example, Wang, 1999; Tang et al., 2002), as mentioned, still adopts victim

44 *Chinese intersectionality*

discourse from the second-wave Western feminism, and thus creates the binary image of 'male abuser and female abused,' focusing on the physical and psychological injury that women have suffered as a result of being abused, ignoring their life complexities and failing to recognize the agency and strengths that 'victims' exhibit. Spivak's (1996) concept of 'strategic essentialism' is useful to explain why Chinese feminists have chosen to use the dichotomous 'perpetrator and victim' perspective for understanding gender-based violence, as it is efficient for them in consciousness raising and establishing temporary solidarity for the purpose of social action in the contemporary moment.

The intersectionality theory is inspiring for this study since it acknowledges not only the gender difference, but the differences between women (Davis, 2011) as well, by including all kinds of lenses of analysis besides gender – class, race, sexuality, state, market, etc. – to capture the complexity and diversity of young people's daily dating experiences, the special locality of Beijing and the socio-cultural particularity of current China. The next huge challenge is how to adapt the intersectionality theory to the Chinese context for understanding gender issues, including gender-based violence; how to understand categories including class, race, ethnicity, etc., in the Chinese context. In this particular case study of dating violence, does the existing Western analytical matrix need to be revised? Are there some categories that need to be added or emphasized which are missing in the model? In different circumstances within dating and intimate relationships, which factor matters more and which less within the matrix? How can I combine the adaptation of intersectionality theory with the current discussion on the interaction between gender, state and market? How can we learn from the experience of interaction between Chinese and Western feminists and their endeavors to do indigenous studies? How can we learn from the postcolonial intersectionality approach to deal with translocal issues within a particular geographical location?

Indigenous endeavor and the dislocation of Confucian ideas

The idea of doing indigenous studies is not only a creation of feminists concerned with gender-based violence, but also an idea running through all Chinese women's studies, sociological studies, and through all the disciplines of social science and humanities. Chow et al. (2004) elucidate:

> Chinese scholars use *bentu* (indigenous) to refer to studies originating in China in contrast to those coming from outside (*wailai*) and use *bentuhua* (literally, to make it indigenous) to refer to the process of critically applying overseas scholarship to the Chinese situation. On one hand, after China reopens [sic] itself, these scholars felt an urgent need to find out what there is Western feminist scholarship [sic]. On the other hand, they are conscious of the threat of China's burgeoning women's studies being

limited, marginalized, and/or colonized by well-developed, well-financed international women's studies or by movements dominated by Western feminism.

(p. 175)

Xu Feng (2009) critically argues that most efforts of indigenization within Chinese women's studies are essentially about contributing to Western theories through rich Chinese empirical data, and that this occurs principally through numerous reports written to international agencies such as the UN and the Ford Foundation. Other scholars, such as Li Xiaojiang (2004), also remind feminists to be aware of the danger of losing the indigenous voice by using the foreign funds and totally following Western theoretical frameworks. Xu Feng (2009) is also right to point out that the desire to indigenize Western theories reflects an understandable anxiety of Chinese scholars to contribute to theory building, so that China is not merely a 'case' against which Western-based theories are tested.

Bentuhua, for Chinese feminists, means establishing Chinese women's studies 'with Chinese characteristics.' Spakowski (1994) raised a suspicion of women's studies with Chinese characteristics based on her Western standpoint and her investigation that Chinese women's studies scholars have not yet provided an adequate justification for why the process of women's studies needs specific Chinese characteristics. Using Barlow's (2004) words to reply to Spakowski's suspicion, 'Chinese feminism is indisputably Chinese and it is feminism' (p. 5). Local and global is a paradox filled with oppositions and consolidations. Tensions and resistances exist inevitably between the Western feminism and Chinese feminism, while doing indigenous studies seems to be an only way out for Chinese feminism, although this strategy is filled with problems as well. On the one side, Chinese feminists would like to learn from Western feminist theory to reflect on Chinese women's issues, but they are worried about being critiqued for copying Western feminism. On the other side, they are keen to establish indigenous studies to resist the hegemony of Western feminism, but they are also worried about being critiqued for self-orientalizing or flag-waving nationalism. Indeed, in their way of establishing indigenous studies, Chinese violence research scholars find Confucian ideas to be a convenient tool to shake off Western thoughts and influence and develop their indigenous studies.

As Hester (2004), in her review article, 'Future Trends and Developments: Violence Against Women in Europe and East Asia,' points out, Chinese scholars have often justified and explained violence against women through recourse to 'Confucian ideas regarding men as dominant and superior, with emphasis on women as virtuous and inferior' (p. 1432), explaining how Chinese women are tolerant of abuse because of the internalization of such beliefs (Gil and Anderson, 1999; Tang et al., 2002; Wang, 1999; Xu et al., 2001). It seems that Hester (2004) is applauding the fact that Chinese 'feminists and others working in the field of violence against women have

46 Chinese intersectionality

increasingly questioned these traditional views' (p. 1432). Instead of simply agreeing with Hester's appreciation of Chinese feminist endeavors, I cannot help but wonder: are Chinese feminists questioning 'these traditional views' or are they just borrowing them conveniently to resist Western feminism? Here I also would like to make explicit that in this study, I prefer to use the concept of 'Confucian ideas' rather than 'Confucianism,' because Confucianism is a complex ethical and philosophical system of moral, social, political, and religious thought.[11] Generally, to use the concept 'Confucianism' as existing feminist studies do would bring the discussion into a paradoxical situation. I argue that feminist appropriation of Confucianism is a cultural dislocation (*cuowei*). In his article 'Background and Dislocation,' Lei Yi (1995) defined cultural dislocation as a betrayal of traditions and a self-orientalism in relation to Westernized globalization, which is precisely seen in the heaviness of the cultural body of local practices and the theoretical bias of a Westernized reading. In the area of gender-based violence research, Confucian ideas as cultural dislocation are fully demonstrated in the following ways.

First, Confucian ideas are regarded as a unique cultural form in China, representing Chinese characteristics; therefore Chinese feminists appropriate them to carry out indigenous studies and to resist the influence of Western feminism. However, the term 'Chinese characteristics' is appropriated from the political ideology rather than an innovation of Chinese feminists. The concept of 'establishing China with Chinese characteristics' ('socialist market economy') was first proposed by Deng Xiaoping in the 1980s in order to incorporate the market into the planned economy in China. Also, adopting the uniqueness of Confucianism to develop indigenous studies was not the creation of feminists, as it echoes the revival of Confucianism in recent years – Confucian ideas of *he* (harmony) have emerged in the national leaders' speech of harmonious society (*hexie shehui*); the 2008 Olympic Games opening ceremony highlighted Confucian themes; the epic movie *Confucius* was being made in 2010; a new statue of Confucius appeared in Tiananmen Square in 2011; and 440 branches of Confucius Institutes have been established in 120 countries.

Second, when Chinese feminists appropriate Confucian ideas to develop indigenous studies and explain the phenomenon of violence against women, it seems that the Confucian sexist ideology, or 'Chinese tradition,' is regarded as the origin of women's oppression through men's violence; therefore, discarding it seems to be a resolution of this situation of oppression. However, the invention of an ahistorical 'Chinese tradition' that is feudal, patriarchal, and oppressive was never the creation of the current Chinese feminists, and may reflect three divergent ideological and political traditions – the May Fourth New Culture Movement, the Communist Revolution, and Western feminist China studies (Li, 2000b). Although Chinese feminists regard this approach as a theoretical innovation to shake off the influence of Western feminism, however, Western gender experts and sinologists have achieved a lot on the interaction between gender and Confucianism (Ko, 1994; Mann, 1997).

Ironically, the viewpoints on Confucian ideas are different among different groups of feminists in China. State feminism regards Confucian ideas of harmony as an effective tool against domestic violence – for example, the ACWF has promoted 'encouraging a social mood where husband and wife can get on in a harmonious atmosphere' (Hester, 2000, p. 159). Xu Weihua, a senior lawyer of the ACWF, explains that 'family with five good values (*wuhao jiating*)' are a part of this 'very traditional programme' to establish harmonious families and prevent domestic violence, which includes emphasizing the mutual respect among marital couples, respecting the old and the young, getting on with one's neighbors and protecting the environment (Hester, 2000). The 'tradition' to which Xu Weihua refers is the Confucian value system based on *li* (ritual). Thus, concerning violence against women, Confucian ideas are either the cause or the resolution, either something valuable representing Chinese culture and resisting Western influence, or something 'feudal' needing to be discarded. The meaning of Confucian ideas gets blurred in the different interpretations of Chinese feminists.

In using Confucian ideas to explore indigenous Chinese women's studies, Chinese feminists project themselves into the state discourses. Using 'harmonious family' to oppose violence in intimate relationships is pretty much like the 'harmonious society' (*hexie shehui*) that former President Hu Jintao preached as an ideal conception to regulate Chinese internal and external affairs. Moreover, establishing women's studies with Chinese characteristics is essentially not very different from the national policy of building a socialist country with Chinese characteristics of the Deng era. The logic of Chinese feminists' appropriation of Confucian ideas to explain violence against women is consistent with the state discourse that women were oppressed in the old semi-feudal, semi-colonial China and liberated in the 'new' China, because Confucian ideas in some way have been turned into signifiers of the sexist ideology and patriarchal society ever since the May Fourth Movement. To all appearances, Chinese feminism and the Maoist discourse provide different images of women: victimized women and liberated women. Behind the scenes, these monolithic images of women are both essential national allegories of the Reform Era and the Maoist Era. When the appropriation of Confucian ideas becomes a cultural dislocation in post-socialist China, Chinese feminists are trapped into lacking their own voice to dialogue with Western feminism or to negotiate with the political system.

In summary, Chinese feminism has danced with bonds among competing discourses and struggled to raise its own voice. Chinese feminists are either influenced too much by Western feminism or have lost their standpoint by identifying with the state discourse. Chinese feminist scholars and activists are deeply influenced by Western feminism. They have adopted the second-wave feminist viewpoint on violence against women and apparently have not caught up with the new theoretical development of intersectionality. At the same time, Chinese feminists also find Confucian ideas to be convenient tools for shaking off Western influence and developing their indigenous studies.

48 *Chinese intersectionality*

However, I argue that purely using 'Confucianism' to explain the roots of violence against women because of the Confucian theme of 'men as dominant and superior and women as virtuous and inferior' becomes inappropriate in multi-faceted post-socialist China, where the discourse of Confucian ideas is one of many competing and multilayered discourses regarding gender, love, sex, and family influence on young people's dating lives. When 'Confucianism' is used by feminists as shorthand for explaining the gender inequality in China, it is an essentialist cultural dislocation (*cuowei*). Just as with the shorthand of the academics, the cultural dislocation of 'Confucianism' also exists in young people's daily lives. In later chapters I will demonstrate in detail how certain Confucian ideas, or 'Confucianism,' are being used for the convenience of these young people, who need to find a moral justification for themselves.

Chinese intersectionality as a new framework

Through a critical review of gender-based violence, the interconnection between gender, the state and the market, the interaction between Western and Chinese feminism, and the cultural dislocation of Confucian ideas, this chapter reconfigures the positionality of Chinese feminists and proposes a new theoretical framework by embedding intersectionality into the context of neo-liberal China: I call it Chinese intersectionality.

Chinese intersectionality inherits the original theoretical standpoints emphasizing that gender analysis alone cannot capture the multidimensionality and complexity of social reality, and that social location and the lived body are epistemically significant. Chinese intersectionality means Chinese feminists' seeking of positionality between the local (post-)modernity and globalization, interlocking the political economy of gender analysis with new dimensions of class, race and ethnicity, and at the same time endowing these terms with their new meanings in China.

The framework pays special attention to three different levels. First, the micro-politics of self and desire, resistance and accommodation, subjectivity and agency. How the individual positions him/herself strategically within multiple and competing discourses and within the matrix of oppression, constructing his/her desire of love, intimacy and belonging, is a core story of young people in urban China. Here I focus more on 'everyday forms of resistance' – a concept inspired by Foucault (1976, 1977) – which focus on small acts of defiance that do not directly constitute a social movement but suggest an individual dissatisfaction with the status quo. Through accommodating and resisting the existing institutional regulations, hierarchies and hegemonies, urban young people construct their intersectional self by demonstrating their subjectivity and agency. Lisa Rofel's (2007) concept of 'desiring self,' Nicholas Rose's (2007) term 'enterprising self,' and Arthur Kleinman's (2011) concept of 'divided self' may facilitate a discussion of the strategies and tactics that young people adopt for establishing intersectional self.

Chinese intersectionality 49

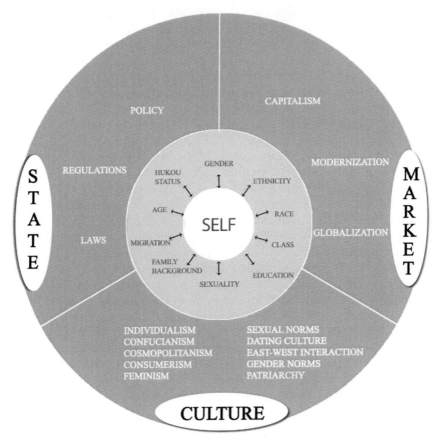

Figure 2.1 Chinese intersectionality

Second, the meso-politics of multiple oppression and interlocking institutional systems – the matrix of gender, class, race, sexuality, race/ethnicity, migration, family, and age. Chinese class stratification has transformed a rigid status hierarchy under Mao into a relatively open, evolving class system in the Post-socialist Era (Bian, 2002; Zhou, 2004). Class stratification in the Maoist Era was rigid, binary, and clear-cut, and included: 1 a rural–urban divide in residential status; 2 a state collective dualism in economic structure; 3 a cadre–worker dichotomy in occupational classification; and 4 a 'revolution–anti-revolution' split in political characterization (Bian, 2002). In current China, the city–rural division has not been changed that much, because the enforcement of the household registration system has not been altered, and hence has become one of the most distinguished factors affecting the class issue in the urban setting. Wang and Zhang (2010) critiqued that class is absent in Chinese feminist activists' narratives, either as a conceptual category or as an issue for activism. However, as I have pointed out in my review,

50   *Chinese intersectionality*

feminist scholars of Chinese gender studies have already included class analysis in gender analysis in their discussions of gender, state and market, though they did not use the concept of intersectionality. In summary, the class stratification[12] in current China has become more complicated and flexible, so that it has close connections with social mobility and status attainment, and age, belongingness, citizenship, consumption, lifestyle and individualization of inequality may become new indicators.

Race is another important construct that has to be understood concerning dating in the urban Chinese context. Dikötter (1992) argues that the construct of race was one of the central elements in Chinese intellectuals' efforts to forge new collective identities over the nineteenth century, since the Confucian symbolic universe declined owing both to internal factors and to the intrusions of expansionist Western powers. 'Yellow race' was articulated as Chinese racial identity and solidarity as an extension of traditional lineage loyalties based on ties of descent, and dire warnings of racial extinction were evoked in its name. Under the influence of globalization, the issue of race extends from the national level into individual lives and cultural consumption. By mid-2011 there were nearly 0.6 million foreigners living in Beijing for the long term, and in 2012 more than 25,000 foreign students came to Beijing for bachelor's and postgraduate studies, both of which phenomena increased the chances of interpersonal interaction between Chinese and foreigners.[13] 'Color' thus becomes a symbolic marker, with categories of yellow, black, and white, and by extension, Chinese/non-Chinese, East/West, developed/developing, or self/other. The issue of race is more imagined and socially constructed in the dating market, which relates to young people's mate selection behaviors in the global world and how they make meaning of their experiences. The factors of nationality, cultural background, personality and social status are interwoven with each other to influence young people's dating choices and their complicated emotions. This study directly connects the race issue with international dating relationships, using young people's choices of skin color in the dating market – yellow, white, or black – as symbolic markers to illustrate the aspirations and struggles within what are called interracial relationships. It is important to look at how young people select their partners by trespassing racial boundaries and challenging the global racial hegemony by their individual choices.

The issue of ethnicity is also entangled with the state discourse. *Minzu* (ethnicity) is paired with the word *zhonghua* (Chinese) to form the term *zhonghua minzu*, a particular nationalized term which in modern China refers to the notion of a 'Chinese nationality' transcending ethnic divisions (Hobsbawm, 1990). This term tends to group all peoples within geographical China as integrated according to a single national, political, and ideologically structured image. Based on the social reality that the Han nationality constitutes an absolute majority of the population (more than 94%), the concept of *zhonghua minzu* constitutes a Han hegemony, in which the voice of the minorities is easily being marginalized and ignored. In this study, because only one informant is of a minority, this issue is not covered; however, a clarification of this issue would still benefit further feminist studies of intersectionality.

Third, the macro-politics of state, market, and cultural hybridity. This chapter has already presented a detailed discussion of how the three characteristics of post-socialist China – the state, market, and cultural hybridity – are entangled with women's images, studies of violence against women, and Chinese feminism and women's studies, and how they formulate a new framework of Chinese intersectionality as three important macro-political factors and discourses influencing young people's experiences of dating violence. As Rofel (1999) argues in her book, *Other Modernities: Gendered Yearnings in China after Socialism*, gender in China is not just 'about' men and women, but is also about the state, the nation, socialism, and capitalism. Indeed, three distinguishing characteristics cannot be missed in Chinese gender analysis: uneven and flexible market and increasing involvement of globalization, the still strong socialist bureaucracy and gradually developed governmentality, and culture hybridity. As Saich (2011) argues, although China's government has greatly relaxed its control over people's daily lives as it has moved to a market-oriented society, the state still explicitly or implicitly mediates individuals' intimate lives and choices (p. 23).

Rofel (2007) argues in her book *Desiring China*, that '[i]t would be misleading, then, to characterize the market economy in China as in opposition to the state, as that which has developed in spite of or around the state' (p. 8). In many circumstances, as the literature review has shown, the state and market have formulated a conspiracy relation to establish barriers to gender equality. I further propose to use culture hybridity to replace the concept of Confucian ideas, which refutes the dichotomy of traditional and modern culture and avoids misleading us into equating the traditional culture with patriarchy and sexism. The concept of cultural hybridity emphasizes the mixture of Confucian ideas, youth culture, dating culture, migrant culture, socialist culture, consumerist culture, and cosmopolitan culture, etc. In this study, I am more interested in how young people appropriate different cultural discourses to justify their behaviors, strategies and choices, rather than how certain 'cultures' impact on young people's everyday lives and practices.

Notes

1 Different studies list 1993 and 1994 as the earliest year that domestic violence was formally regarded as a social problem, when the term was accepted academically. Wesoky argues that the term domestic violence does not appear in any of the surveyed magazine article titles until 1993, and this article, in *World Women's Vision*, was in reference to an American case of domestic violence (Ye, 1993, quoted in Wesoky, 2002). The Maple Women's Psychological Counseling Center's (2001) report on domestic violence shows that Chinese society began to regard domestic violence as a social problem to be researched in 1994.

52 *Chinese intersectionality*

2 In detail, different types of violence include the following concrete behaviors. Verbal aggression, including insulting or swearing at the partner, sulking or refusing to talk about an issue with the partner, stomping out of a room or house, and doing or saying something to spite the partner. Sometimes verbal violence and psychological aggression are cross-linked with each other (Straus et al., 1996). Physical assault includes both 'minor' and 'severe' violence. The former is defined as throwing something that could hurt, twisting, pushing or shoving, grabbing and slapping probably without physical injury; the latter includes using a knife or gun, punching or hitting, choking, slamming, beating up, burning or scalding, and kicking (Straus et al., 1996). Psychological aggression includes insulting, saying things to upset, saying mean things, criticizing, calling names, making the other person feel guilty, making the other person feel inferior, giving the other person the cold shoulder, degrading, and hurting feelings (Stets, 1991). Sexual coercion typically ranges from unwanted touch, molestation, and sex with verbal manipulation (insistent arguing, false pretense, threats to terminate a relationship, or threats of physical force), attempted rape, to forced physical aggression and rape (Kelly and Radford, 1996; Koss, 1989; Lonsway et al., 1998; Ottens and Hotelling, 2001; Russell and Oswald, 2002).

3 Personal conversation.

4 *Women's Voice* is a good-will weekly newsletter established in 2009 by Media Monitor for the Women's Network. The newsletter collects and edits extensive information about women's development and gender equality, and sends it to readers through a website and emails.

5 This study is available from the website Stop DV, Chinese Law Society: cyc6. cycnet.com:8090/othermis/stopdv/index.htm.

6 Hua Mulan is a heroine who disguises herself as a man to serve in the army in her father's place. While serving, she is recognized as a courageous soldier and is offered a government post.

7 Daji and Baoshi were concubines of historical rulers and were regarded as evil beauties who destroyed the rulers who fell irrevocably under their spells.

8 The double burden refers to the workload of women who work to earn money, but also have responsibility for unpaid domestic labor. Especially in Chinese families, the dual-job couple is the most common arrangement; however, the woman often spends significantly more time on household chores and care work, such as child rearing and care for the sick, than does the male partner.

9 *The White-Haired Girl* is regarded as a story paying tribute to Chinese liberation. It was a novel first and then was adapted into a ballet, an opera, drama, film and all kinds of art forms. 'Although the plot has been repeatedly altered over the years, no one ever tampered with the basic role structure. Xier, the fiancée of Wang Dachun and daughter of Yang Bailao, is abducted by the landlord, Huang Shiren. Xier's father dies shortly thereafter. Dachun cannot rescue her and leaves the village to join the Red Army. In the Huang household Xier suffers horribly. When she discovers that Huang is about to sell her, she manages to escape and disappears into the mountain wilderness. Years later Dachun returns. The revolution defeats the landlord, and Dachun finds Xier and brings her home' (Meng, 1993, p. 120).

10 Personal conversation.

11 In the process of writing, I am very careful about the term 'Confucian ideas,' which is used in different places with different meanings, and I want to make it explicit and clear. In making the critical review on Chinese feminist scholarship on violence against women, one of the most important critiques that I make of current Chinese feminist scholarship is that 'Confucianism is used as shorthand for explaining the entire unequal situation between men and women.' When I quote these feminists' arguments, I have to quote the word 'Confucianism,' as it appears in their original texts.

12 According to (Lu, 1989), in rural China there are eight different classes: rural cadres, 7%; private entrepreneurs, 1%; managers of township and village enterprises, 1.5%; household business owners, individual industrialists and those in commerce, 6%–7%; professionals, 2.5%; employees in collective industry and migrant peasant workers in cities, 16%–18%; wage laborers in the local private sector, 16%–17%; and peasants, 48%–50%. According to Bian (2002), in urban China there are generally six stratified classes, but each class can be divided into more subgroups: peasant peddlers and household businessmen; working class; administrative and managerial cadres; capitalist entrepreneurs; intellectuals; and middle classes.

13 *Beijing Statistical Yearbook* (2011, 2012), tongji.cnki.net/overseas/engnavi/HomePage.aspx?id=N2010090572&name=YOFGE&floor=1.

3 Dating landscape, power struggles, and love geography

This chapter is all about young people's everyday dilemmas, struggles, and negotiations in dating relationships, such as how they choose their partners and what their criteria are for doing so, how they start and end their relationships, how they perceive love and what kind of lives they lead within their dating relationships. If violence is one of their strategies for gaining power in intimate relationships, then it must be related to all of these issues.

Based on their personal narratives, this chapter illustrates the dating landscape of young Beijing people, the interaction of their personal dating choices with a range of social-cultural discourses and forces, and the power struggles within dating relationships, and between the individual and society as well. The following subjects are addressed: first, how to map out young people's interests, motivations, attitudes, feelings, and experiences in dealing with their intimate life; second, how young people attempt to attain individual autonomy and create spaces for the intersectional self in which they can build meaningful dating relationships; and third, how they negotiate notable social-structural institutions and cultural rules they encounter in finding partners, negotiating power, and sustaining dating relationships.

The distinction between Beijingers and *waidiren* (outsiders) here serves as a framework to examine the cultural and socio-economic differentiation of dating practices. We further complicate this framework by highlighting the internal heterogeneity of *waidiren*, including four groups: college students, new Beijingers, young professionals without Beijing *hukou* (household registration certificate), and rural migrant laborers. We argue that our participants' narratives reflect a desire for autonomous partner choice and fulfilling love relationships; we also demonstrate how the *hukou* system, competition in the neo-liberal market place, differential access to education, rural–urban division and the difference between Beijinger and smalltowner may interact to create opportunities and obstacles for young people's personal choices.

Existing research tends to emphasize the retreat of the state and the importance of the post-socialist marketplace in shaping young people's dating relationships (Farrer, 2002). In contrast, we highlight how our participants' intimate relationships are constructed through a matrix of cultural rules and institutional demands, such as the rules of competition in the dating market, the *hukou* system, access to education, and cultural interpretations of the rural–urban divide, Beijinger and smalltowner. For the young people we interviewed, socio-economic and cultural hierarchies between Beijingers and the four groups of *waidiren* mentioned above worked to create distinctive obstacles and opportunities in the construction of fulfilling dating relationships. We simultaneously point to the ways our participants worked to achieve autonomy in their personal choices in the face of such structural boundaries.

The Italian Marxist Gramsci (1998) used the term 'hegemony' to refer to the particular way in which the dominant authorities in society, through a process of 'intellectual and moral leadership,' seek to manipulate the consent of the subordinated group. Grewal and Kaplan (1994) raise the concept of 'scattered hegemonies' and remind us to notice the transformation from a hegemony located primarily within a culture of modernity that is spread out all over the urban global to another, ongoing hegemony experienced by practices of social postmodernity. These 'scattered hegemonies' offer a historical site for Chinese feminist study: among them one may identify the nature of resistance and compromise, and the unfolding pursuit of subjectivity by young people in post-socialist China. Although 'intellectual and moral leadership' once represented the distinctive characteristic of Beijing, it has ironically been replaced with the progressive empowerment of a newly fashioned symbolic 'leadership' initialized by, and commodified within, the political economy and historically changing circumstances of Beijing. This hegemony indeed shows us a process within which exchange and negotiation among the state discourse, the market, and young people's dating lives take place. This process also can be examined to analyze different types of conflicts and violence in dating relationships in contemporary China. In many cases, power struggles extend from the interpersonal tension between men and women, and these represent and refract the conflicts between the individual and society, as young people endeavor to achieve upward mobility, though they may be frustrated by the unattainability of desires within the dating hegemony and within consumer society.

Dating: pattern, process, and hierarchy

There were heterogeneous dating modes among the participants. Among 43 participants, 15 of them had had only one dating relationship, 19 had had two to four different dating relationships, and seven had had five or more different dating relationships with different persons. 22 had had monogamous dating relationships and 19 were either actively (11) or passively (eight)[1] involved in multiple dating relationships, including triangular dating. There were still many other dating practices, such as: two participants with experiences of a one-sided relationship (*danlian*); four who had established dating relationships through the Internet (*wanglian*); eight who had maintained long-distance dating and four who had broken off relationships because of long-distance

56 *Dating landscape, power struggles, love geography*

dating; seven who had experienced one-night stands (*yiyeqing*), three of whom had been involved in extra-marital affairs as third parties; two women who were dating men ten years older than themselves (*wangnianlian*); and three who had had international dates with white and/or black men.

There is a Chinese folk expression saying that for a man to chase after a woman is as difficult as climbing a high mountain, while for a woman to chase after a man is as easy as piercing a piece of paper. Though the narration of 'falling in love at first sight' emphasizes the mutuality of spontaneous 'falling,' practically, the power struggle between a couple starts almost at the very first moment when they meet each other. Deng Li narrates her experience of dating different men:

> At the beginning, they chased me ardently, and then I looked down on them, ignored them. After some time, when I felt touched and began to have feelings for them, they had already lost their patience and left ... I did not understand why, once they had said that they were attracted to me, I felt privileged and had more power in the relationship.
>
> (Deng Li, F, 33)

The action of chasing provokes a flux of power in the dating market, which implicates an imbalance of power within a dating couple. The fluidity of power stemming from chasing exists because one person can be completely in love with another while the other is either uninterested or, if interested, emotionally guarded. The delay or mismatch in emotional intensity often leads to an imbalance in perception and emotional identification that can further lead to heartrending pain, dissatisfaction, and, in the extreme, obsessive behavior (Jankowiak, 1995). It seems that women somehow are given privilege in the process of being chased, although it may not last forever, as Deng Li's story demonstrates.

'Usually, people feel that girls should date up, while boys should date down,' as Qin Cui (F, 31) claims. In the dating market, there are some unspoken hegemonic dating modes, such as men preferring women who are younger, shorter, and who have achieved less socially, while women prefer men older, taller, and with higher achievements. Similarly, it seems that it is more appropriate for a man to chase after a woman than for a woman to take the initiative and chase after a man. In the particular context of Beijing, Beijingers prefer Beijingers rather than *waidiren*, and so it is difficult for a *waidiren* to date a Beijinger.

Outwardly, Deng Li is in the advantageous position of 'being chased,' but behind the scenes, the illusionary superficial power still has been created by patriarchal dating hegemony: it is the norm for a man to chase a woman. In contrast, Nanyue is brave enough to pursue her love by chasing a man, but she still feels a certain discomfort as a woman in regard to her initiation of the dating relationship:

Dating landscape, power struggles, love geography 57

After all, I chased after him first, so I feel that I have lower status in the dating relationship.

(Nanyue, F, 22)

Nanyue's narrative shows the ambiguity that she faced in the dating process: on the one hand she had the courage to take action to challenge the hegemonic discourse that only men can chase a woman, but on the other hand she was not totally confident of her action and even had some negative feelings about it. 'Chasing' creates a gender-biased romantic relationship; 'breaking up' is another critical moment that provokes ambivalent feelings in the love-utopia narration by going against the ideal of being 'loyal and faithful to the one you love from beginning till death.' Pragmatically, threatening to break up is a strategy commonly used in dating relationships, and Wen Jie illustrates how she successfully uses it to transform her boyfriend from a 'male chauvinist' to a tender lover:

His personality looks open, but in essence he is very conservative, even a male chauvinist ... Sometimes I cooked for him but he just sat there and did nothing ... Once I just asked him to put something back in its place; he glared at me, angrily. In his mind, how could I 'order' him to do anything? He thought that all trivial things should be done by me, not him. I was extremely angry, and I could not accept this typical male chauvinism. So I told him that in my family, my father not only worked hard outside (*zhuwai*) but also did chores inside (*zhunei*), and a good man should be like this. If he couldn't change, I would insist on breaking up with him. Because I believe that no man is too good to lose ... Insisting on breaking up is lethal for him, and an effective tool for me to pursue equality.

(Wen Jie, F, 26)

Wen Jie achieves her goal because she is very determined and has a strong belief in herself, and sticks to her own criteria of selecting a good man: *work hard outside and do chores inside*, which is a pragmatic way to ask men to share the double burden with women. Sometimes, however, if threatening to break up is used by (wo)men for attention seeking, the more it is used, the less useful it becomes. Deng Li described a scenario that happened quite often before she broke up with her ex-boyfriend:

I had no intention to break up with him. I just wanted him to spoil me. For example, the first time, I said that I would break up with him, he would cry and feel sad. The next time I said that, I expected that he would cry even harder, I would feel satisfied. While in reality, he got used to it and gradually wouldn't cry. Finally, one day, he said, okay. I was shocked but too proud to reconcile with him.

(Deng Li, F, 33)

58 *Dating landscape, power struggles, love geography*

Although it seems that women are in advantageous positions when they are chased or when they threaten to break up, more strategic work needs to be done to keep the advantage. The actions of chasing and breaking up emphasize individual endeavor and capacity in pursuing intimate relationships, which did not exist in the era of arranged marriage. Chasing and being chased, breaking up and reconciling are dramatized and romanticized power performances in the dating geography. As Jankowiak (2002) suggests, every dating selection is typically a compromise between fantasy ideal, personal preference, and the realities of the dating market. All dating choices are made implicitly or explicitly based on a conditional comparison (*tiaojian bijiao*) which includes many aspects of a person's life, such as appearance, family background, education, career, money, future development and so forth. Romantic love and individual preference are emphasized as personal choice, which undermines the hidden materialistic and pragmatic factors and agenda. If the actions of chasing and breaking up weaken the materialized dating relationship by purifying and spiritualizing romantic love and expressing individual subjectivity on the surface, the mushrooming of mate selection agencies (*hunyin jieshaosuo*), dating websites, and match-making TV programs all over China more directly shows the power of new arranged, commodified dating based on direct comparisons of material balance.

The difference between Beijingers and *waidiren* stood out as one of the most important general features for understanding young people's practices of partner choice and dating. 'Beijingers' refers to those who were born in Beijing with Beijing *hukou*, while *waidiren* is a general term for people who were not born in Beijing, but have come to the city to live there for study and/or work. The 43 participants include 15 native Beijingers and 28 *waidiren*. In turn, the 28 *waidiren* can be divided into four different types. The first type encompasses college students (15) who have temporary Beijing student collective *hukou*, which means that all the students' *hukou* were managed by the university for the study period but were not assured of permanent Beijing domicile after their graduation. The second type is the new Beijinger (seven), who has Beijing *hukou* through migrating to the city, obtaining higher education and securing a professional job, but who may still sometimes be regarded as a *waidiren* or 'outsider' by native Beijingers since (s)he speaks with a non-Beijing dialect or accent. Third are young professionals without Beijing *hukou* (three), all of whom are well educated but who face considerable limitations in terms of their access to goods, welfare, services, and participation in public life because of the *hukou* status. Fourth are migrant workers (three), rural *hukou* holders who come to the city as laborers without access to Beijing *hukou*. As Zhan (2011) argued about the exclusion of migrant workers, the distinction between Beijingers and *waidiren* through the *hukou* system implicates the intersection of two types of identity dichotomy: on one hand, the distinction between non-locals and locals, and on the other hand the differentiation between rural and urban. Zhan (2011) also argued that 'while *hukou*-based legal exclusion requires state intervention and endorsement,

Dating landscape, power struggles, love geography 59

identity-based exclusion can operate in the absence of state regulations, even when the state outlaws such practices' (p. 261).

In addition to the emphasis on the intersection between non-local/local, and rural/urban, we found that education played a significant role in creating hierarchies in the dating market. Along these lines, 'Beijing,' as a cognitive location, prefigured our participants' choices of intimate partners, constituted a pattern of stratification according to the outlined types of *hukou* possession, and formulated the subsequent dynamics of their relationships: most Beijingers dated Beijingers and most *waidiren* dated *waidiren*. Among our participants, only four of 15 Beijingers had had the experience of dating *waidiren* and only three of 28 *waidiren* had dated Beijingers. All *waidiren* involved in dating relationships with Beijingers were well educated or had what were clearly well-paid jobs. Among the migrant workers we interviewed, no one had dated a Beijinger or even a person belonging to the other three types of *waidiren*. This shows the basic structure of dating in Beijing.

At first glance, 'Beijinger' is just a word stemming from a geographical location; however, it has become a privileged identity and is a powerful metaphor in the dating market. The division between Beijingers and *waidiren* constitutes an institutional dating hierarchy closely associated with the household registration system, within which there is a *hukou* (household registration certificate) quota for entering Beijing (*jinjing zhibiao*), and with the city–rural division, under the influence of state policy for developing cities.

Using the concept of 'sexual geography,' Farrer (2002) describes 'dating lives, personal sexual stories and public narratives' in his book *Opening Up: Youth Sex Culture and Market Reform in Shanghai*, providing a modern discussion of 'how the local context shapes the possibilities of sexual discourse and interaction in the city' (p. 31), where the distinct geographical, 'dramatistic account of Shanghai' (p. 19) reveals 'one process of cultural transformation in particular historical circumstances' (p. 6). The notions of dating landscape and love geography are particularly linked to the cognitive locality of Beijing, which is in a special position, culturally and territorially located between lingering policy-based repression and the increasing 'liberation' brought on by individual practices within the free market atmosphere. The geographically based hierarchies are closely associated with these institutional hierarchies. Beijingers and *waidiren* or urbanites and smalltowners are commonly distinguished in terms of their social status on the basis of such geographic hierarchies. Long-distance relationships and transnational dating attempt to transgress the geographical limitations; however, such endeavors are both limited and encouraged. The new media-mediated relationships have considerable power to counteract geographical limitations, at least at the beginning.

In this chapter, mapping dating landscapes represents more than an effort to understand how the local context shapes patterns, social stratification, the possibilities for dating; and gender and sexuality discourses and practices of

60 *Dating landscape, power struggles, love geography*

interaction in relation to the city. It also offers an entry point for examining the struggles entangled in dating violence by penetrating the geographical and ideological structures that are veiled within Beijing. Deutsch (2000) reminds us to be aware that 'the discourse' is modified by 'urban sexual geography,' which affects the way people 'negotiate with the urban terrain' (p. 70). This urban space-related discourse is intimately related to what young people want and what Beijing provides, and these in turn are highlighted by the inter-sectionality between the spatiality of the changing urban society and an emerging individuality.

College students: the matrix of job selection and dating choice

For Beijinger college students, whether to date a *waidiren* or not sometimes involves practical considerations: first, as to whether the *waidi* college student will be able to find a job and stay in Beijing after graduation; and second, considerations of 'face.' In this sense, the institutionalized differentiation of domicile through the *hukou* intrudes upon young Beijing people's personal lives by structuring the subjective interests that inform their choices. The women and men we interviewed selected their partners and later chose whether to remain with them or not based on an array of interests – that is, sets of beliefs, values, and feelings, on the basis of which they chose certain courses of action. Apart from the pursuit of ideals of love, interest in maintaining face vis-à-vis one's family and peers and in attaining economic security were prominent in our participants' narratives. Shen Juan is a Beijinger, and her dating relationship is hidden from her dorm-mates because her boyfriend is a *waidiren*:

> Girls in my dormitory are all Beijingers, and they feel that they should find Beijingers as dating partners. Because my peer classmates come from all over China, and they may not find a job and stay in Beijing after four years' college, so my dorm-mates somehow look down on them. My boyfriend is a *waidiren*, so I avoid telling them.
>
> (Shen Juan, F, 21)

Shen Juan studies at a university where most of the students are Beijingers. However, at other state-run universities, an intimate relationship such as hers would not be that obvious, since students come to them from everywhere in China. Shen Juan's narrative illustrates a significant conflict of interest: having chosen her boyfriend for love, her interest in maintaining 'face' with her classmates and her awareness of the problems her boyfriend will likely confront in finding employment locally have led her to keep her relationship secret. While her conflict of interest is deeply personal, it nonetheless highlights the intrusion of the state into her personal life through the *hukou* system. The *hukou* system entails a pattern of socio-cultural stratification that places Shen Juan's boyfriend in a disadvantaged position in regard to herself, because when he graduates he may or may not be able to obtain a Beijing *hukou*.

Hukou status is also strongly related to his chances of finding a good job and becoming successful in Beijing. The urban job market has become increasingly competitive, as many more college graduates are produced every year than can be absorbed by employers. According to statistics from the Ministry of Education, China's college and university student registration rose from 1,083,600 in 1998 to 6,750,000 in 2011. According to Chen and Yao (2012), of 6,082,000 college graduates in 2011,[2] 570,000 were unemployed. College students in Beijing joke about the claim that 'graduates come in four grades' in terms of job seeking: the first grade consists of male students who have household registrations in Beijing; the second grade consists of female students, also with household registration in Beijing; the third grade is made up of male students with other urban *hukou* registration, or (especially) with rural *hukou* registration; and the fourth grade consists of female students with other urban *hukou* registration, or (especially) with rural *hukou* registrations. In a highly competitive job market, every small advantage over others can make a big difference – the intersection of gender, Beijing–other city division, and the rural–urban division is vividly displayed within the alleged 'ranking.' Tong and Su (2010) conducted a survey on job seeking among 2,964 college students in April and May 2009, since in or before April and May every year, job searches of college seniors in Beijing are usually settled. They found that students with rural household registrations were the most disadvantaged group in the college students' job market:

> From the urban-rural perspective, the fewest employment agreements were signed with students with rural backgrounds. The rate of signed or about-to-sign job agreements was 32.9 percent for college students originating from within Beijing, 32.2 percent for college students from other cities, but only 16.5 percent for college students with rural backgrounds.
>
> (p. 93)

In the era of the planned economy, all college graduates were assigned jobs by school and state, without individual choice. Many senior dating couples in universities had to break up after their graduation if they were distributed to different cities. Even today there exists the phrase 'love at dusk' (*huanghunlian*) on campus, which especially refers to the phenomenon of two seniors dating each other and facing a future break-up after graduation because of their forced and reluctant spatial separation. In the era of the market economy, the official policy towards college students' employment is that of mutual choice, which means that the employing companies/institutions have the right to make decisions on who they want and the college students also have the right to make the choice of what they want to do. Thus college graduates have much more flexibility and mobility than before. However, there are still many barriers for *waidi* college students, the most important issue being that of inclusion in the *hukou* quota for entering Beijing, which involves getting a permit for entering, staying, and working in Beijing.

62 Dating landscape, power struggles, love geography

Since 1955 China has implemented strict control through the household registration system, which restricts immigration between the cities and rural areas. In her paper on Beijing migrant school children, Woronov (2004) gives a detailed description of the system:

> Every resident of China was classified as either a rural or urban household through a household registration certificate (*hukou*). Although analysts differ on the motivating factors that led to these decisions, the effect was to create a 'caste-like system of social stratification' (Potter and Potter, 1990) between urban dwellers and the rural peasantry. As Solinger (1999) describes in great detail, a Chinese person's classification as a rural or urban *hukou*-holder not only determined place of residence, but also the benefits s/he would receive from the state.
>
> (p. 291)

State-supported benefits of urban dwellers were slightly different in the Maoist Era than they are in the Post-Mao Era. Under the impact of the market, life-long employment and subsidized housing are no longer guaranteed. However, compared to the rural peasants, urban dwellers still have access to many more state-supported benefits, including free or lower-cost medical care, social security/retirement pensions, the opportunity to buy economical housing (*jingjishiyongfang*), and the fact that their children can inherit the urban *hukou* and enjoy better educational opportunities.

The *hukou* quota for entering Beijing was born in the era of the planned economy, in the 1950s. At that time the rigid household registration system excluded college students from other places from Beijing. However, as the political and cultural center of China, Beijing needed a lot of well-educated college students to staff the national bureaucracy and institutions, and so the *hukou* quota for entering Beijing was established. Before 2000, a *waidi* college graduate needed to be included under both the quota for staying in Beijing (*liujingzhibiao*, issued by the Education Department of Beijing City) and the *hukou* quota for entering Beijing (as determined by the Personnel Bureau of Beijing City) before (s)he could get the chance to work in Beijing. In the era of the planned economy, for college graduates, not to be included in these quotas virtually meant that they could not get official jobs and make a living in the city.

Right now, although mutual choice as a policy has been implemented, only the quota for staying in Beijing has been abolished; the *hukou* quota for entering Beijing is still maintained. In effect, this means graduates of universities and colleges in Beijing can stay as long as they like, but with no guarantee of becoming Beijing *hukou*-holders. According to a report by the Beijing Development and Reform Commission,[3] there were more than 200,000 graduates (including undergraduates and postgraduates) in Beijing in 2010, but only 60,000 annual permits to remain under the current *hukou* quota were issued. Most permits were tied to public-sector employment,

Dating landscape, power struggles, love geography   63

rather than to work in the private sector, although 'the private sector has contributed more than two-thirds of GDP [gross domestic product] output' (Kleinman, 2011, p. 3). As public-sector jobs are rare, with applicants far outnumbering available positions, the competition for permits is intense. In addition to being included under the *hukou* quota through official channels, some *waidi* college graduates can attain Beijing citizenship through purchasing inclusion under the quota on the black market, thereby obtaining Beijing *hukou* and increasing their opportunities for job hunting in the high-paying private sector. *Beijing Youth Daily* published an article in October 2013,[4] which narrates that two college graduates spent 280,000 and 720,000 RMB, respectively, to purchase a *hukou* within the *hukou* quota for entering Beijing through the agency of the black market, and that the Beijing police department arrested eight related suspects for selling the national legal documents.

However, the high-flying housing prices since 2003 have made Beijing one of the most expensive cities in the world. Osnos's (2014) book, *Age of Ambition: Chasing Fortune, Truth, and Faith in the New China*, states that 'between 2003 and 2011, home prices in Beijing, Shanghai and other big cities rose up to 800 percent' (p. 56), and 'by 2012, a typical apartment in a Chinese city was selling for eight to ten times the average annual income nationwide' (p. 267). Too many college graduates are produced every year, and their social status drops from 'pride as a son of heaven' (*tian zhi jiaozhi*) to '*yizhu*' ('ant tribe,' that of college graduates who cannot find a job or can only find a low-paid job, who rent dorm-like living places located in the villages of the suburban area) and '*fangnu*' (slave of the apartment – the price of apartments is too high and the young buyers become 'slaves,' working hard to pay mortgages). According to Lian Si's (2009) estimations, there are at least 100,000 college graduates living as *yizhu* in the suburban area of Beijing. They are well educated, but for some of them the day of graduation becomes the day of beginning to live between jobs. They may always be changing jobs; most of them work in retail, food services and in other temporary jobs, with average monthly salaries lower than 2,000 RMB (around US$320), similar to or even less than what a working laborer can earn. Even for those college graduates who are lucky enough to find decent professional jobs and escape the misfortune of being *yizhu*, being *fangnu* is often another step waiting for them. For many Chinese young people, owning an apartment entails a sense of settling down, a sense of home, a desire to be middle class, a feeling of modernity. Nowadays buying an apartment has become an important precondition for marriage in urban China and the criterion for mothers-in-law in picking their sons-in-law, while obtaining an apartment and a car has become young people's materialistic 'Chinese dream.' Some young people act against the preconditions and get married without house or car, but they are mocked as having a '*nuohun*' (naked marriage) – '*nuo*' (naked) indicates their economic insufficiency. Moreover, recent city policies for real-estate purchases in 2012 make the situation of *waidiren* even worse, as they mandate that a *waidiren*

64　*Dating landscape, power struggles, love geography*

can buy a house or apartment in Beijing only on the condition that he or she has been working in Beijing and paying tax in Beijing for more than five years. Though the policy is intended to keep housing prices down, it exclusively affects *waidiren*. As a result, there is a new trend of 'fleeing from Beijing' among young college students who take the initiative to leave the city after completing their studies to avoid becoming either *yizhu* or *fangnu*.

Shen Juan's boyfriend thus faces a great challenge if he is to remain in the city and become successful. Conceivably, he just might not make it. Shen Juan's story is reflective of those of seven other female interviewees from Beijing, all of whom have some sort of reservation about dating *waidiren*. Among our nine original female Beijinger interviewees, only two had dated *waidiren*. Shen Juan chose to keep quiet about her relationship in response to cultural norms that make the prospect of economic achievement an important element of sexual desirability. It is important, however, to note the ambiguous meaning of Shen Juan's silence. By not disclosing her relationship to others, she seeks to keep face, thus ostensibly acknowledging and reinforcing the values that make her boyfriend a poor match. Her silence could nonetheless also be interpreted as a strategy to subvert these norms, insofar as it allows her to avoid a situation in which criticism and pressure from others might end her relationship. Shen Juan might be seen as carving out a temporary space in which her personal feelings and the choices based on them trump the socio-economic barriers created by the *hukou* system.

The *hukou* system may therefore differentiate life situations in ways that affect the prospects of non-Beijinger college students' attainment of success, stability, and love in the city. Competition in the job market resulting from the *hukou* regulations becomes associated with competition in the dating market, engendering a power matrix that may weaken the popularity and attractiveness of *waidi* college students. For the college students we interviewed, dating remains a contested site of sexual expression in which Beijingers and *waidiren* often cannot feel truly free to choose each other as partners, and in which personal considerations about love may be continuously challenged. Here we can see the shadow of the traditional *mendanghudui* (a mate selection between families of equal social rank) mate selection practice at work, though it may be hard to notice for young people. Even though young people like our participants may think they are pursuing free love and dating, their partner choice may be implicitly informed by the notion that they should find someone of equal social status. Nonetheless, young people may still find spaces in which intimate relationships based on love and companionship, rather than on socio-economic considerations, may survive. At least in Shen Juan's case, however, such relationships seem fragile and their future is uncertain.

'Looking forward' or 'looking only at money'?

The free market has washed away the Maoist Era issues of political performance and class conflict as criteria for partner selection and set up alternative parameters. On the one hand, the neo-liberal reforms of Chinese society have created potential spaces within which young Chinese can autonomously renegotiate gender relations and attempt intimate relationships built upon love and sexual attraction. On the other hand, urban China's transition to the open market has given rise to a set of discourses, which alongside the implications of state policy just outlined, serve to curtail the degree to which such potential autonomy can be expressed.

Shen Juan's case again serves as a case in point. Her complaints about her boyfriend show how new criteria for date selection play a role in her dating relationship:

> He always says that, in contemporary society, a man should be successful, and a woman should be beautiful. Every time he sees other girls prettier than me he feels unhappy. He often says, 'I'm just a small potato now. If I have money I can find anyone I want.'
>
> (Shen Juan, F, 21)

Her boyfriend's attitude points to a commodification of intimate life, where men's success may be traded for women's beauty. It echoes as a universal standard throughout the global world. American sociologists Buss and Shackelford (1997) found that the level of young US women's mate retention behavior was positively related to a partner's income and status striving, while that of men's mate retention was positively related to a partner's youth and physical attractiveness. This suggests that women's beauty and men's financial resources are likely to attract the opposite sex universally.

A range of cultural and socio-economic factors, including a woman's beauty and a man's wealth, are fashioned into a cultural hierarchy that differentiates individuals' desirability as sexual partners. Women prefer dating up – taller, richer, older, and better-educated men are desirable, and the phrase *gao fu shuai* (tall, rich, and handsome) characterizes the best dating choice. Conversely, men prefer dating down – shorter, younger, prettier, and less-educated women are desirable, and the phrase *bai fu mei* (rich, pretty with a white complexion) designates the best dating choice. Here we need to note that the above two idiomatic expressions have *fu* (rich) as a desirable quality for both men and women, as the market force of economic status has been complicating the original simple rule of 'dating up and dating down.' As *gao fu shuai* are the most desirable men's qualities in the dating market, the opposite concept of *diaosi* has been created recently to describe the 'losers,' who feel themselves to be disadvantaged in the dating market and use self-deprecating humor – 'short ugly poor' (*ai cuo qiong*) – to make fun of their situation and empower themselves in the process. Partner choice may thus be driven by a range of material interests – wealth, sexual attractiveness, and so forth – in relation to which it is possible to estimate the worth of both oneself and one's potential or actual partners in a competitive dating market. The

66 *Dating landscape, power struggles, love geography*

characteristics of the *diaosi* parody precisely this materialism and interest in superficial physical beauty.

In the present case, Shen Juan's boyfriend feels at a loss when he uses her beauty to measure his own value. When 'develop and improve the socialist market' and 'the basic goal is to improve living standards and let a group of people get rich first' became primary elements of the state discourse after 1989, 'success' suddenly became closely related to career and, more directly, to money: being rich, having political status, or being famous in intellectual life or in the entertainment business (Jankowiak, 2002), so that now being rich and successful has emerged as a notion of the 'Chinese dream' (Yan, 2011, p. 44). In a study of Beijing young professionals born in the 1980s, when asked for the definition of success they listed material success as the basic requirement – to have money, an apartment, and car – and then listed recognition and promotion in a career as the inevitable way to achieve success (Lü and Wang, 2012).

The old-fashioned heroes of the Maoist Era have given way to new market economy heroes – especially CEOs such as Ma Yun (Jack Ma/Alibaba Group), Pan Shiyi (SOHO China), Wang Shi (China Vanke), Zhang Chaoyang (Charles Zhang/Sohu Inc.), etc. in the Internet and real-estate industries, and cultural figures like Ai Weiwei (contemporary artist), Gong Li (actress) and Han Han (writer), etc. The widely disseminated images of the new heroes exemplify how the urban discourse of interregional economic linkage produces a cultural identity that may facilitate the re-territorialization of the capitalism of the free market. Money, or rather the desire for money, has subsequently played an increasingly prominent role in initiating, developing, and maintaining dating relationships.

Postgraduate student Yue Feng has an interesting explanation for the trade-off between men's success and women's beauty:

> Career is men's biggest capital, while youth and beauty are the most important capital for women. When they're young and dating each other, men lack, while women have. Naturally, women in their twenties are in a powerful position, and thus they're so bitchy. Therefore, women can't complain that men in their thirties and forties have money and turn worse [by having affairs, seeking prostitutes, divorcing and marrying a much younger girl]. Same reason! [In their thirties to forties, the gendered advantages are reversed, which means that men have the capital that women lack.]
>
> (Yue Feng, M, 24)

Here, modern love has come to be conceived of in the same terms as capitalist economic exchange, entailing instrumentally rational choices about intimate partners based on their perceived economic and erotic capital, respectively. Another participant, Xiao Hong (M, 26), made the economic dimension of dating still more explicit in his statement that men must have four big *zi* in their lives: *chezi* (car), *fangzi* (house), *piaozi* (money), and *mazi*

Dating landscape, power struggles, love geography 67

(women). It seems that, within the powerful narrative of neo-liberal capitalism, he commodifies women as objects whose meaning is analogous to that of cars. At the same time, he commodifies himself: car, house, and money turn into factors measuring his own value in the dating market, and they define the interests based on which he chooses a partner.

In this study, most informants date their classmates, colleagues, or friends of a similar, young, age. Therefore it is relatively easy for girls to occupy an advantageous position. Yue Feng mentions:

> At that time, she lived in conditions that were not good. So I comforted her [with the boast] that I would have a bright future. But she just said indifferently, 'I can't wait.' Her words frustrated me! It sounded like I had no ability to have my beloved woman lead a better life.
>
> (Yue Feng, M, 24)

Yue Feng is a postgraduate student at one of the most prestigious universities in China, and ordinary Chinese would regard him as having 'potential stock' (*qianli gu*) in the dating market and being worthy of investment. However, for Yue Feng's ex-girlfriend, the vision of an imaginary bright future is not enough to improve her current problematic situation and she has no patience to invest her time, energy and love in him. Yue Feng's conundrum points to the emergent duality of the 'enterprising' and 'desiring' self commented upon by authors such as Yan (2010), Rofel (2007), and Rose (1992, 2007). His girlfriend's categorical 'I can't wait' is suggestive of the need for young professionals to reflexively strategize their upward social mobility in a hypercompetitive setting, and to revise and adjust their personal plans and relationships according to the markers of desirability that prioritize economic attainment over personal feelings. No wonder the girlfriend quickly broke up with Yue Feng and left him heartbroken. Later on Yue Feng chose not to believe in love and frequently had casual sex with different girls as a means of revenge. As a current popular saying goes, the eyes of the Chinese are supposed to look forward, but in reality they are set only on money (in Chinese, 'looking forward' and 'looking only at money' are pronounced in exactly the same way) (Chu and Ju, 1993). At the same time, Yue Feng's clear commitment to his 'beloved woman' shows that such strategizing is easily complicated by the emotions of romantic love.

Uncle–Lolita Complex

The role of reflexive strategizing in the pursuit of social mobility in dating choices is further underlined by the cases of two, Wang Fang and Xia Bing, of the total of 29 female participants, who dated men much older than themselves. Xia Bing was a college student, who cohabitated with a successful businessman ten years older than her. She says:

68 *Dating landscape, power struggles, love geography*

> I have an auntie, a successful single woman; she's very liberal, and she hopes that I can turn out just like her. She told me that I should try to date different men and then would have different experiences. She told me that I should make use of the man as much as I can, not depend on him and that, anyway, dating was an exchange of interests.
>
> (Xia Bing, F, 20)

In ordinary people's eyes, Xia Bing's cohabitation can be defined as *bang dakuan*, which means that a young woman dates and financially depends on a rich older man – a relatively new social phenomenon in post-socialist China. Behind the age difference there exists a gendered capital exchange between different social classes in terms of men's success and women's beauty. Scholars call this 'eating spring rice' (*qingchun fan*, also translated as 'the rice bowl of youth'), which is a phrase to describe how women lead the desirable life that they are eager for by making their youthful, feminine, and urban bodies consumable. 'Eating spring rice' is a Chinese phrase to describe their attitude and lifestyle, and is 'a metaphor for young girls living off youth and beauty that will not last forever' (Hyde, 2001, p. 159). Hanser (2005), in her book on the sexual politics of service work in urban China, emphasizes that young women convert their youth and beauty into employment opportunity by 'eating spring rice'; however, this strategy is also applied in intimate relationships, and women's beauty and men's success become closely related to their femininity and masculinity, respectively. Zhang Zhen (2000), in her paper on 'the rice bowl of youth' in urban China, points out how the phenomenon signals new ways of sexual politics for exchanging femininity and masculinity in current China:

> The rice bowl phenomenon signals the formation of an urban mass culture and a new sexual politics. It is also the object of an underlying structural anxiety about time, in which feminine youth – fashioned as the timeless object of male desire – is simultaneously the trope and implement of modernization and globalization with Chinese characteristics.
>
> (p. 97)

On the one hand, women's beauty and men's success become women's and men's vehicles to partially get out of the dating hierarchy created by state policy; on the other hand, they involve a new process of classification by the market, in which both women's bodies and sexuality and men's value are commodified, actively and passively, for the consumption of partners.

Recently a new term has been created to describe girls like Xia Bing: UncleCon (*dashu kong*), which is an abbreviation of 'uncle complex' ('complex' stems from the Japanese 'コン' (con), which means passionately obsessed with somebody or something). UncleCon refers to girls around 20 years old who are eager to date men aged 35 to 40. Some of these girls are influenced by Japanese comic books, especially those romantic stories of older men with younger girls, and they feel insecure about themselves, and have special affection for mature men. As for the 'uncles,' they may or may not be married, but they must be successful in career, mature and wealthy enough to take care of others, and have a taste for a romantic, high-quality, bourgeois lifestyle. In a national survey on attitudes about dating and marriage among Chinese men and women carried out by the match-making dating website Shiji Jiayuan[5] in 2013, 70% of women aged from 18 to 25 reported that they had an UncleCon, and 17% of them had had a real experience of dating 'uncles.' They also reported that the three huge barriers to dating 'uncles' are: 1) parents' disapproval; 2) uncles' current marriages; and 3) the feeling of being in a disadvantaged position and without the capacity to control either him or the romantic relationship because of their age difference.

UncleCon is related to the Lolita Complex (*luolita kong*), from the character Lolita in Vladimir Nabokov's novel *Lolita*, 12-year-old Dolores Haze, with whom middle-aged literature Professor Humbert is obsessed and becomes sexually involved after becoming her stepfather. In China, the Uncle–Lolita complex (*dashu luoli kong*) borrows the translation of 'Lolita' and adds the word *dashu*, which refers to intimate couples with male partners at least ten years older than female partners.

There is a joke widely spread in China: Chinese men have the highest-quality loyalty in the world: when they are 18 they love girls who are 18; when they are 28, they love girls who are 18; when they are 38, they love girls who are 18 – until they are 88, when they still love girls of 18. Many well-known high-achieving CEOs get married to much younger girls who are in their early twenties and become 'role models' to the general public – only men with fame, money and power are capable of being such desirable 'uncles.' For example, the well-known musician Gao Xiaosong talked about his 19-years-younger ex-wife and his marriage with the following comments: 'When she came together with me, she was too young to enter the society, so her basic worldview was formulated by me. I am a huge influence to her – on how she views the world, what kind of music she listens to, what kind of movie she watches, etc. – so basically we think the same and this way makes me very happy' (Chen, 2014). Underlying this comment, we can see clearly the patriarchal male fantasy of fostering young, pure, pretty, innocent girls as partners according to the man's ideas, allowing him feel a sense of ownership and control.

Li Yinhe (2014b) argues that the emergence of UncleCon is a sign of returning tradition. Interestingly, Fudan University's survey on dating and marriage (Hu et al., 2014) in the Yangtze River Delta shows that among existing marriages, the uncle–Lolita type of marriage has the lowest level of satisfaction and happiness. The survey did not explain why, but from the story of another informant, Wang Fang, we can see that the different expectations of the relationship may be a reason for conflict and even violence – for the 'Lolita' girl hopes to be spoiled by finding somebody to depend on and rely on, while the 'uncle' hopes his girl will be submissive, listen to him and

70 *Dating landscape, power struggles, love geography*

respect him. Wang Fang (F, 25) has a boyfriend ten years older than she is, and they have constant conflicts and violence within their relationship. She feels that it is not fair for him to treat her like a child rather than as an independent woman:

> He always said that I am only a kid. I feel that it is unequal for him to call me a kid. I try to tell him that I am an adult too and have my own thoughts. But he always mocks me that I act, behave and think like I am only 12.
>
> (Wang Fang, F, 25)

In contemporary intimate relationships, both women's bodies and sexuality and men's valuation of 'success' may be commodified, actively and/or passively, for the 'consumption' of their partners. The uncle–Lolita type of relationship is an extreme orientation of the pattern of 'women dating up and men dating down' that makes the trade of 'men's success for women's beauty' particularly visible and the unequal power relationship between men and women particularly obvious. However, most women included in this study have realized that in China's neo-liberal market society, 'beauty' is merely a bonus helping women to achieve an advantageous position in both intimate relationships and career development. Young women may learn to convert their youth and beauty into employment opportunities by 'eating spring rice,' but they understand clearly that the fulfillment of self-directed material interests is even more important than being beautiful, and that they have to acquire higher education and move beyond the barriers established by the *hukou* system for entering Beijing if they are to secure for themselves a better life. Xia Bing's story points to a possibility of the disembedding of the participants' dating practices from traditional institutional patterns and illustrates a pattern of choices which, on the one hand, may allow young women like her to overcome barriers to social mobility in Beijing society. On the other hand, this pattern of choices seems to validate and reinforce these barriers, insofar as it translates the stratification of individuals according ownership of a Beijing residency permit, wealth, and sexual attractiveness into one according to a set of material interests, on the basis of which intimate partners are selected.

Peacock girl and phoenix boy: dating between Beijingers and *waidiren*

'Peacock girl and phoenix boy' (*Kongquenü yu Fenghuangnan*) is a very popular Internet phrase to describe an intimate relationship between a city girl and a rural boy who has successfully bypassed the *hukou* barrier through higher education, has finally secured a middle-class job, and has become a new Beijinger. However, because peacock girl and phoenix boy are born with different family backgrounds and have different viewpoints on love, intimacy, marriage, and family, they experience all kinds of conflicts and contradictions. In this sense, 'peacock' and 'phoenix' have different metaphorical meanings:

Dating landscape, power struggles, love geography 71

the former means that the city girl is 'peacocky,' selfish, and arrogant; the latter indicates the rural boy's long-suffering willingness to accomplish the transformation from crow into phoenix. Sometimes, being a phoenix is what a 'peacock girl' might call 'super-excellent,' as Zhang Fan said during our interview:

> If the *waidiren* want to date Beijing girls, they need to be *super-excellent*. Compared to us, they may feel low self-esteem.
>
> (Zhang Fan, F, 27)

In reality, the Beijing girl Zhang Fan did not have any experience of dating *waidiren* and had no willingness to do so. In this sense, the above quote most of all illustrates some Beijingers' feelings of superiority, as well as the struggles *waidiren* may face in becoming accepted. On their way to super-excellent status and finding love in Beijing, *waidiren* may need to pass through several barriers: first, becoming at least a well-educated college graduate; second, passing through the boundary established by the *hukou* quota and the household registration system to stay and work in Beijing; third, becoming successful in his or her career, or at least to have the potential to become successful, with a high-paying job, a house, and a car; and finally, stepping up to marry a Beijinger. Since such individuals obtain domicile (i.e. official registration) in Beijing, we can call them new Beijingers. Such *waidiren* have the chance to enter the elite class, and some of them – especially those from better family backgrounds and other cities – are in fact currently actively involved in important institutions in Beijing. Nonetheless, in the eyes of those born in Beijing, they are always *waidiren* because they were not born in Beijing and do not speak the Beijing dialect. According to statistics from the Beijing Civil Affairs Bureau covering the period from 2004 to 2009, Gao Ying and Zhang Xiulan (2011) found that 45.5% of registered marriages are between a Beijinger and a *waidiren*. However, it is interesting to note that it is much more common for Beijing men to marry *waidi* women (32.8%) than for Beijing women to marry *waidi* men (12.7%). These figures echo our earlier argument that the hierarchy of 'men date down and women date up' does persist in the dating and marriage market today. Also, these findings highlight the struggles between 'peacock girls' and 'phoenix boys,' as well as the difficulties *waidi* men may face in becoming 'super-excellent' and marrying Beijing women.

When it comes to partner choice, the inferior status of *waidiren* vis-à-vis Beijingers is often solidified through parental influence and control over dating relationships. While such relationships are ostensibly motivated by love and sexual attraction between intimate partners, the parents' approval continues to be regarded as pivotal to a relationship's long-term success. In sum, the patterns of social stratification sustained by the *hukou* system and the criteria of success in the marketplace shape the perceptions Beijing parents may have of their children's intimate partners.

72 *Dating landscape, power struggles, love geography*

The case of Deng Li, a successful business owner and *waidiren*, illustrates this point. Although she is beautiful, successful, and well educated, she fails to be a 'super-excellent' *waidiren*, as she does not have Beijing *hukou*. In the past, children's *hukou* was inherited from the mother, but the policy was changed in 2006. Now children's *hukou* can be inherited from either the mother or the father, which has rapidly encouraged marriage between Beijingers and *waidiren*. According to the change in the policy, Deng Li's future children would be able to become Beijing *hukou*-holders. However, the boyfriend's parents still use her *hukou* status to oppose her:

> His ex-girlfriend was a *waidiren* too; she borrowed from him a big amount of money, and didn't pay him back even though they broke up. Ever since then, his family didn't allow him to date *waidiren*, because they are Beijingers. They think *waidiren* are liars. I'm a *waidiren*, so his parents don't allow him to date me.
>
> (Deng Li, F, 33)

This narrative shows how the personal bonds of family may come to internalize the social hierarchies brought about by the *hukou* system to constrain the degree of choice young men and women come to have in their intimate lives. In Deng Li's case, her boyfriend's family endorses the cultural hierarchy of Beijingers and *waidiren* created by state discourse, and disrupts free dating between their son and Deng Li. Although many current studies focus on the retreat of the state and the growth of the market (e.g. Farrer, 1997, 2002; Ferry, 2003a, 2003b; Pei and Ho, 2006; Knight, 2003), Deng Li's attempt to achieve 'super-excellence' through the market is still challenged by the disruption of the *hukou* system and traditional family hierarchical authority structure, and state discourse and policy powerfully manipulate her dating life. However, a subjective desire for autonomous choice remains a powerful force in Deng Li's life, entailing the decision to maintain her relationship with her boyfriend regardless of these pressures. Dating relationships in this sense may manifest young people's resistance to the interpenetrating hegemonies of family and paternalistic state control.

Lin Ping is an only daughter of a Beijing family, and she explained the reason why a *waidiren* seems a good choice for her: 'I'm an only-child, and my parents are old. He's alone in Beijing, and then he has time and energy to take good care of my parents' (Lin Ping, F, 31). Lin Ping explains in this way why she wants to choose a *waidiren* with a Beijing *hukou* as her preferred future husband. Being 'alone,' in her explanation, symbolically cuts him off from his original family-ethic relationship by making him a member of her family. Here the geographical division of local Beijinger and outsider *waidiren* influences the expression of power in the dating relationship and signifies an acceptance or rejection of the family relationship.

However, sometimes Lin Ping feels insecure about the future success of this marriage arrangement. The reasons for her insecurity parallel the arguments

Dating landscape, power struggles, love geography 73

in a heated debate currently taking place in Chinese mass media and on the Internet about the family situation of 'phoenix boy' and 'peacock girl.' This debate is about the high expectations 'phoenix boy' has of 'peacock girl' in terms of tenderness and kindness, while he turns their family into a city reception center for his extended family, thus focusing on supporting his family of origin rather than his relationship with his wife. The tensions in marital life that such split loyalties may occasion were a significant concern for Lin Ping at the time of our interview. Here we see that family ethics may work together with the big forces of urbanization, migration, and state discourse to intervene in young people's choices within dating relationships, imposing yet a further level of pressure on the relationship between dating partners.

The narrative of 'peacock girls' and 'phoenix boys' points to the limited persistence of regulative familial bonds and attendant norms in relation to which young people may define their interests in dating relationships. These norms and attendant parental efforts to impose themselves on their children's intimate lives have clearly been re-embedded within frameworks of meaning derived from relatively recent formations of state and market. At the same time, however, our participants' efforts to pursue intimate relationships of their choosing, in spite of the barriers they face, suggest an incipient individualism in the form of partner choice based on personal, rather than purely familial or socio-economic, interests. This is evident in the idea of being 'super-excellent,' through which achievement in the face of significant structural barriers is translated into an element of personal attraction and a criterion for partner selection.

Thriving in the cosmopolitan city? New Beijingers' everyday conflicts

This struggle for emancipation within the contested space of dating relationships is evident in the significant conflicts some of the participants reported. Their subjective experiences of dating and partner choice were often structured as much by a push and pull of competing pressures as by love and desire. It is often only through conscious choices in spite of or challenging these pressures that our participants found it possible to maintain relationships with their intimate partners. Equally, however, conflict and violence between intimate partners may come to be a focal point of the tension between interests in, on the one hand, a love-based intimate relationship and, on the other hand, material achievement and security in the context of the patterns of stratification imposed by state and market. For new Beijingers, their dating is often associated with pressure and competition in their everyday lives. Living far away from their parents, they are particularly dependent on themselves, and strive more for a better living than local Beijingers do. As Qin Cui narrates:

> If a Beijinger loses his/her job, (s)he can stay with parents, rest for several months and then find a job. Kids from the outside are different. If they did not work today, they may have nothing to eat and no place to live.
>
> (Qin Cui, F, 31)

74 *Dating landscape, power struggles, love geography*

The exploration of such conflicts illuminates the tensions that may be inherent in experiences of individualization. On the one hand, the waning of traditional patriarchal controls may entail heightened ambitions for love, romance, and personal success, while, on the other hand, the direct pressure to achieve material success in a hypercompetitive market may painfully restrict the attainment of these personal dreams.

There are seven new Beijingers among our interviewees. Zheng Xin's story illustrates the relationship dynamics some of them encountered. Zheng is a postgraduate student and her boyfriend is a new Beijinger who works as a middle-school teacher. They have a long developmental plan for their lives in Beijing. Usually Zheng Xin lives in the school's dormitory. On weekends, she goes to her boyfriend's place. Zheng Xin has suffered from physical abuse, and sometimes her body is black and blue. Most of the time, the problem of the couple's material conditions becomes the last straw, setting off girlfriend battering, such as in the last serious episode of physical violence before the interview:

> He lives in a basement, only ten square meters, very small and crowded. It's inconvenient for either cooking or taking a shower. The bathroom is shared by many other people. That night, I wanted to have a shower. At 9:00 pm the bathroom was occupied. At 10:00 pm I went to it again – still occupied. When I came back to his room, I was a little bit upset and told him, next time, you should rent an apartment with a kitchen and bathroom. Then he lost his temper immediately and said that I put a lot of pressure on him – we quarreled with each other, and he suddenly said, 'If you dare to talk back again, I'll slap you.' Then I said, 'Slap if you dare!' He really did, slap, slap, slap – till his hand hurt too. Then he began kicking me, and my face turned into 'red bread.' He threw things at me. My neck bled a lot because my necklace was pulled apart.
>
> (Zheng Xin, F, 23)

Serious violence broke out because Zheng Xin's complaint challenged her boyfriend's self-esteem and masculinity, which were closely related to his capacity to be successful and make money. In Zheng Xin's explanation, if the man cannot bring enough money home and make life comfortable, the woman has a right to complain. At the same time, the man needs to understand that the complaint is only an innocuous one without the further meaning of blaming him. In order to justify her complaint, Zheng Xin emphasized that she was a person who could eat bitterness, by giving an example of dining:

> We seldom go out for lunch or dinner, and just eat at the canteen in his school. One meal, 10 RMB [around $1.5], is enough for both of us. His colleagues often dine out, but we just stay in his basement and eat leftovers. I don't feel bitterness at all.
>
> (Zheng Xin, F, 23)

Eating bitterness means that one must work hard and suffer in order to reap the benefits of one's labors at a later time. Frugality has long been recognized as a traditional Chinese virtue. In the old days, Chinese children were taught to be diligent and frugal, because survival in traditional China very much depended on those qualities (Chu and Ju, 1993). Eating bitterness is particularly regarded as revealing the high spirit of Chinese womanhood, which is mediated precisely by the virtues of self-sacrifice, self-effacement, and a responsive understanding of others, especially of their suffering (Chow, 1993; Kristeva, 1986). One of the leaders of modern Chinese enlightenment, Liang Qichao, argued that 'the individual has a dual-self, the small self centered on personal interest and the great self based on the interest of the nation; the small self should always be secondary and submissive to the great self' (Kleinman, 2011, p. 9). In the Maoist Era, the notion of 'divided self' was used to call on people's willingness to 'eat bitterness' and to call on them to sacrifice personal interests for the collective purpose of the party, country, and society. However, now the concept of 'divided self' can be understood as multi-dimensional, as 'the self can be divided by a number of "dividers," such as past versus present, public versus private, moral versus immoral, and so on' (Kleinman, 2011, p. 5). 'Enterprising self' becomes young people's strategy of paying more attention to investing in, and disciplining themselves in pursuit of, success; 'desiring self' becomes their way of constructing their inner self, and therefore 'eating bitterness' has become an entrepreneurial strategy of new Beijingers in order to lead better personal lives in the future.

For young people, a feeling of institutionalized unfairness is strong, and sometimes the purity of romantic love becomes the last salvation of their everyday lives. In their justification, 'eating bitterness' is worthwhile if it preserves 'true love.' 'Falling in love at first sight' (*yijianzhongqing*) and 'being loyal and faithful to the one you love from beginning till death' (*congyi'erzhong*) are commonly listed as the ideals of love, which articulate ambivalent and paradoxical discourses of romantic love in contemporary materialistic society. The concept of 'falling in love at first sight,' influenced by the romantic love discourse in the West, involves physical attraction and sexual arousal at first sight and becomes a fairy tale-like entry point for pursuing the love journey. In contrast, 'being loyal and faithful to the one you love from beginning till death' is a concept with deeper historical and cultural connotations, and is more like a measurement of love with the characteristics of a sociological institution. It stems from the Confucian ideas of imperial China and was a restriction to discipline women to maintain chastity and submit to their husbands throughout their lives. Both male and female informants used the phrase to express the expected happy results of ideal love, yet their responses also show that the one-way compulsory loyalty of women to men in imperial China has turned into an imagined mutual commitment for couples nowadays. It directly links dating with inevitable marriage, using a spiritual description to commit a heaviness of loyalty through which to

76 *Dating landscape, power struggles, love geography*

construct a picture of 'happily ever after,' an 'after-image' of dating. Ironically, this image combines an inheritance of Confucian ideas of life-long commitment, the romantic love discourse of ownership and exclusivity, and the widespread monogamy with modern Chinese characteristics, and thereby empowers an old-fashioned sexual discipline within the love utopia, which transcends class, social strata, race, ethnicity, rural–city division, and Beijinger–*waidiren* division, at least on the expressional level.

Nevertheless, in a consumer society filled with all kinds of seductions, it may be hard to continue eating bitterness, especially when the pure ideal love encounters interpersonal problems and institutional unfairness; those who date may feel emotional emptiness and that they are at a loss, and they may doubt what is true love, while others cannot help but be trapped into making calculations concerning their relationships:

> I think I am somehow traditional. I think men should not spend women's money. But in his opinion, gender equality means men can ask women for money. He is the type of guy, if I don't give money to him, he will not be happy. If I do give him money, he will be very sensitive. Once I asked him to do something for me, he said that he is not my imperial long-term laborer (*changgong*) and warned me not to feel so arrogant just because I give him some money.
>
> (Ding Yi, F, 22)

> He hasn't bought me any gift. Although my birthday was in the winter holiday and he wasn't in Beijing, after he came back he didn't make it up to me. His birthday was in the winter holiday too. I bought him a watch, but I didn't give it to him. On one side, I felt that the watch was not very nice; on the other side, I was thinking: why should I give him a gift? He didn't give me anything.
>
> (Shen Juan, F, 21)

Money and gifts become two important ways to measure love in the consumer society. Gift giving becomes an important way to express love and makes love visible and exchangeable, while the desire for money and the reality of lack of money become reasons for conflict between dating couples. Men's poverty turns into one of the most unacceptable situations in the dating relationships, and it is even worse if the man does not mind using women's money. In Ding Yi's story, although the boyfriend uses 'gender equality' to justify that a man can use his girlfriend's money just like a woman can use a man's, his sensitivity shows that he cannot fully justify this reasoning to himself. Here he borrows the term 'imperial long-term laborer' to signify power and control within the dating relationship, as the term refers to the relationship of domination and subordination between master and slave in pre-modern China.

Two years after the first interview, I interviewed Zheng Xin and Ding Yi again. Both of them had graduated with master's degrees, found well-paid

Dating landscape, power struggles, love geography 77

jobs, obtained Beijing *hukou*, and were living without dating violence. Deng Yi had broken up with her former boyfriend and was cohabiting with a new man. Zheng Xin was going to be married to her formerly abusive boyfriend and had bought an apartment together with him. I asked them directly whether the change of material conditions had any relation to the cessation of dating violence. Both of them affirmed that material conditions had no relationship to violence in the dating relationship. Deng Yi emphasized that her new boyfriend had a better personality, while Zheng Xin thought that she and her boyfriend had both learned how to communicate and improve their relationship. In Zheng Xin's narrative, one external force was especially influential in stopping her boyfriend from abusing her – he had become a Christian, under the influence of a foreign friend. Thus Zheng Xin, either intentionally or unconsciously, ignored the fact that she now lived in a newly bought apartment with a private kitchen, bathroom, heat and hot water, so that the lack of these amenities were no longer an issue to fight over. She preferred to locate herself in a global world in which the influences coming from a foreign friend were more precious than the change of material conditions.

Schein (2001) elucidates the transition of Chinese cities under capitalism and globalization:

> That the city, however conceived, has become an object of increasingly intense desire in the era of reform is closely linked to a burgeoning consumerism. Cities, especially megalopolises such as Beijing, Shanghai, and Guangzhou/Shenzhen, are widely viewed as glittering markets for a world of goods imported from the catalogs and store shelves of global modernity.
>
> (p. 226)

Meanwhile, as Dirlik and Zhang (2000) argue, the mutual movement of both the world market's spread into China and China's willingness to enter it enables Chinese consumers to encounter fully a world of difference, unevenness, inequality, and hierarchy on a larger scale, often delineated in terms of nation-state borders. The power of global capitalism involves at least two desires: the desire of global capital to enter China, making an impact in every corner of young people's ideas, beliefs, and lives; and the desire of young people to be freed from oppression and suppression and to enter into the bourgeois lifestyle of which they dream. Pun Ngai (2003), in her paper on consumer revolution in 'globalizing' China, states that:

> For Chinese urbanites, the dream of a middle-class lifestyle already fills their imaginations. The only problem is to determine when and how these dreams will be fulfilled … Their not being able to consume is not a problem; what is important is the power of the desiring machine to incite them to dream and to produce further desire.
>
> (pp. 475–477)

78 *Dating landscape, power struggles, love geography*

New Beijingers, as a group with stronger desire and fewer resources than those of Beijingers born in the city, need to depend on themselves to fight for a bright future and fulfill their dreams. The feeling of institutionalized unfairness is inevitably strong, which projects into their emotional lives as a big disparity between pure ideal love and cruel social 'reality.' The pure ideal love fused with the promising future becomes something that they desperately dream of, just like those glittering decorations that hang on the huge Christmas tree in the fancy shopping mall – they can see it, smell it, even touch it, but never get hold of it. Wang Mei, a 25-year-old postgraduate student, complained that her boyfriend was reluctant to show his commitment to the relationship:

> We do not have a future, and he did not give me a promise. We just drift along. He doesn't care about the future. He always says, 'What the future will be like, let's think about it later.' I try to tell him that I don't care about money. But he said, without the material basis, it's a waste of time to talk about love.
>
> (Wang Mei, F, 25)

Such disagreements among dating couples reflect wider cultural tensions around youth's expressions of post-traditional individualism in contemporary Chinese society. There are so many luxurious houses and fancy cars and there is so much fashionable clothing, and all these seem so close to the young, while it remains so difficult for them actually to acquire and consume them. When all these material interests are displayed in dating relationships, the idea of the 'desiring self' (Rofel, 2007) is replaced by material pursuits, resulting in frustration and confusion. Of course, there are particular situations that need to be considered, such as family background. A new Beijinger with millionaire parents or parents who are high-ranking in other cities officials may lead a much better life than a local Beijinger with parents who are laid-off workers (*xiaganggongren*). On the other side, although most of these new Beijingers may frequently lead harder lives than most of their Beijinger peers, they also have much more freedom, as they are far away from their parents' direct surveillance. As Beijinger Zhang Fan says:

> I have some friends not originally from Beijing, their living conditions are different from ours. They have no parents around them, they need boyfriends or girlfriends to support each other, can cohabit and lead an independent life easily. They need to take care of everything by themselves and make a living on their own. But me, I still live with parents, everything is taken care of by them.
>
> (Zhang Fan, F, 27)

In this sense, without parents' direct surveillance, new Beijingers have much more potential and space to develop and establish a youth sub-culture for doing gender and sexuality, and they have more freedom for risk-taking and are more willing to try different romantic and sexual adventures. It may be easy for them to fall in love at first sight because they are young and passionate, while it is much more difficult for them to maintain the lifelong relationship of 'ideal love' because there are so many barriers and seductions. Eating bitterness is no longer as desirable and attractive as enjoying life, and drifting along may be one of the ways of appreciating their life.

Floating population: out of place

On the way to becoming a 'super-excellent' *waidiren*, higher education plays the role of a filter and helps a 'candidate' to move beyond class stratifications, the urban–rural divide, and the division of Beijingers and *waidiren* institutionalized by state discourse and policy. In Beijing, there exists another category of *waidiren*, a category of 'otherness forever': that of the 'floating population,' as Zhang Li (2001) has labeled it. Usually, members of the floating population are rural *hukou*-holders with little education, who come to the city to work as laborers in the factories, as construction workers and factory workers, and in service industries, as catering staff, security guards, domestic helpers, etc. The opening of the market economy and the availability of geographical mobility within China has made a great many rural migrants rush to the cities to work as laborers. The household registration system constrains their self-development in Beijing, which makes it extremely difficult for them to obtain local *hukou*-holder status and become new Beijingers. Often having only limited educational and professional qualifications, they have to sell their physical labor to make a living in the city.

Only three *waidiren* who were working laborers have been included in this study: Long Qun (M, 22) was a security guard, Chu Yu (F, 22) was a typist in a company, and Ai Ling (F, 24) was a domestic help first and became a salesgirl in a clothing market later on. All of them came to Beijing in their teenage years after completing middle school, and none of them has had the chance to date a Beijinger, or even a new Beijinger. Their dislocation in the city marginalizes them in social and cultural terms and excludes them from the dating market by rendering them undesirable according to the material interests outlined in previous sections. In practical terms, they have limited choices when it comes to dating – lack of time, money, and space tie them down, limiting both their chances in the dating market and their opportunities for upward social mobility. Long Qun works ten hours a day, six days a week, while Ai Ling explained that shifts of 13 hours were common for salesgirls. Long Qun earns only 500 RMB (around $80) per month, most of which he sends home to his family, while Chu Yu and Ai Ling earn around 1,000 RMB (around $160), but spend half their income on rent. In 2005, the average monthly salary of Beijing citizens was 2,849 RMB (around $455),

80 *Dating landscape, power struggles, love geography*

according to the *Chinese Statistical Yearbook* for 2006,[6] so their incomes were much lower than the average. Long Qun lives in an eight-person shared dormitory, Chu Yu shares a one-room apartment with a colleague, and Ai Ling shares a two-bedroom apartment with three single friends.

On top of the obvious constraints imposed by these precarious living arrangements, the mobility and instability of their working conditions also make it difficult for laborers from different places and provinces to maintain romantic relationships. Thus, all of them have had very limited dating experiences. For example, while Long Qun has worked in Beijing for more than five years, he has had only one brief romance, with a cook, lasting a total of three months.

May's (2011) work in the Changbai Mountain community of Huangbiyu illustrates a very different but no less creative set of agencies. Here, young men and young women migrate on a temporary basis to local towns, but for different reasons. The men leave their villages to accumulate the money needed for their future marriages in their villages, while their sisters migrate to spend money on themselves in order to attract an urban husband with a better set of life opportunities. Intriguingly, the fact that the Cinderella story so rarely transpires in real life seems to be little impediment to the popularity of this particular aspiration.

Gender difference also exists in this part of the study: for the male working laborer Long Qun, it seems that saving money for future marriage back in his rural area is the only feasible way to establish an intimate relationship:

> I only spend 50 or 100 RMB each month [the job provides a dorm and three meals a day] and then send the remaining salary back home. [My] parents will save all this money for my future wedding. It's not so common for a female laborer to date a male laborer, because our jobs have a strong fluidity: when one leaves [the city], then the relationship is naturally over. You know, people come from different places – doing labor (*dagong*) is just temporary, for when we're young, and finally we'll go back home and get married.
>
> (Long Qun, M, 22)

However, the two female working laborers, Chu Yu and Ai Ling, both somehow manage to establish some romantic relationships in the city with *tongxiang* (peer working laborers from the same hometown). For Chu Yu, during the past seven years of staying in Beijing, she has only had one on-and-off 'relationship' with her *tongxiang*, who was her middle-school classmate and who went to high school but did not pass the college entrance examination, and later came to Beijing and became a soldier in the army. However, the *tongxiang*'s infidelity traps her in loneliness, self-doubt, and emotional trauma, which makes her wonder whether this relationship is only her one-sided fantasy. For Ai Ling, two years before the interview, one *tongxiang* introduced her to another *tongxiang*, who was a truck driver. After a

Dating landscape, power struggles, love geography   81

short period of consideration, Ai Ling began to date the *tongxiang* and established a close intimate relationship with him.

The reason why *tongxiang* become a common choice is because they have a limited network in the city, and it is difficult for them to know somebody outside their circle. *Tongxiang*, because they come from the same place and may have similar culture, dialect, history or experience to share, are therefore persons who feel mutually close and who can rely on each other. According to a report on Beijing's population, at the end of 2012, there were 20.69 million people living in Beijing, among whom 7.7 million belonged to the floating population, and had increased by 0.31 million from 2011 to 2012 (Beijing Population Development Research Center, 2013). The three cases of working laborers presented are thus like drops of water in the enormous sea. Their existence as sojourners in the urban society is due to the opening up of the market, which has attracted a lot of rural migrants to the cities to serve as laborers. However, all three of them only have middle-school education, and although they may have a chance to become exposed to the urban life, the rigidity of the household registration system prevents them from becoming local *hukou*-holders, and therefore legalized Beijingers. They may repress their sexuality and desire for an intimate relationship and hope for the future, they may date their *tongxiang* and have a dream of striving together with them and making a fortune in the city, and they may say that they finally will go back to their hometowns – but at the same time, they desperately want to stay in the city, despite the fact that the city has a 'glass ceiling' for them. Most of the time their incentive for remaining in the city is more a matter of hope and imagined possibilities than of 'reality.' Beijing is a symbolic site of opportunities for them to develop and become participants in the exciting modern urban world, and therefore to become modern men and women. As Yan Hairong's (2003) paper on migrant female laborers shows, their hope may turn into despair in the face of the cruel 'reality' of the city:

> The city proved not to be a high place of hope; it merely displaced her old despair with a new despair. The conundrum persists: between the country and the city, these young women have no place to pursue a modern personhood.
>
> (p. 590)

Tamara Jacka (2005), in her paper on rural women in Beijing, argues that the migration of people from rural to urban areas is emblematic of the twentieth- and twenty-first-century modernization and globalization of contemporary China:

> At the macro level, rural-to-urban migration is a key outcome of the strategies of 'flexible accumulation' of both domestic and international capitalists, enabled by a state that has tried to promote rapid economic growth and integration into the global market by stimulating

82   *Dating landscape, power struggles, love geography*

geographical and social mobility on an individual level while at the same time maintaining the key institutions of social differentiation and control such as household registration system. For individuals, movement across rural/urban divide in China results in experiences of dislocation and the multiplication of different, often clashing, subject positions, that are typical of the experience of modernization and globalization.

(p. 54)

Although the floating population makes great contributions to the modernization, urbanization, and marketization of Beijing and seems to challenge the household registration system, the latter remains an overwhelming authority for social exclusion. Both the household registration system and the *hukou* quota for entering Beijing only give green lights to college students, and higher education plays the role of a filter and only helps well-educated people go beyond the division of urban and rural, Beijinger and *waidiren*. For the floating population, like Long Qun, Chu Yu, and Ai Ling, their lack of higher education becomes a huge barrier to a change in their identities, and to obtaining Beijing *hukou*, achieving upward mobility, and finally adding to their attractiveness in the dating market.

Judd (2011) argues that the *hukou* system has softened in the Reform Era but that it still functions to tie rural people to specified rural areas for administrative purposes and remains the locus of remaining and emerging safety net provisions. Without totally abolishing the social policy of the household registration system enforcing the urban–rural division, the sexuality of the subordinated sojourners in urban Beijing will remain suppressed. As Zhang Li (2001) argues in the paper on the floating population in Beijing mentioned above:

> People who do not fit in the existing categorical order of things tend to be viewed by most societies as 'out of place' and thus a source of danger and pollution (Douglas, 1996) … In China, peasants who have left the farm and 'float' in the cities are regarded as perilous and threatening because they do not occupy a proper structural position in the existing national order, which denounces spatial mobility.
>
> (p. 209)

The interaction between Beijinger and *waidiren* illustrates a distinct piece of dating geography created by the intersection between gender, state, and market. Although the state discourses and policies are still overwhelmingly powerful, the market as a rising force confronting, negotiating, and struggling with the state politics co-maps young people's dating lives and creates alternative dating geography. Meanwhile, young people attempt to create and practice a utopia-like ideal love in their daily lives; however, they often fail to conquer the uncertainty and so compromise with the repressions of the state and market.

Dating landscape, power struggles, love geography   83

When state policies result in a hierarchy in the dating market through the household registration system, and the market constructs rules of dating by resisting the existing hierarchy and establishing a new classification, there are other practices associated with the dating geography, which expand it further. On the one hand, under the impact of globalization, international dating and marriage are mushrooming (Farrer, 2002). Although the locality of these international dating stories is Beijing, these dating practices have the significance of transnationalism and cross-cultural interaction. On the other hand, long-distance relationships are very common among informants, and young people lead trans-city relationships and spread Beijing's dating geography to other cities. Both foreigners and people living in other cities are *waidiren*, in a broad sense.

International dating: choice of skin color

In this study, three female informants had experienced international dating, while no male participant had. Here I note that nationality and ethnicity would be very important in considering young people's dating lives. However, unfortunately, this project has not included sufficient data to address these issues. Ann Mah's article entitled 'Beijing's New Beautiful People' in the *International Herald Tribune*, May 19, 2005, argued that Beijing's foreign women regarded dating Chinese men as the biggest challenge because of cultural barriers, particularly concerning different concepts of romance and intimacy. The argument is not so convincing, because cultural barriers definitely also exist in romantic relationships between Beijing women and foreign men, which are increasing and are becoming commonplace in Chinese urban societies (Clark, 2001; Farrer, 2002). According to the *Beijing Statistical Yearbook*, [7] by the middle of 2011, there were nearly 0.6 million foreigners living in Beijing long term, and in 2012, more than 25,000 foreign students came to Beijing for bachelor's and postgraduate studies. According to Huang's (2010) study on the foreign population in Beijing, in 2007, the male to female sex ratio of foreigners working in Beijing was 392:57. This is a statistical reason for the fact that international dating in Beijing seems to be becoming more a practice for Chinese women than for Chinese men.

The other intriguing phenomenon is that all three female informants who have experienced international dating are Beijingers, and all have the experience of dating Caucasians. It seems that Beijingers have more chances to date foreigners than *waidiren* do; however, I cannot draw this conclusion based on the limited information of international relationships in this project. At any rate, among the three, Meng Xi is the one with the most complex story.

Meng Xi, aged 27, had undertaken various jobs, and was the storekeeper of a small clothing store when the interview was conducted. Meng Xi had had various boyfriends and sexual partners with different skin colors, including Chinese, black and white men. She expressed the power of her body through

84 *Dating landscape, power struggles, love geography*

the choices that she made about the skin color of boyfriends and lovers. At one point Meng Xi dated a German, and narrated the situation as follows:

> When I was with him, I always felt that I tolerated him unconsciously [because of the hidden notions of Western superiority and the fact that he is a white man and I am a yellow woman]. But I got compensated. When I was going out with him, I felt proud and did not feel any pressure [from family, friends, and people on the street].
>
> (Meng Xi, F, 27)

At the time of the interview, she was dating an African-American. In the following, Meng Xi explains the pressures that are associated with dating black men in China:

> In the world, 90% of people are affected by racial discrimination. When I walk with him on street, all of the Chinese men look at me as if I were a *chicken* [slang term for a prostitute].
>
> (Meng Xi, F, 27, emphasis mine)

In the Western psychological tradition, the Freudian notion of 'the gaze' theorizes voyeuristic desire as a form of sadistic mastery over a masochistic object (Freud, 1977). Meng Xi also said:

> If Chinese men knew that I had had black boyfriends before, they would not want me to be their girlfriend.
>
> (Meng Xi, F, 27)

The two reasons she offered may be real to her but sound like many elements of racial stereotype and racial discrimination. She thinks that she has become 'dirty' from the point of view of Chinese men since she has been with African-American men, and she also believes that Chinese men feel sexually inferior to Westerners. Foucault's 'gaze' has two dimensions: the figure of authority turns its gaze on the 'victim,' and the 'victim' looks back (MacCannell and MacCannell, 1993). The 'look' that is given in public, especially by many Chinese men to a woman, initiates two encounters that construct the two different power spaces of public and private. Meng Xi's experience with her German boyfriend offered her so-called public pride and private inferiority, whereas her experience with black men resulted in a discriminatory public gaze and private superiority (Wang and Ho, 2007b). Although the classification of skin color (white/black) is a manifestation of archetypal dominant power roles, Meng Xi's version of 'looking back' was to choose to be intimate with black men. This appears to be an act of resistance, because in the competition between public pride and private power, she finally chose private power:

Dating landscape, power struggles, love geography 85

My body shape is also an important factor. I have an *oriental* face and a plump figure. They [black men] are more stimulated by and attracted to my body shape ... In the beginning, I chose him just because it was easy for me to control him. In fact, they [black men] are *easy*. They are lonely. If they get a chance, they will hang on to you. They are *easy* and I don't want to waste my time.

(Meng Xi, F, 27, emphasis mine)

Meng Xi seeks out intimate experiences with black men not only to assert her sexual appeal as an 'oriental' woman but also as a way to assert the social superiority of her own ethnicity, thus transforming the body from a physical entity into a symbolic marker. 'Oriental' is often used to indicate particular and stereotypical qualities of women: restraint (*kezhi*), steadfastness (*jianren*), reserve (*hanxu*), and dignity (*ningzhong*) (Barlow, 2004). Although the male gaze is perceived as a threat to her subjectivity, by returning the gaze she reinforces her desire to bring about a new sense of self and express the power of her body in two ways. On the one hand, she turns her 'oriental' face into a symbolic marker to attract non-Chinese men, and especially black men, and on the other hand, she transforms the meaning of others' judgmental 'cheap' into her pragmatic 'easy' with the conception that if the process of finding a partner becomes easy, then obtaining sexual satisfaction becomes easy.

Meng Xi's dating story clearly demonstrates a young woman's struggle in globalizing Beijing. Young Chinese women use their physical bodies as a weapon to gain power in international dating relationships through the choice of their partners' skin color and by making use of their 'oriental' face. Although this seemingly subjective process resists the archetypical racial hierarchy, at the same time it unconsciously submits to the dichotomy of white/ black and orientalism in the materialist society that has emerged under globalization. However, international dating geography implicates the co-existence of women's individual dating choices, sexual pleasure, and implicit power struggles according to skin color. In urban Beijing, the context of dating is hyperactive but is not sufficiently free, and the choice is essentially between submission to the extremely materialistic society or the employment of extreme psychological strength to resist it. Though the choice of skin color is often associated with cultural, status, and economic power, it is still a woman's choice that is entangled with a dilemma in contemporary urban China. The data of international dating in this study are limited and the above single case cannot be generalized to the female population in Beijing. However, as I have observed, in urban China, the transnational intimate relationship among highly skilled and mobile middle-class professionals is gradually becoming a fashionable trend, which is different from a lot of existing studies that have tended to emphasize 'catalog marriages,' marriages of convenience, and so forth, in the global setting.

In the introduction to their book, *Distant Love*, Ulrich Beck and Elisabeth Beck-Gernsheim (2014) write of 'the global chaos of love,' characterized by

86 *Dating landscape, power struggles, love geography*

'every conceivable kind of relationship at a distance: mixed-nationality couples, people who migrate for work or marriage, women who rent out their wombs, and the utterly normal tragedies of Skype-mediated love relationships' (p. 2). They directly place their discussion of such 'relationships at a distance' in the context of their analysis of the individualization of intimate life, characterized by the waning of traditional norms and values and the emergence of new, precarious ways of living together: 'Increasingly, the husband is replaced by the partner of the moment, single mothers and fathers have become more common, and patchwork families ... have emerged as the consequence of successive marriages and divorces' (p. 2). How Chinese dating couples deal with relationship at a geographical distance will be the focus of the next section.

Long-distance relationships: can love stand the separation?

Like international dating relationships, long-distance relationships are another 'relationship at a distance.' Among the 43 informants, 12 had, or had had, the experience of long-distance dating, which is too common to be ignored. Usually, the partners lived in two different cities and met each other only on vacations. This phenomenon has peculiar socio-cultural meaning in the Chinese context.

In China there exists the ancient fairy tale of Niulang and Zhinü, who were forced to live on two different sides of the Milky Way galaxy and could only meet each other once a year, on July 7 by the lunar calendar. The story of Niulang and Zhinü became a symbol of faithful love, and until now the bird bridge (*queqiao*), the place where they meet every single year, is a term extensively used to refer to a dating introduction. July 7 by the lunar calendar has become the Chinese equivalent of Valentine's Day. These spatially separated couples often quote the Song Dynasty poem *Fairy of the Magpie Bridge* (*Queqiao Xian*) by Qin Guan to encourage themselves to hang on to the relationship: 'If love between both sides can last for an age, why need they stay together night and day?' This poem romanticizes the spatial separation and the individual suffering from the conflict between society and individual, and becomes a 'theoretical basis' for long-distance relationships.

In the May Fourth Era, the writer Lu Xun (1881–1936) and his student and later partner and mother of his son, Xu Guangping (1898–1968), published a book of their love letters, which recorded their five months of courtship in 1925 and their three later brief separations, *Letters between Two* (*Liangdi Shu*). The collection of letters became a model for maintaining a long-distance relationship.

During and since the Maoist Era there have been a lot of husbands and wives living in different places, so that family separation (*liangdi fenju*) has become a particular term to describe this phenomenon. During the Maoist Era personal family life was not at all important compared to a career for the party-state. In 1968, the state launched the 'up to the mountain and down to

Dating landscape, power struggles, love geography 87

the countryside movement' (*shangshan xiaxiang*), and encouraged young educated people to 'go to the rural area, go to the grass roots, and go to the place that the country needs you most.' The movement lasted for the next decade and caused a lot of separations because of the need for 'revolutionary work.' Moreover, a lot of former politicians and intellectuals were displaced to the labor camps as 'counter-revolutionaries' and 'anti-socialist elements' to get re-education through labor from the people from the 1950s to 1970s, causing a lot of forced separation among family members. In summary, the rigid household registration system, job assignment system, and work unit (*danwei*) system under socialism gave people little flexibility to choose where they wanted to live. According to Zhang Yuehong (2005):

> Once the job was assigned, it was very difficult to switch work units even in the same city, not to mention between two cities. It was extremely difficult to switch work units to a bigger city or to a city of higher administrative rank. It was nearly impossible to switch work units from other cities to Beijing.
>
> (p. 8)

As I have mentioned, many senior college couples had to break up before graduation because of spatial separation in the Maoist Era; however, some dating couples choose to maintain their relationships despite being assigned to different places after graduation, and they have to live with and deal with the spatial separation. Till now, though work unit and job assignment systems have become less rigid, the household registration system has continued to be strong, and solving the problem of family separation through the government bureaucracy is still a time- and energy-consuming project that includes a lot of paperwork. Luckily, unlike before, a young person can choose to live in the city as long as he or she does not care much about *hukou*, and forced long-distance relationships brought on by the job assignment system have gradually become history.

In Lu Xun's age, letter writing was a method to express affection and love, but nowadays love letters are a cultural relic and letter writing has been replaced by much more convenient new technology – phone calls, cell phone messages, MSN, QQ, email, blogs, WeChat, WhatsApp, etc. New technology allows dating couples to contact each other almost at any time and place, and the development of public transportation makes traveling between cities much easier. High-speed rail services have been quickly developed in China since 2007, and their daily passenger numbers grew from 237,000 in 2007 to 1.33 million in 2012. In 1993, commercial train speeds in China averaged only 48 kilometers per hour (km/h), but 20 years later the high-speed train speeds reach up to 380 km/h, almost 8.5 times the original speed.[8] However, all these changes cannot make up for young people's feelings of loss, loneliness and isolation due to separation, and sometimes long-distance affection just cannot compete with the happiness of closeness and togetherness.

88 *Dating landscape, power struggles, love geography*

Sometimes long-distance relationships are closely related to suspicion, distrust, cheating, breaking up, and therefore violence. Zhong Qing makes it clear that dating is different from marriage and that she can stand long-distance dating, but not family separation (long-distance marriage):

> Now we are all students, long-distance dating is no problem. But when I work, I hope we won't have such distance. Work will cause pressure, and both men and women need somebody to support them. Dating in different cities is acceptable, but if you get married, I think it's better to stick together.
>
> (Zhong Qing, F, 21)

Zhong Qing and her boyfriend were high school classmates. At the time of interview, she was an undergraduate student at a famous university in Beijing, while her boyfriend was a student at a junior college in Tianjin. There is a two-hour train journey (30-minute high-speed train journey) between the two cities. She was determined to stay in Beijing or at least to go to Xi'an (the capital of her original province) after graduation, while her boyfriend might go back to their hometown, a small city in Shaanxi Province, because of his lower educational level. She told me:

> I will never go back [to the hometown]. If he insists on going back, then I will have to break up with him.
>
> (Zhong Qing, F, 21)

While Zhong Qing's break-up was being prepared to solve conflicts in the future and was just in her imagination, Wang Mei's break-up had already happened:

> I had a boyfriend. We appreciated each other, loved each other, and cared about each other. But he could not come to Beijing. He came here once, stayed here nearly one year, we lived together. Finally he went back to our hometown, you know, his college was so-so, and major was so-so, he couldn't find any good job in Beijing. And then there was so much pressure. Then we broke up.
>
> (Wang Mei, F, 25)

Although Wang Mei claims that her love for her ex-boyfriend was the best love she had ever experienced in her life, neither she nor Zhong Qing were willing to give up their development and *hukou* status in Beijing to pursue their relationships. Besides, Wang Mei's boyfriend was an only-child of his family, and his parents really wanted their only son to stay close to them. On the one hand, he could not find a good job in Beijing because of his unremarkable credentials; on the other hand, his parents mobilized their social network and helped him find a stable job as a public servant in the local government. The perfect love thus seems helpless and vulnerable when facing

Dating landscape, power struggles, love geography 89

the axes of the Beijing *hukou* system, life pressures, parents' requirements and spatial separation. It seems that the only right way for Wang Mei's ex-boyfriend was to leave Beijing and leave regrets in both their hearts.

Xiao Wei is a postgraduate student in Beijing and his girlfriend is a freshman in Tianjin. Their severe physical violence stems from his complaint of loneliness without her company:

> I texted her, 'Now I feel very lonely, sometimes I am bitterly disappointed. I miss you very much, and hope you always stay with me, but when I think that we will still be three years more apart, then I feel I could not stand any second. I would like to cry.'
>
> (Xiao Wei, M, 22)

Xiao Wei's text message caused his girlfriend's antipathy, so that she avoided him and even fabricated another boyfriend to make him jealous and angry. When Xiao Wei went to Tianjin without informing her first and saw her with a male friend in a cafeteria, his jealousy went out of control. The girlfriend was determined to play the fake boyfriend games until the end: she accused Xiao Wei of not loving her, not caring about her, and only putting pressure on her, while the fake boyfriend was the one who really loved and cared about her. Though Xiao Wei used the long distance to justify himself, his outrage made him blind, so that he believed his girlfriend's lie and could not stop himself from using physical violence to get revenge. When the girlfriend finally told the truth, a sense of regret, remorse, and guilt took hold of him, and he got down on his knees to beg for forgiveness. However, from that moment, their love changed, and their world became different. Bruises may only remain on the body for a short while, but emotional hurt is buried in the heart for a long time.

Only faked betrayal exists in Xiao Wei's story, while in many other long-distance relationships real cheating occurs. Xia Yu narrates the following, an episode that happened with her ex-boyfriend:

> At that time, I worked in Beijing, and he was in Liaoning. Once I visited him and found some clues of the existence of another woman. I did not say anything and waited. Later, after receiving a phone call, he went downstairs in a hurry, and then I watched from upstairs. To my surprise, a woman was just waiting for him downstairs, they even kissed and hugged right under my eyes. I picked up my stuff quickly and waited at the door. After a while, he came back. As soon as he entered the door, I gave him a big slap and left for good.
>
> (Xia Yu, F, 29)

If Xia Yu's narrative is from the side of being cheated on due to a long-distance relationship, Chen Bing's narrative is from the point of view of an active participant in infidelity, whose girlfriend lives in the dark:

90   *Dating landscape, power struggles, love geography*

I think the arrangement is perfect for me, she is in Tianjin and I am in Beijing, and our relationship is stable for marriage. She cannot control what I am doing here. I have plenty of chances to fool around and have one-night stands.

(Chen Bing, M, 29)

Although long-distance intimate relationships have been a common popular practice in China, the reasons have changed fundamentally – from being a celebration of romantic love, resistance to the household registration system, repression of sexuality, political punishment, and contributing to the country in the Maoist Era, to nowadays emphasizing individual development, focusing on personal need, career choices, and the pursuit of sexual desire in post-socialist China. Young people no longer regard long-distance relationships as a romantic arrangement, or as a test of their true love and commitment. They prefer the warmth of sticking together and have lost the patience for loneliness and separation, though the developments in communications and transportation provide much more convenience than before. Long-distance relationships are no longer desirable but have become a rich soil for conflicts, jealousy, infidelity, and even violence.

Conclusion

This chapter portrays dating landscapes in three ways. First, a within-Beijing dating geography, in which dating is stratified by the state policies of the household registration system and the *hukou* quota for entering Beijing, which have established a dating hierarchy within Beijing society. Second, there is an alternative geography, in which the market endows women with beauty and men with success and the power to penetrate the existing dating hierarchy in Beijing and engage in upward mobility. Third is a cross-border geography, which extends from Beijing to other cities/places (long-distance dating), from other cities/places to Beijing (new Beijingers dating), and from Beijing to other countries (transnational dating). In summary, our participants' intimate lives had been disembedded, to a notable extent, from traditional social mechanisms of choosing a partner and maintaining a relationship. The social bonds of family and the concerns voiced by parents still played a part in some interview narratives (see the next chapter). However, their significance as a psychological force of moral self-regulation and devices of external social control had receded. Instead, the participants found themselves rather directly confronted with the demands of state, labor market, and consumer society when negotiating dating.

The influence of class is demonstrated clearly in the social stratifications of the dating hierarchy, especially for *waidiren* who are working laborers. The race issue is vividly displayed in the international relationships under the influence of globalization, and I argue that some Chinese women learn to emphasize their subjectivity and choice, leading to the subversion of the racial

Dating landscape, power struggles, love geography 91

hierarchy. It is also clear that some concepts stemming from traditional Chinese culture, such as 'eating bitterness' and 'being loyal and faithful to the one you love from beginning till death,' have gained new meaning and are reinterpreted in young people's lives to emphasize individual autonomy and desire.

As a result of this process of biographical re-embedding, young men and women like our participants may face significant constraints in constructing intimate relationships, and the intersectionality of gender, class, race, age, state, and market is fully demonstrated in this chapter. The interconnection, negotiation, and competition of state and market co-exist everywhere in the dating lives of young people. The patterns of stratification imposed by state and market cut across the dating lives of the young people I interviewed: in their positions within the dating market, in the material interests they bring to bear upon their choice of partners, in their perceptions of ideal love, in their emphasis on individual subjectivity and desire, and in changes in their views of lifestyles. In particular, the state continues to intrude directly in our participants' private lives, with the *hukou* system serving as a paramount agent of stratification in the dating market. The Beijinger–*waidiren* framework constitutes powerful power struggles and social stratifications in the dating market, within which Beijingers occupy the most advantageous position, and with new Beijingers obviously a group with much more upward mobility and flexibility than *waidiren* who are working laborers, who hold the lowest rank.

In line with other studies (e.g. Farrer, 2002), this study confirms the role that participation in the neo-liberal marketplace may also play in young people's intimate lives. Nonetheless, this study departs significantly from these studies in highlighting the persistent role of the state in the organization and stratification of personal life. These patterns of stratification placed our participants in social positions from which the attainment of a fulfilling dating relationship is relatively unproblematic for some, but becomes fraught with uncertainties and obstacles for others. It has to be noted that there is not just one kind of dating hegemony, or dominant mainstream discourse, that affects young people's lives. This is also the reason why dating practices are filled with complexity and contradiction: choosing a *waidiren* as a partner is not only a practice of consciously resisting the predominant status hierarchy, but also a rational consideration in terms of providing care for aging parents; rejecting a white man and choosing a black man is not only opposition to the dichotomy of white/black, but also emphasizes individual subjectivity of sexual choice and satisfaction; and choosing a long-distance relationship may not be a celebration of romanticized loyalty, but a convenient way to maintain multiple relationships.

The findings point to the prevalence, among many of our participants, of highly materialistic and simultaneously strong gendered attitudes, through which material success and beauty may become pivotal to relationship satisfaction and shape an array of material interests based on which partners are chosen and which relationships are maintained. It is intriguing to find that young people resist the dating hegemony on the one hand and take part in

92 *Dating landscape, power struggles, love geography*

conforming to and redefining it on the other. Their individual subjectivity is rising to challenge the dating hierarchy through education, upward mobility, and the purity-of-love discourse. At the same time, they compromise with the overwhelming hegemonic discourses of gender, love, and dating by pursuing eye-appealing happiness and desire, even establishing alternative hegemony, such that women's beauty and men's success can be vehicles to resist the dating hierarchy, although they also set up a new hegemony in terms of market domination of dating practices. The findings may be suggestive of a burgeoning consumerism among China's new middle classes in the context of the country's sudden and rapid opening to capitalism, but they may also be illustrative of broader, international cultural trends in the era of global neo-liberal hegemony (Illouz, 2007); and maybe both.

The need to navigate this dating landscape largely on their own, without compelling moral guidance from family and community, had significant consequences for our participants' subjectivity. The participants' general interest in unfettered love and dating presumes the rise of 'a desiring self,' as evocatively described by Rofel (2007). Love, sex, and intimate attachment may be sought as ends in themselves, bringing pleasure, happiness, and fulfillment. Equally, they may be commodified as means of satisfying other (for instance material and financial) interests. In any case, it is an autonomous, reflexive self that pursues dating to such ends. Moreover, discussing their dating practices, our participants generally exhibited a high level of reflexive awareness of the range and limits of their agency, and the development of strategies for the circumnavigation of these limits often played a central role in their stories. Such enterprising selves, strategizing in the pursuit of self-fulfillment, in spite of their seeming obduracy, needs to be and can be worked through institutionalized hierarchies and boundaries.

While talking about dating geography, I describe how international dating is emerging under globalization, and the choice of skin colors becomes a symbolic marker signifying women's individual choice and desire in the global market. However, in this study, only three women mentioned their romantic relationships with foreigners and therefore the information is not rich enough and the discussion is not deep enough to capture the complicated situations of international dating in China. When I highlight skin color as symbolic marker of imagined race, I have to point out further that the issue of imaged race needs to be followed by discussion of nationality, such that whether black men are Nigerian or African-American may make a difference, or whether white men are American, European, or Turkish also may make a difference. Moreover, the symbolic markers of yellow, white, and black are too clear-cut to include those foreigners who may not exactly fit into the classification, such as Thai, Arabs, Japanese or Koreans. However, these types of international dating, especially dating between Chinese women and Japanese and/or Korean men, are also active in Beijing. Even the 'yellow' Chinese also includes the diversities of Taiwanese, Hong Kong, and American-born Chinese, etc. International dating should definitely be further studied as an individual topic, in which the intersection between the imaged races, femininity, masculinity, and nationality is an unavoidable issue.

Notes

1 These people wanted to have monogamous dating relationships, but their partners were unfaithful and so they were passively involved in multiple relationships.
2 www.shanghairanking.cn/Greater_China_Ranking/Greater_China_Ranking2014.html.
3 Beijing Development and Reform Commission, 2006–10 statistics of university and college graduates in Beijing. www.bjedu.gov.cn/publish/mainmain/1439/2011/20110120170408286543993/20110120170408286543993_.html. 2006–10 statistics of postgraduate graduates in Beijing. www.bjedu.gov.cn/publish/mainmain/1439/2011/20110120170007711414974/20110120170007711414974_.html.
4 epaper.ynet.com/html/2013-10/15/content_16385.htm?div=-1.
5 Shiji Jiayuan: www.jiayuan.com; Shiji Jiayuan 2012–13 annual dating and love report: dl.jiayuan.com/doc/marriage_views/20122013yearly.pdf.
6 *China Statistical Yearbook*, 2006, www.stats.gov.cn/TJSJ/ndsj/2006/left.htm.
7 *Beijing Statistical Yearbook*, 2012. www.bjstats.gov.cn/nj/main/2012-tjnj/index.htm.
8 en.wikipedia.org/wiki/High-speed_rail_in_China.

4 Sassy girl and tender boy
The transformation of doing gender

> I like *My Sassy Girl* because sometimes I feel that I'm violent too – I remember
> once when I learnt that my boyfriend had had three girlfriends before me, I was
> mad at him and asked him, 'Why didn't you tell me?' Then I kicked him many
> times.
>
> (Chen Lin, F, 24)

Although the Korean film *My Sassy Girl* was not publicly released in Mainland China, it is very popular among young people. The film was selected as
the fashion symbol of 2002 by Chinese Avant-garde Rank, a campaign organized
by *News Weekly*, Sina.com, *Sun TV*, and more than 40 other media institutions.
The movie *My Sassy Girl* is a love story: Gyeon-woo, a male college student,
falls in love with a pretty girl, but as their relationship progresses, he begins to
discover how crazy she really is: she exhibits a good deal of 'wacky' behavior,
she is often angry, and she always wants Gyeon-woo to please her, even if it
means that he will come across as a complete idiot in public places or that
he will get beaten by her.[1] The movie establishes a new model of dating: girls
are assertive, willful, and aggressive, while boys are loving, tender, and fragile.
The film seems to offer an implicit or invisible message to women: their violence
is 'acceptable or even glamorous' (Worcester, 2002, p. 3192).

I used the movie as stimulus material to break the ice in the focus groups
among male and female college students, to encourage them to talk about
their opinions and experiences of violent dating relationships. This movie
became an excellent entry point for the participants in the focus group to
lower their guard and to discuss freely the subject matter. Psychological
research, popular media, and our own everyday understanding associate
aggression very closely with the masculine gender (Squire, 1998); however, the
media image of the sassy girl offers an interesting entry point for exploring
both men and women's aggressive behavior, and new images of masculinity
and femininity. This chapter shows that the intersectionality of competition,
and multilayered discourses on gender, state, and market, leave some space
for young adults to justify women's aggression as socially acceptable.

This chapter addresses the following research questions. How do young
people perceive the image of the sassy girl? How do young women and men

Sassy girl and tender boy 95

make sense of their own or their girlfriends' violence? How do they do their gender, sexuality, and intimacy (Plummer, 2003; West and Zimmerman, 1987) through aggressive behaviors and interactions? How do young women negotiate the multiple expectations and demands that their boyfriends, parents, and the society impose upon them? What are the discourses that have made women's aggression in dating relationships socially acceptable? What are their tactics of resistance to establish autonomy and pursue love and freedom against normative gender roles and expectations? To what extent does women's aggression create new images of men and woman in dating relationships in contemporary China? How is the theory of intersectionality helpful for understanding their gender stories?

Pattern, types, and interpretations

This study shows that violence permeates extensively the different dimensions of young adults' dating lives: among the 43 participants, 39 had experienced dating violence of some sort, including physical assault (29), psychological aggression (31), and sexual coercion (17), either having inflicted it or having received it, and including both minor and serious violence. The other four participants had not experienced dating violence mainly because they had had little dating experience. It is worth noting that psychological aggression is predominant among violent dating behaviors, and more participants reported experiences of psychological aggression than physical and sexual violence. In this chapter, I will focus on physical violence and psychological violence, and how young men and women do their gender through their violent behaviors. Sexual violence and other sexual practices will be the focus of the next chapter.

In this chapter, I follow Straus et al.'s (1996) classification of physical assaults as either 'minor' or 'severe' violence.[2] In this study, eight of 29 participants reported they had experienced severe physical violence, the other 21 having experienced minor physical violence. The violence reported had different forms. 1) Serious girlfriend-battering occurred, in which boyfriends acted as perpetrators and girlfriends were hit and injured. Two of the eight severe cases belong to this category. Serious girlfriend-battering is not as common as mutual violence. 2) Mutual violence is the dominant phenomenon among dating couples with violent behavior, including both severe and minor violence; five of the eight cases of severe violence were mutual, while six of the 21 minor violence cases were mutual, and the participants concerned tended to claim their mutual violence was 'play-fighting.' 3) Women's aggression was quite common for both severe violence and minor violence, played a huge role in cases of mutual violence and was extremely obvious in cases of minor violence. For 21 cases of minor violence, 12 participants reported that their dating relationships involved women's aggression only. These data present a different image from that of 'women as victims' in existing studies, and show that women's severe and minor violence were

96 *Sassy girl and tender boy*

distinguished in all but two severe girlfriend-battering cases, as well as in four cases involving men's minor aggression. It is not clear whether this is because the dating period is the most powerful, brilliant, and exceptional time in the life of a woman, as some scholars have argued (Lloyd and Emery, 2000), and so may empower women, to some extent, and establish the grounds from which women's aggression may emerge. While the study of men's perpetration of violence is a long-term commitment of feminist mission, it is necessary for feminist scholars to pay attention to women's aggression, research this phenomenon, and compare it with men's abusive behaviors, given these existing data.

In English-language scholarship, the school of social conflict was the first to acknowledge women's aggression. Many quantitative studies of dating violence have revealed that reciprocal or mutual violence is more common in dating relationships than it is in domestic arrangements (Capaldi and Crosby, 1997; Straus, 2004) and claim that women's violence also widely exists within intimate relationships, and is therefore a major social problem in the USA. Radical feminists, who focus on the use of the wheel of 'power and control' to explain why women are abused in patriarchal society, criticize the school of social conflict as practicing 'victim-blaming' (Kurz, 1993), and showing a 'grudging acceptance of the extent and range of men's use of violence towards women and children' (Kelly, 1996, p. 35). These feminists tend to see women's violence only within the context of self-defense (Dasgupta, 2002; Schwartz and DeKeseredy, 2000) or as a reaction to years of abuse (Saunders, 2002), thereby creating the myth of 'non-aggressive women' (White and Kowalski, 1994), which implies that aggressive women are either *bad* or *mad* (Gilbert, 2002). This standpoint of second-wave feminists makes conducting research into women's aggression difficult because of the pressure on researchers to be 'politically correct' (Saunders, 2002, p. 1425), which means to handle men's violence first and to avoid discussing women's aggression. Some scholars point out that the second-wave feminists' lack of attention to, or denial of, women's aggression 'will damage the credibility of feminist scholarship and interfere with the future development of feminist theory' (Stith and Straus, 1995, p. 9).

The new generation of feminists has attempted to examine the myth of 'non-aggressive women' (White and Kowalski, 1994) in relation to real gender inequalities that exist between women and men (White et al., 2000). On the one hand, they have inherited the critique of the patriarchal system and argue that intimate relationships can be sexist, patriarchal, and therefore involve exploitation and violence. On the other hand, they want to take violence by women seriously 'without losing sight of the general patterns in intimate partner violence that need to guide antiviolence work' (Worcester, 2002, p. 1391) and deconstruct the notion that self-defense is the only framework through which to understand women's aggression (Sarantakos, 2004). This chapter adopts this standpoint (Sarantakos, 2004; Worcester, 2002) to understand Chinese women's aggression, and explores how it is possible for Chinese women to make use of different discourses (including 'Chinese' discourses and 'Western' discourses, state discourse and the market influence) that offer positions of resistance from which women can seek to change the power of male dominance and gain social acceptance of their own aggressive behavior. Furthermore, this chapter extends the understanding of gender-based violence in its intersection with other unequal social-structural arrangements (of class, race, ethnicity, age, and so forth).

The paradox of *My Sassy Girl*

The film creates an attractive but aggressive image of a woman, and this image can be found in many other recent cultural products that also integrate the two seemingly contradictory concepts of love and violence in single visual presentations. The music video of the Taiwanese pop song 'Xiao Wei' by male singer Huang Pin-Yuan shows the male actor being slapped by different women more than 50 times in less than five minutes. A popular Chinese novel, *Never-flowers in Never-dream* (*Meng li hua luo zhi duoshao*) by Guo Jingming, presents the love stories of two young women who are brave and kindhearted but violent, and who talk dirty. These media images, as emblematic manifestations of broader cultural narratives, may simultaneously work to cement and challenge hegemonic gender relations and impact on young people's everyday lives.

Many of the women participants explained that not only did they like the movie, but they also felt that they themselves were 'sassy' to some extent. As for men, they seem to have a different view regarding women's willful behavior. One film critic (Wu, 2005) has pointed out that 'owning' a sassy girl is just a masculine fantasy. In real life, men want to be the audience rather than the main character of the story. During data collection, many of the men stated that they would not put up with a girlfriend as aggressive as the woman in the film. It seemed that they wished to separate media entertainment from real life as they all preferred to have a 'traditional' girlfriend. Wen Jie said her boyfriend did not like the movie:

> He said that he would never have that type of girl as a girlfriend – what he wants is a tender and considerate woman. He likes girls with traditional values, such as moderation, goodness, and taking care of the family.
>
> (Wen Jie, F, 26)

The paradoxical perception of *My Sassy Girl* has penetrated young men and women's dating experiences and practices, especially at the site of women's aggression and men's reaction: women use the film to justify their own violent behavior, while men blame the film for encouraging women to be more and more aggressive. Apparently, the young women's identification with the 'sassy girl' in the movie shows that they welcomed the use of an attractive and aggressive image to redefine the image of traditional Chinese women, and

98 *Sassy girl and tender boy*

had a more positive and proactive attitude about their power and rights in dating relationships. Women like Chen Lin would like to identify themselves with the 'sassy girl' and use the image to justify their violent behavior. Men would like to blame the movie for turning women into aggressive beings. As Sei put it:

> It's all *My Sassy Girl*'s fault, that's the reason why girls turn more and more aggressive.
>
> (Sei, M, 20)

The young men's rejection of the image of the sassy girl shows that they still want to preserve the conservative concepts of femininity and masculinity as the ideals and feel that their girlfriends should maintain all the traditional virtues of Chinese women: 'tenderness, goodness, moderation and humility, austerity, tolerance' (*wen liang gong jian rang*) and be 'virtuous wives and good mothers' (*xianqi liangmu*) (Barlow, 2004, p. 261).

Although the young men and women had different attitudes and opinions about the movie, they seemed to agree on one point: they did not think that the sassy girl's behavior in the movie should be counted as violence. In a focus group of several female college students, the young women expressed their opinions as follows:

R: What do you think about the violent behavior shown in *My Sassy Girl*?
WANG: (19): Does it count as violence? Or is it just play?
ZHANG: (20): I feel that it isn't violence. The key point is that the man was beaten but happy, so I don't think it is violence.
LI: (19): Just because of the girl's personality. She is *renxing* (willful)
QIAN: (18): I don't think so; ... it is just being playful with each other.
SUN: (19): That's their mode of communication.In another focus group of five male college students, the following comments were made by three participants:
R: Does it count as violence?
MAO: (23): No.
HU: (24): In dating relationships, boys often indulge girls. After getting married, things will change.
R: If a boy adopts the entire behavior of the sassy girl toward a girl ...
YANG: (23): ... then, it's violence.
R: If a girl does all those things to a boy ...
YANG (23): ... then it doesn't count.

The two sets of participants in the two focus groups reached the same conclusion: that the violent behavior depicted in *My Sassy Girl* did not count as violence – they gave different reasons for why they felt this was so. The female group was inclined to define the act of hitting a man as playful behavior. The male group held a double standard regarding violence: the behavior that is violent when a man displays it toward a woman, and it is not violent when displayed by a woman toward a man. They seemed to be saying that such aggressive behavior on the part of women is just playful: men do not find it painful and they even feel happy about it; they can never be defeated by such mild challenges and they can deal with it. Both focus groups pointed out that women's aggression has many functions: it is a form of playful fighting, an expression of emotion, a communication mode, and even a way of increasing their intimacy and affection.

Willful and therefore 'normal'

The idea of willfulness (*renxing*) has often been used to explain women's exertion of violence in dating relationships. Among 29 female participants, 19 of them see themselves as 'willful' in some way. Among 14 male participants, 11 of them think that their girlfriends are 'willful' in some way. Therefore, 'willful' is a common expression used by both women and men to describe women's aggressive behaviors. In the words of two female participants, willfulness means 'what he wants me to do, I definitely will not do, and meanwhile, what he doesn't want me to do, I will definitely do' (Zheng Xin, F, 23), and 'What I ask him to do, he must do it right now, and meanwhile, what he asks me to do, I do it or not according to my willingness' (Deng Li, F, 33). Generally, willfulness describes people's impulse to engage in emotional actions and just to follow their will to do whatever they want. Such people are often regarded as somewhat childish and spoiled, which means they have less responsibility even if they do something wrong. In 2014, 'rich and a bitch' (*youqian jiushi renxing*)[3] became a buzzword on the Internet and in Sina weibo and WeChat friends' circle, and many people proudly proclaimed themselves to be like this. The popularity of the new buzzword gets rid of shame and adds glory to being a bitch (willful), as long as you have financial resources as a precondition. The notion of willfulness has strong implications for the hierarchies and dynamics of power within intimate relationships, and now money becomes one important factor of this matrix. In this study, it was found that not only did men and non-violent women define violent girls as willful rather than violent, but also violent women identified themselves as willful. Since women's aggression is just an act of willfulness, it is due to a childish personality and thus is no big deal:

> If I saw a girl hit her boyfriend, I would feel she is very willful, but I wouldn't call her violent.
>
> (Nan Yue, F, 22)

Sometimes women's willfulness is due to the fact that they are spoiled by their boyfriends. In describing her ideal dating relationship, Wang Mei (F, 25) emphasizes that she wants to be spoiled:

100 *Sassy girl and tender boy*

> Maybe because I'm a little bit willful, what I really want is just to be
> taken good care of and be spoiled – that is nice.
>
> (Wang Mei, F, 25)

Ding Ling (F, 22) described how her boyfriend's pampering behavior
turned her into a willful girl:

> He is the kind of person who treats me unbelievably well, does everything
> that I ask and tolerates me all the time. In fact, I feel that my willful
> personality is just a result of him spoiling me so much.
>
> (Ding Ling, F, 22)

According to these women's logic: first, having money and being pretty
would be huge capital for young women to be willful; second, being spoiled
by a boyfriend is a criterion for mate selection and has become a symbol of
attractiveness; third, being spoiled by a boyfriend makes them become even
more willful; last but not least, since their aggression is just a result of their
boyfriends spoiling them, their boyfriends should be willing to accept it and
neither of them should consider such behavior between consenting adults as
violence, but as 'normal.' Deng Li (F, 33) described how she used aggression
toward her boyfriend:

> After we quarreled with each other, I always told him to apologize to me.
> If he refused, then I would keep making trouble – I'm always violent
> toward him, but I only pinch him. I asked him to apologize; if he didn't
> comply, I would pinch him. Once, because I pinched him really hard, he
> pushed me away. I was very short and slim, so with just a little push, I fell
> to the ground. I thought that he was beating me up; I was very angry.
> Then I picked up a stone from the bookshelf, a very rare and expensive
> jade that he collected, and threw it at him. He ducked and the stone
> smashed through the window, leaving a big hole. It was not violence. It
> was just normal.
>
> (Deng Li, F, 33)

Deng Li pinches and throws stones when she is fighting with her boyfriend,
but she adopts the word 'normal' to justify her own behavior, maybe because
traditional Chinese femininity still has a strong influence on her and she
cannot afford to see herself as violent. As Deng Li said, 'I am fundamentally
a conservative woman who wants to be a virtuous wife and good mother.'
Here Deng Li plays a time trade-off: to be a 'good' woman most of the time
and to be a spoiled, willful woman some of the time. Labeling herself a feminine woman has perhaps prevented her from acknowledging her violent
behavior, so that emphasizing her aggression is only a way to assert herself
and demand an apology.

Transformation of aggressive women images

In China, women's aggression is not a new phenomenon, and different historical eras have different aggressive woman images. 'As feminists have recently theorized, gender identity is never fixed but is rather contingent on practice, performance, and context' (Rofel, 1999, p. 49). The stories that follow show how aggressive women in China have enacted their radically transformed identities.

In traditional China, the image of *hedong shihou* (the lion roars) existed, and even now it is very popular among the general public for describing an aggressive, jealous, and controlling wife. It stems from a story from the Song Dynasty. The eminent writer Su Shi had a good friend named Chen Jichang. Mr. Chen liked to give parties and invite female singers to entertain. His wife Liushi was a very jealous and fierce woman, who would shout and yell if Mr. Chen dared to invite female singers. Sometimes she even drove away his guests, so he was afraid of her. Su Shi wrote a poem and used 'the lion roars' to mock Mr. Chen for his fear of his wife, which became a literary quotation from the story. In ancient China, under the gaze of Confucian patriarchy and hierarchy, 'the lion roars' established the image of an undesirable woman. 'The lion roars' thus represents an 'otherness' among 'virtuous wives and good mothers' in ancient China, which appeared during the Song Dynasty, when an extreme emphasis was placed on women's 'three obediences and four virtues.'[4] It ironically demonstrated a subversive force against Confucian femininity.

In the Maoist Era, one image of aggressive women cannot be avoided: that of the female Red Guards (*nü hongweibin*), who participated in the widespread violence that accompanied the Red Guard movement in the Cultural Revolution. They 'cut their hair short (or more daringly, shaved their heads), donned army clothes, marched barefoot through city streets' (Honig, 2002, p. 255), and were as violent as their male peers towards father-like figures (schoolmasters, cadres, and so on). Generally, people think 'the especial eagerness of female Red Guards was noted in a movement that was supposedly all about class' (Laqueur, 2002). However, Honig (2002) argues that Red Guard violence was closely related to gender construction:

> On the surface, Red Guard violence was gender blind: there was nothing gendered about either its perpetrators or victims, whose class identity and political affiliation were far more salient. Beneath the surface, however, personal accounts and memoirs of the Cultural Revolution reveal that its violence was in fact deeply gendered, sexualized, and enmeshed in contested notions of masculinity and femininity. This does not mean that violence was about gender, but rather that its practice and representations had clearly gendered dimensions.
>
> (p. 256)

102 *Sassy girl and tender boy*

Young (1989) mentions that her female Red Guard informants reflected proudly on their personal violent acts, such as beating up a boy or man on the street. In fact, it is hard to say whether, at that time, it was their missing femininity or their enjoyment of the power they had in the name of class struggle, or both, that allowed and pushed them to adopt a 'masculine' disguise. Since the Cultural Revolution, Chinese feminists have put a lot of effort into critiquing how the Maoist Era deprived women of their femininity, and have called for the return of femininity as a way of liberating women. However, the reemphasis on gender difference and femininity is sometimes merely a disguise for a commodified femininity under the male gaze and the impact of the free market, and once again trivializes individual women's voices.

The female Red Guard and Chinese sassy girl show a transformation of an aggressive women image from the Maoist Era to the Post-socialist Era through the adoption of different strategies of doing femininity. The female Red Guard was a product of the Maoist discourse that 'men and women are the same' and that 'women hold up half the sky,' which was taken to mean that women had to give up a feminine appearance, act and work like men and compete with men, and finally articulate an 'iron girl' image in order to gain social power. The female Red Guards only existed in a public space, in a stage of class struggle, and in a collective and unitary style, whereas their private lives and individual voices were invisible and inaudible. The Chinese sassy girl is more sophisticated: she may look very feminine and sexy, but she acts in provocative, assertive, and willful ways. She may label herself a traditional woman rather than 'the lion roars,' but what she does is competitive and ambitious. She may or may not label herself a feminist, but being equal and respected is her greatest concern in intimate relationships. She may be aggressive in many ways, but she is submissive, vulnerable, and fragile in other ways. It seems that 'sassy girl,' both in the film and in reality, refers only to her individual emotional life, but is also closely associated with the changing urban environment and with different discourses. The image of 'the lion roars' tells the 'sassy girls' that the cultural core of Chinese femininity is to be 'virtuous wives and good mothers,' interpreted according to Confucian ideas, and is still expected by men in the present, and they know when and where they need to perform in this way. They have also inherited the spirit of the female Red Guard, but they have changed the battlefield from the public to the private, and express themselves willfully in the name of love rather than in that of class struggle. The state discourse and their parents' expectations make them understand the importance of being independent and educated. The open market, bourgeois lifestyle, and consumer society push them to the idea that being a woman means being glamorous, fashionable, desirable, and (un)available.

Rey Chow (1993) uses the term 'virtuous transaction' to describe Chinese women who learn to give up their own desire in exchange for their social place, and although they fulfill their part of the social contract they are still victimized by the patriarchy of imperial China. In the Maoist Era, women in the novel *The Ark* (Zhang, 1988) realized that the 'virtuous transaction' that socialist society expected of them had no necessary connection with their own well-being. Ng (1993) interprets 'virtuous transaction' as a social conformity. Women have two means of expression: either to adopt male speech directly or become implicit in the male production of the fantasy female. The female Red Guards' action was just like the 'virtuous transaction' of adopting male speech and involved a sacrifice of her feminine appearance to fulfill the national task. However, the Chinese sassy girl, for the first time, turns this 'virtuous transaction' to her advantage and can achieve her own well-being either by aggressive behavior or by her performance of virtue, though the danger of 'male production of the fantasy female' is arising under the free market.

On the other hand, aggressive women in China are also a response to the new trend of 'girl power' locally and globally. Based on his fieldwork in Xiajia village in northeastern China, Yan Yunxiang (2011) argues that there is a rising of girl power and a waning of patriarchy in rural China, especially in the setting of mate choice and courtship. He argues that 'youth autonomy in mate-choice is reflected mainly in the increasing power of young women' (p. 135), and young women persistently pursue freedom and intimacy in terms of decision making in mate selection. On the international level, Aapola et al. (2005) argue that:

> Girl Power draws on previous women's movement but argues a new, 'girl-centered' feminism. It reclaims the word 'girl' and sometimes focuses on young women's anger as feminist tool. It seems that many major issues still face young women, especially regarding body and sexuality. At the same time, it emphasizes autonomy, sassiness, and is sometimes depicted as sexy and assertive.
>
> (p. 203)

The cute but powerful girl-woman has become a pop culture icon: she is a heroic overachiever – active, ambitious, sexy and strong, offering an alternative cultural presentation of young people's everyday practices. In the Chinese context, aggressive women prefer to understand femininity as feminine appearance rather than as inherently submissive and passive behavior. Even their 'virtuous' performance is another justification of their aggression.

'Harmless' due to love, tolerance, and arrogance

From the interviews, I noticed that some male participants seemed to be more than willing to accept and endure their girlfriends' aggression. Li Qiang, an 18-year-old male college student, thought that an aggressive girl was a good dating choice. He argued in this way:

104 *Sassy girl and tender boy*

> Aggressive women are more direct and expressive, and therefore more lovable. It's easy to get along with them because I do not need waste my energy to guess what they want.
>
> (Li Qiang, M, 18)

Huang Mei, a 33-year-old nurse, quoted her male colleague's labeling of women's aggression as 'small temper,' and that it had a function of increasing affection between couples. He Rong, an undergraduate student, was slapped by his girlfriend quite often, especially when she was not satisfied with him. He did not feel ashamed when he told me the story, but felt quite proud of himself:

> I feel that a girl was born to be spoiled and to be loved by men. This is the way I love her – after she slaps me, no matter who is wrong, I'm always the one to say sorry.
>
> (He Rong, M, 23)

According to O'Keefe (1997), both sexes are more accepting of females' use of dating violence than that of males. It seems that this also is the case in the Chinese context. When the men talked about the movie, they clearly rejected the image of the sassy girl as violent and hung on to the ideal images of femininity and masculinity. However, when they deal with real-life situations, their attitudes may actually change and they may show more willingness and flexibility to adopt and accept different images of masculinity. They claimed that they would not regard women's aggression as violence, in order to build up a sense of both mental and physical superiority. Physically, males have certain advantages. As one male informant put it: 'after all, [women] are disadvantaged groups and do not have enough strength; if they want to hit us, they are just asking for trouble' (Yue Feng, M, 24). Mentally, they disdain to fight with a woman because they believe that 'it's shameful' (Chen Bing, M, 29) and universally unaccepted behavior. They want to maintain a certain image of themselves as modern men who are tender, generous, and tolerant, qualities that have been increasingly important criteria for young women when choosing dating partners.

Statistically speaking, the male to female sex ratio at birth in China was 111.3 to 100 in 1990, 118.0 in 2001, and 120.5 in 2005 due to the one child policy (Li, 2007), and therefore in the current dating market there is a surplus of young men relative to their female peers, which makes young women even more valuable in the dating market. According to the 2010 Population Census by the National Bureau of Statistics of the People's Republic of China,[5] there exists a huge imbalance between unmarried men and women, and the longer the situation goes on, the more serious it becomes. The sex ratio between unmarried men and women born in the 1990s was 110:100, while the ratio was 136:100 among the unmarried born in the 1980s and 206:100 for those

Sassy girl and tender boy 105

born in the 1970s. In the age group of 30 to 39, there were 11.959 million unmarried men, but only 5.82 million unmarried women. In this situation, a lot of older men have had to find a mate among younger groups; moreover, the practice of 'women date up and men date down' makes the competition for younger women even more intense. As I described in the last chapter, many well-off older men are interested in twenty-somethings, either looking for girlfriends or wives, or are interested in searching for mistresses, second wives or affairs, and so the Uncle–Lolita Complex has become a dating fashion. However, there are pretty, well-educated, financially secure thirty-something women who will not date younger, poor men. Young males in their twenties may feel disenfranchised and sexually frustrated because of the 'dating up' culture and the intensive competition from more successful older men.

Moreover, having a girlfriend is one of the most important issues in establishing masculinity, especially for young straight male college students. For them, the campus is like an imaginary dating market filled with temptation and competition, and having a girlfriend shows success. At the time of the interviews, several college male students told me similar stories: when they had a girlfriend, the first thing that they liked to do was to walk intimately with their girlfriends on campus, which became a gesture to show off the fact that they had a girlfriend, sometimes with the hidden agenda of warning competitors that the girl 'was taken.' Dating relationships fulfill their need for intimacy, sexuality, and masculinity, and so young men in their twenties do not want to give them up easily; thus being 'tender' and 'warm' becomes their major strategy to attract female peers. At the same time, it is important for them to see their girlfriends' aggressive behavior as harmless.

A new word, *nuan nan* (sunshine boy), was recently created and listed as one of the ten most popular phrases in 2014. The word became the label for the most desirable men in intimate relationships. It describes the type of men who can provide a sense of warmth for their partners, who can spoil their partners, who have high sensitivity in understanding women, and at the same time have a sense of leadership to direct the intimate relationships. *Nuan nan*, in a way, echoes the 'tender boy' that I have described in this chapter. However, it is still a very patriarchal term, describing a category of men with a superficial tenderness and warmth and deep-down firmness – which means that although they may have improved their communication skills and sympathy levels, they have not changed their view of women and do not regard women as equals. This study presents a picture quite different from the stereotyped gender images: women can be aggressive, dominant, willful, and selfish, while men can be tender, tolerant, and spineless. The young men's tolerance of their girlfriends' aggression shows that they are learning to cope with changing social norms and to be tender, because for modern men, tenderness, cleanliness, and being supportive are becoming ideal qualities. It turns out that justifying women's aggression is their method of developing an image of themselves as modern men who are charming, desirable, and highly valued.

106 *Sassy girl and tender boy*

'Can you just do what I say?'

Sassy girl and tender boy becomes a new dating mode; however, there is never a one-dimensional picture in the complex and fast-changing city. Such young women expect their boyfriends to be tolerant of their willfulness and aggression, but this does not mean that all their boyfriends are prepared for it. Some men are reluctant to accept their girlfriends' willfulness and complain about it, while others may use the demand to '*tinghua*' (do what I say) as their weapon to fight against women's aggression or to demand their girlfriends' submission, which often brings serious violence that no one would like to see.

In Jankowiak's (2002) description of the gender stereotypical configuration of women from the Chinese men's point of view, in addition to being gossipy, anxious, and sentimental, 'being inclined to make a fuss out of nothing' is on the list. This latter trait vividly describes some men's attitudes and reactions to women's willfulness. Chen Bing, a university lecturer, dated a girlfriend five years younger than himself, and thought that the relationship was tiring since she was quite demanding of attention while he was looking for freedom and affairs, at the same time, maintaining a long-distance relationship with the girlfriend. He said:

> Sometimes I do not know whether I am dating a girlfriend or nurturing a daughter. You know, it is so tiring to have to take care of her like this.
>
> (Chen Bing, M, 29)

The metaphor 'nurturing a daughter' reveals that he is helpless when facing his girlfriend's willful behavior – though he tries hard to cope, behind the scenes it is just like the term *tinghua*, which treats women as children rather than adults and displays men's superiority to obey their demands. It seems that, in this situation, men and women develop two sets of logic about *tinghua* and willfulness, which can be appropriated by different people to justify their divisive purposes. The game of the pairs of contradictions is played as if they were practicing sadomasochism (S&M)[6] in their everyday lives, the difference being that participants in S&M know that they are playing domination and submission, while young people may not. Thus it is more risky for them to play at crossing the line and the situation may sometimes carry something playful into disaster.

Tinghua is a strong term in Chinese and carries the sense of 'obey me and do what I say!' It is usually a requirement that the 'listener' accept what is being said and be submissive, and this constitutes a contradiction with women's willfulness in dating relationships. When their boyfriends cannot accept women's willfulness and hope they will be obedient, the disparity becomes obvious between being assertive/aggressive/willful and being a 'good woman' under men's patriarchic eyes and requirements. Both Qiu Ye's (F, 23) and Huang Mei's (F, 33) stories are highlighted to explain how their

Sassy girl and tender boy   107

boyfriends cannot accept women's willfulness, and therefore *butinghua* (not doing what I say) is first used as an accusation by their boyfriends and then becomes a prelude to violence and even a justification for men's violence. Qiu Ye is an office worker, who narrates a conflict with her ex-boyfriend that caused them finally to break up:

> He said, 'You are my girlfriend; you have the obligation to *tinghua*.' I said, 'My parents do not control me, how dare you?' He said, 'You are mine. Only belongs to me.' I was angry and told him that I never belong to anyone, I own myself. I stormed out and told him my decision to break up.
> (Qiu Ye, F, 23)

The requirement '*tinghua*' implies a hierarchy, wherein men have the power to ask women to be obedient and submissive. To go further, it demonstrates a struggle of 'the concept of ownership of a person': does the man own the woman or does the woman own herself? The concept of ownership is a rather modern notion in China, and falls under the bourgeois discourse of individual right and autonomy (Zhang, 2005). Qiu Ye found breaking up to be her way out, while Huang Mei was stuck with the serious abuse triggered by her 'not listening,' according to her boyfriend's accusations.

Huang Mei was a nurse, who had dated her boyfriend for two and a half years at the time of the interview. They pooled their money and bought a two-bedroom apartment in suburban Beijing, and planned to get married. Everything seemed perfect. One day they went to a building materials market and planned to buy some materials for home decorating. However, on the way back home, they got into an argument about what kind of home they would like to have. The boyfriend insisted on bringing some old furniture into the new apartment in order to save money. However, Huang Mei insisted on having a brand new home without any old furniture, especially any that had been used by the ex-wife of the boyfriend. They could not come to an agreement, and suddenly the boyfriend moved from anger into violence:

> He suddenly pushed me from behind, it was so hard, and I almost fell to the ground. I was surprised and asked, 'What are you doing?' He did not say anything but kept on pushing me, I fell, stood, and fell again – I did not want to go back [to] the apartment with him, he pulled me by force – it was summer, the buttons of my shirt were broken and I was humiliated and embarrassed since a lot of people were there. I wished somebody could come up and offer some help, however, nobody seemed [to] care. I suddenly felt so scared and did not know what would happen next. In the elevator, I tried to hint to the security guard with my eyes [hoping he would intervene], however, the security guard turned his back to me and he [her boyfriend] began to scold me violently and abusively. As soon as we got to the apartment, he started to push me to the window. The

108 *Sassy girl and tender boy*

apartment was on the 17th floor, and he threatened to drag me to jump from the window with him –

(Huang Mei, F, 33)

This was not the first time that Huang Mei had experienced violence from her boyfriend, but this was definitely the most serious and damaging incident. She was beat up and raped, and her body was black and blue. One traumatic part was that Huang Mei felt that the once-dreamed-of new wedding apartment was turning into a nightmare and her once-handsome fiancé was turning into an unstable monster who could explode at any time, anywhere. For her, the most unacceptable element of the violence was that the boyfriend had perpetrated violence to her in the community, in public spaces, where a lot of neighbors witnessed it, but no one provided any help, which deeply influenced her sense of self-esteem, face, and dignity. She lost her interest and excitement in decorating the new apartment, and for quite a long time afterwards, every time she went to the apartment, or even set foot in the community, she could not help but remember the violent scene, cry, and want to break up with the boyfriend. She even thought of selling the apartment. She sought help from a psychological counselor and attended all kinds of lectures on how to improve intimate relationships. She became quite reflective concerning her relationship with her boyfriend:

I was thinking: Why could he require this of me? How he could shout at me and ask me to keep silent? Sometimes I tried to talk back. Then he said, 'You are a woman, I am a man. Man acts like this, woman should be tender, listen ...' He lost his temper very easily ... after he hit me, he said sorry to me. He also said that it was difficult to change me and make me listen to him.

(Huang Mei, F, 33)

In the logic of the boyfriend, it was not his fault that he used violence, it was Huang Mei's disobedient behavior that provoked him to lose his temper, and his temper escalated into physical abuse just in order to make her 'listen' and train her in submissive and traditional femininity. In his eyes, Huang Mei was a willful woman who provoked his violence rather than a victim of dating violence, as the general public usually would perceive it. Hence, willfulness becomes a double-edged sword: on the one side, it is used to justify women's aggression as normal; and on the other side, it is used by men to justify their violence by accusing women of willfulness. From both Huang Mei's and Qiu Ye's stories, we can see clearly that demanding their partners to *tinghua* actually is a strategy by men to confine women within the feminine, submissive gender norm, therefore emphasizing men's domination and superiority.

Zheng Xin (F, 23) is another woman who experienced severe violence from her boyfriend. The first time I interviewed her, I was surprised to find that she managed to keep smiling while talking about her experience of being

Sassy girl and tender boy   109

physically abused. The second time I met her, maybe because we knew each other better, she started to describe more details of the abuse than she had the first time. When she mentioned that her boyfriend forced her to get down on her knees (*gui*) when he was hitting her, she could not help but cry, because getting down on one's knees has a special meaning for Chinese people, symbolizing absolute obedience and unavoidable hierarchy. She described the scene:

> When he hit me, he told me to get down on my knees, but I did not. The room was so small, it only had one table and one cabinet. He started to push me, punch me, and grab anything to throw at me. I was so afraid when he threw an iron chair at me; luckily, he missed, otherwise I would be paralyzed. He insisted that I get down on my knees, while I said I would not. We were trapped into a stalemate. Whenever I said I would not get down on my knees, he would hit me even harder, kicked my legs, stomped on my legs ... [long crying] ... No one ever treated me like this, my parents, grandparents love me very much. When I was little, during the Spring Festival, other kids need to kowtow to get the red pocket money, but I never did that ... [long crying] ... I fled from his room when he needed to go out, I have been hiding for several days.
>
> (Zheng Xin, F, 23)

Huang Mei and Zheng Xin were the two participants reporting the most severe physical violence in this study. Their stories share many similarities with domestic violence cases, especially in the 'cycle of violence' (Walker, 1979, 2000) of experiencing the tension-building phase, explosion phase, and the honeymoon/reconciliation phase. Every time, after the bad incident of physical violence, their boyfriends used all kinds of strategies to reconcile with them – apology, gifts, excuses, romantic gestures, promises that they would never do it again, etc. – and the 'honeymoon' period would last until the next round of tension-building and violence broke out. Huang Mei attempted to convince her boyfriend to attend couples therapy but he constantly resisted. After six months of an on-and-off relationship, Huang Mei finally decided to leave the relationship for good.

However, Zheng Xin experienced cycles of violence many times, over a longer period, during her relationship with her boyfriend. Over the last ten years I have interviewed her many times, and witnessed her reconciliation with, marriage to, and divorce from the same man. After her boyfriend converted to Christianity, they did manage to maintain a peaceful life together for quite some time after they got married. Two years after the marriage, cruel violence exploded again, when Zheng Xin found her husband had cheated on her and she questioned him about it. The physical abuse was unbearable, and this time she chose to run away for half a year. She finally made a decision never to go back, hired a lawyer and sued for divorce. Though she presented evidence of domestic violence and the infidelity of the husband, the court granted the divorce but provided no favorable judgment. She lost the

110 *Sassy girl and tender boy*

apartment that she had financially contributed to buy and for which she had shared in making the down payment and the mortgage payments, which had risen in value more than three times at the time of divorce, and for which she received only limited compensation. Her story shows that it is extremely difficult, and takes a very long time, for abused women to break the evil cycle of violence and finally get out. Moreover, the current institutional context, for example the actions of the courts, ignores the situation of abused women and does not offer just treatment.

Taormina and Ho (2012) compared dating, engaged, and married individuals in China, and found that married people reported lower satisfaction in their relationships than single or engaged individuals in every dimension, with the engaged always reporting the highest satisfaction. This suggests that dating people make initial investments in new relationships while engaged people make even stronger commitments to their partners, perhaps in anticipation of the joys of marriage (p. 39). Another study, by Stets and Straus (1989), compared violence in the three intimate relationships of dating, cohabitation and marriage, and found that the male-only violence rate was highest for cohabitation, and female-only violence was highest in (non-cohabiting) dating relationships. These two studies, however, employ different classifications, especially of 'engaged' and 'cohabitation,' the former study emphasizing the intensity of commitment, while the latter just describing the living arrangements of 'moving in together,' which may or may not include a vision of the future and strong commitment.

For example, Huang Mei and Zheng Xin were both cohabiting with their boyfriends at the time of the interviews in 2004, when Huang Mei was engaged but Zheng Xin was not. Young Chinese couples do not practice the customary ritual of proposal which symbolizes that the relationship is moving to the next stage of engagement, as their Western peers do, which makes 'cohabitation' maybe a more precise concept for classifying different intimate relationships among them. The first article mentioned above does not pay attention to violent elements in the intimate relationship and seems to over-romanticize the satisfaction brought by commitment. In China there is an old saying: 'If you are dating, that's a matter of two, while if you are going to get married, it's a matter of two families.' The commitment surely can bring enjoyment, togetherness, and happiness, while causing stress, anxiety and uncertainty at the same time. This study echoes Stets and Straus's (1989) finding, in that the most severe violence occurred among the 18 cohabitating individuals among our 43 participants.

The anxiety of money in the highly competitive and commercialized metropolis also plays a role in stirring up violence. In Zheng Xin's story, her boyfriend's low-paying job and their poor living conditions – an underground room with shared kitchen and bathroom – sometimes led directly to their arguments, which escalated into physical violence. In Huang Mei's case, her boyfriend did not have a stable job and was living on his savings, mainly from the stock market, which was decreasing in value constantly at the time of the interview. Such financial insecurity challenged his sense of masculinity since the market society uses financial 'success' as almost the only criterion for assessing a man's value. This made him hesitate to join in Huang Mei's excitement and aspiration to have a new home and new life together.

Masculinity in flux

In January 1997, the famous Taiwanese writer Lung Yingtai wrote an article entitled 'Ah, Shanghainese Men,' which was published in a local Shanghai newspaper (*Wen Hui Bao*). This article eulogizes the loveliness of Shanghainese men, who can 'go to the food market and bargain for every penny, wash clothes and cook meals willingly and skillfully.' The article presents an image of 'new good men' (*xin hao nanren*), celebrates the achievements of the CCP's policy on gender equality, and draws the conclusion that tenderness is the most important quality for being a liberated modern man. However, contrary to Lung Yingtai's intention, this article is misread as mocking Shanghainese men's lack of masculinity and has been critiqued fiercely by many male writers in Shanghai.

The debate on Shanghainese men is in resonance with the process of reconstruction of Chinese femininity and masculinity in the Reform Era. After the Cultural Revolution, as women began to shake off their masculine appearance and seek the missing femininity, another trend, 'looking for the real man,' enlivened the general public. In the 1980s, a stage play, later adapted into a film, entitled *Looking for the Real Man*, presented an 'old' single woman who attempted to find 'a real man' but failed. The drama and film raises questions within society: 'Why does China lack "real men"'; 'Why is the society turning into a rise of the feminine and a decline of the masculine (*yinshengyangshuai*)?' According to Zhong Xueping (2000), the 1980s were a tough time for Chinese men, who felt that their masculinity was 'besieged,' and therefore reconstructed their masculinity. The open market allowed the general public to project their ideal of masculinity onto the hero images created by Japanese actor Ken Takakura, French actor Alain Delon, and American actor Sylvester Stallone in the movies: this included 'toughness, courageousness, and decisiveness' (Louie, 2002), therefore 'hegemonic masculinity' as Connell and Messerschmidt (2005) described it. Thus Chinese masculinity became trapped in a fantasy of Western masculinity.

Since the middle of the nineteenth century, China has been feminized in the Western imagination (Brownell and Wasserstrom, 2002; Chow, 1993) and therefore Chinese men have also been feminized under the 'hegemonic masculinities' (Chen, 1999; Connell and Messerschmidt, 2005). The discussion in these accounts concerns the relationship between different kinds of masculinity and the ways in which issues of sexuality and embodiment are featured. Within the framework of 'hegemonic masculinity,' there are specific relations of dominance and subordination played out between groups of men. For example, Chinese men were called 'the sick men of East Asia' (*dongya bingfu*)

112 *Sassy girl and tender boy*

by the Western imperialists in the semi-colonial, semi-feudal China, and the image of individual men was associated with the weakness of the nation. It is interesting to note that it was at exactly the same time that the Kang-Liang reformers used the weakness of China's women to represent China's national vulnerability and regarded educating women as a route to national salvation. The strong West and the weak China, 'masculine Western men' and 'feminine Chinese men,' innovative Chinese radical intellectual reformers and weak Chinese women – all these dichotomies enmeshed Chinese femininity and masculinity with nationalism at the beginning, when the concept emerged. Special attention needs to be paid to the fact that Chinese intellectual reformers rejected their own stereotyped image of 'sick men' under the Western gaze and focused on the vulnerability of Chinese women.

Even now, a few existing studies on Chinese masculinity still focus on how Chinese men make efforts to improve their masculine image and reject their feminine image; unfortunately, they are going farther in the wrong direction by intensifying the stereotyped image of Chinese men. However, Kam Louie (2002), in his book *Theorising Chinese Masculinity*, resists the hegemonic masculinities in the global world and advances the dyad *wen-wu* (cultural attainment and martial valor) as an analytical tool and theoretical construct for conceptualizing the Chinese masculinity matrix. He describes the dyad in detail:

> The core meaning of *wen-wu* still revolves around cultural attainment and martial valour. However, in practice *wen* can refer to a whole range of attributes such as literary excellence, civilized behavior, and general education, while *wu* can refer to just as many different sets of descriptors, including a powerful physique, fearlessness and fighting skills. I have shown that as a cultural construct, the *wen-wu* ideal must reflect the multifarious social conditions that produce it.
>
> (p. 161)

In this way, we can understand 'being tender' as just a by-product of civilized behavior and general education in China, and not a creation of masculinity in the Post-socialist Era but developing far back in the history of Chinese masculinity. In China, there have long existed 'talented scholar/beautiful woman' (*caizi jiaren*) stories, and Louie (2002) theorized this concept by using the hybrid Chinese/English term 'wen masculinity.' Kipnis (2011) renamed it 'literacy masculinity' and pointed out that academic success is an attractive characteristic of both male and female students in the current Chinese educational system, especially for boys. Just like in the old days, talented scholars (*caizi*) were allowed to achieve social and political power through success in the imperial examination system (*keju kaoshi*). Moreover, there are numerous narratives in Chinese tradition depicting a female desire for sensitive, slender, pale, and studious boys (Kipnis, 2011). In a way, 'tender boy' is not only the creation of current dating subculture and revising gender relations, but has a long cultural

Sassy girl and tender boy   113

tradition of acceptance. According to Rofel (1999), the ground of masculinity has shifted from that of the Maoist Era to that of the Post-socialist Era:

> Official and popular discourses alike represent the gendered activity that will bring modernity not, as with Maoism, as a transgression of feminine identity in the state sector via labor, but rather as an assertion of a natural masculinity in the market via risk-taking exploits. As Lyn Jeffery (1995) has argued, the post-Mao imaginary of modernity feminizes the state sector as the realm of passive inactivity and loss, while market economy signifies masculine prowess.
>
> (p. 97)

Maoist heroes of the collective era (such as soldier Lei Feng and iron worker Wang Jinxi) have given way to new heroes – the athlete, the rock star, and the wealthy businessman (Jankowiak, 2002). When the market portrays 'success' as one of the most defining qualities of masculinity, for young men in their twenties who have not acquired 'success' and become new heroes, tenderness becomes the one significant quality to win the hearts of women. Chinese masculinity is hybridized by modernity and globalization: when hitting women becomes an abusive behavior disdained by almost all of society, men may learn other ways of establishing their 'martial' valor, such as by going to the gym and building up a tough body. As being 'successful' becomes the final criterion for measuring Chinese masculinity, tenderness becomes the modern young man's extra quality in becoming a modern man. In this situation, Chinese men develop flexible tactics to cope with all kinds of love crises in 'reality' while formulating a strong nostalgia for men's ultimate power in the context of past patriarchy, especially concerning the issue of whether women should go back home to be housewives.

When (imaginary) cheating happens

I notice how money (lack of money, undesirable material conditions) and infidelity (jealousy, betrayal, and cheating) become two important areas of power struggle within couples and are closely associated with violence. However, it is important to look into the whole set of circumstances to understand the power struggles in dating relationships, as different couples definitely having different issues and reasons for arguing, conflict, and violence. The following section will focus on how young men and women deal with infidelity, and how psychological aggression becomes predominant in such situations.

Different people have different perceptions of violence and subjective feelings of experiencing violence. Even the same act, inflicted or received by different people, may be perceived differently – some may see it as harmless and feel it is no big deal while others may take it seriously and feel hurt. For example, Yan Li (F, 25) expressed that 'words [verbal aggression] can be much hurtful than physical [violence],' because she thought that some of her

114 *Sassy girl and tender boy*

ex-boyfriend's words deprived her of self-esteem. This is the reason why I do not stick to the typology of dating violence in existing studies, but instead pay more attention to the experiences and stories, the context of violence, and the interaction between the couples. It is intriguing that several participants mentioned that their experiences of their partners' infidelities were their most hurtful experiences, and they were willing to label them as emotional betrayal, and therefore psychological abuse.

Cyber-stalking

He Yi was a 22-year-old male college student at the time of the interview, who had had a pretty girlfriend, originally from Shanghai, during his sophomore year. One day he bet with one of his friends that he could court and charm another Shanghainese girl within a week, who coincidentally was his girlfriend's close friend since they came from the same city. He Yi had a little feeling for the new girl but was determined to win. He started to make moves by sending flowers and chocolates, and it was no surprise that his girlfriend immediately found out what he had done and asked to break up. He Yi was regretful and asked for her forgiveness by renouncing the bet; however, the girlfriend thought that what he had done had violated her lowest acceptance of tolerance and humiliated her self-esteem. She was too proud to take him back. At this point, He Yi started to suspect his girlfriend of cheating on him, and started cyber-stalking her. He Yi paid a computer expert to set up equipment on his computer with the power to stake out his girlfriend's computer: whenever and however she used her computer online, he would know; he could copy any file from her computer; he could even write directly on her computer screen from his own. He waited online for many days but did not find that she had done anything suspicious. Just before he was going to give up, one night he found that she was chatting with her male high school classmates online and had even complained of his recent behavior to a classmate. He Yi suddenly felt that he had caught something, and impulsively wrote a sentence on her computer screen: 'Bitch, do you think I do not know what are you doing now?' I cannot imagine the feeling of shock, anger, hurt, and anxiety that his girlfriend must have experienced when the sentence suddenly popped up on the screen of her computer. At the time of the interview, He Yi confessed to me:

> I think that what I did was emotional abuse. Now I feel deep regret, but I cannot undo what I have done. I think this had some bad impact on her. She asked quite a long sick leave from school afterwards. Later on I noticed that she had a new habit that, whenever she chatted online, she always deleted her chatting records at the same time. She hid from me and never talked to me again. I went to Shanghai during her sick leave, I was hoping that we could reconcile but she just did not come out to see me.
>
> (He Yi, M, 22)

He Yi's story is strangely enmeshed with both 'performed infidelity' (he made moves to the other girl for a bet) and 'imaginary infidelity' (his unreasonable suspicion of his ex-girlfriend and his overacting by cyber-stalking). He Yi defined his behavior as emotional harassment, because his stalking was not physical but was through an invisible cyber format, which may cause even serious emotional terror and damage.

Cold war

Emotional abuse and manipulation becomes a very dominant form of violence within young dating couples. Follinstad et al. (1988) find that verbal harassment/criticism, isolation, and jealousy/possessiveness are the forms of psychological abuse most frequently found within intimate relationships. When infidelity is involved, whether real or imaginary, it is the most dangerous time for emotional aggression to arise.

Wang Mei (F, 25) was an office worker at the time of interview. One day she went home and surprisingly found her boyfriend would not talk to her. She was confused and later on she learned that her boyfriend had peeked at her online chat records with her male colleague and found some content to be flirtatious. She attempted to explain that it was only for fun and nothing really had happened, but her boyfriend did not listen and treated her coldly for several days. Wang Mei was frustrated and also furious about not only his covert fidelity management but his 'giving her the cold shoulder' as well:

> I would rather have physical violence than 'cold war,' I wish we just got into a fight and then get over it. Not talking to each other is just unbearable.
>
> (Wang Mei, F, 25)

For Wang Mei, 'cold war' was all about emotional oppression, and physical violence was a 'hot war' expressing emotion. She thought that the former definitely brought more emotional torture for her, and wondered if minor physical violence would be a quicker and better way to fix the problem. However, Wang Mei never questioned who authorized the boyfriend with the right to peek at her chat records, or whether privacy is allowed even in an exclusive relationship. It seems that she accepts her boyfriend's reaction and her own 'guilt' because of love, and what she wants to change is the form of punishment.

Emotional blackmail

Sometimes break-ups and infidelity are the fertile soil for nurturing emotional blackmail, especially when one party wants to break up and the other does not, and if a third party is involved in an intimate relationship, things can get pretty ugly and complicated.

116   *Sassy girl and tender boy*

Luo Ting was a 24-year-old senior postgraduate student at the time of interview. She had a boyfriend who was a classmate and they had dated for five years. During her internship with a foreign company, she met a supervisor who seemed mature and charming. They started to flirt, one thing led to another, and she spent a night and had sex with the supervisor. She thought it was a harmless mistake of youth and decided to keep it secret, treat it as a one-night stand and move on with her life with her boyfriend. However, the supervisor did not want to let it go and seduced her to have one last farewell sex session. She agreed. He induced her to speak a lot during sex and audiotaped it. Afterwards he threatened that if she dared to leave him, he would upload the recording online, send it to her boyfriend, the department that she studied in and the job placements for which she was applying. Thus, she was trapped.

The other tactic used quite widely is 'rumor-mongering and character assassination' (*zhaoyaozhongshang*), which means to use slander and make false accusations to the partner within his or her neighborhood and/or workplace. This tactic has strong Chinese characteristics, because in the Maoist Era the work unit system (*danwei*) deeply penetrated people's private lives, and flaws in personal character and behavior could become fatal obstacles to career achievements. Though now the work unit does not pay as much attention to employees' personal lives as before, this socialist practice still remains in the market-oriented society.

Mei Gui was a 27-year-old housewife at the time of interview, and her marriage had encountered numerous resistance from her husband's family. Mei Gui and her husband were high school classmates in a small town in Henan Province. After the college examination, Mei Gui went to a vocational college and later became a policewoman in the township, while her husband (then her boyfriend) was admitted to one of the top universities in Beijing, with everyone predicting a bright future for him. The boy's family thought that their son was way out of the league of Mei Gui and worried their dating relationship would jeopardize his career development, and therefore they did whatever they could to sabotage their dating relationship. His father went to Mei Gui's home, scolded her parents for not raising their daughter properly, and threatened that he would never allow or approve their marriage. His older sister spread a rumor about Mei Gui to her friends, community, and police station to accuse her of 'seducing her brother, cohabitating with him in order to get pregnant, therefore forcing him to marry her.' In a rather closed, conservative small town, this type of accusation meant great moral damage to a single woman. Under the great pressure of the disapproval of the boyfriend's family, they broke up for a while to avoid further direct confrontation between the two families. However, when Mei Gui reconciled with the boyfriend and found out that he had had a brief dubious relationship with another woman during their break-up, to my surprise, she did exactly the same as her boyfriend's sister had done to her. She called the other woman, her friends, and her company to spread rumors and humiliate her. When she told me this story with the joyfulness of defeating her opponent, I wondered

Sassy girl and tender boy 117

whether it had ever occurred to her that her actions had caused similar pain and humiliation to that which she had once suffered, therefore making her feel a sense of guilt, remorse and sympathy. Why, when her boyfriend was cheating on her, was her first action to condemn the other woman and not her boyfriend? It seems that she had already established a code of 'first wife,' just like in her defense – only the other woman was the seducer to make her man make the mistakes that all men would make. Once a victim of this kind of emotional torture, she suddenly became a perpetrator with 'expertise.' She may have learned it from her own experience, but it was definitely a vicious cycle of violence.

Punishment or opportunity?

Sometimes infidelity in intimate relationships may become the last straw for physical violence. Xu Ling's story perfectly demonstrates this point. Xu Ling, a 24-year-old office worker at the time of interview, had dated a man for more than one year. After she found out that he had cheated on her, she decided to break up with him. The boyfriend did not want to end the relationship, so he apologized, bought gifts, said sweet things and tried pretty hard to win her back, but she was not touched and felt it was unfair. Their relationship had become so enmeshed that she found she could not end the relationship. Thus, she found that violence was a way out:

> One day I slapped him as hard as I could. The week before last, I choked him for a long time. Last week, I pinched him black and blue all over his body. Yesterday, when I was mad at him and started hitting him without thinking, his waist bumped into the door and it's still hurting him, and I spilled some hot water onto his leg. I am afraid that I am getting used to violence, and it became the only way for me to solve problems. The guilt that I felt when I used violence the first time has gone – I don't know what I can do.
>
> (Xu Ling, F, 24)

Unlike other women who use 'playful,' 'willful' or 'normal' to describe their aggressive behavior, in this situation of her partner's infidelity, Xu Ling used the word 'violence' more directly and more readily to define her aggressive behavior. Many Western studies of women's violence often examine it within the context of self-defense and see it as a result of long-term suffering of being abused. Here, women's aggression seems like self-defense, but it is not. It is more aggressive and proactive. It is a type of punishment: women such as Xu Ling feel that they have the right and the moral power to punish their boyfriends, who deserve it because of their cheating behavior.

Since 1949, polygamy, adultery, and pandering have been sharply condemned by the state discourse of communist morality (Kristeva, 1986), which consolidated the exclusivity in dating relationships directed towards marriage and set up a high moral standard to refute any sort of sex outside marriage

118 *Sassy girl and tender boy*

and clearly distinguish 'right' from 'wrong.' The romantic love discourse emphasizes that exclusivity and jealousy are accepted as expressions of love and so they are legitimate grounds for women's violence (Borochowitz and Eriskovits, 2002; Fraser, 2003, 2005; Jackson, 2001). Zhang Na et al.'s (2012) study was based on a national probability sexuality survey in 2006 with data on 3,567 people aged 18–49 years old who were in a marital (89%) or dating/cohabiting (11%) relationships. In attitudes, extra-marital sex was completely unacceptable to 74% of women and 60% of men, and either somewhat or completely unacceptable to 95% of women and men. Most (77%) women wanted severe punishment of men's short-term commercial sex and women's jealousy was equally elevated by their primary partner's episodes of commercial and non-commercial sex. Both discourses and statistics offer women an ideological basis to justify their aggressive behavior, and the guilt that men feel because of their infidelity also makes both of them see the violence as justified.

He Rong, a 23-year-old college student, referred to his girlfriend's cheating as a form of psychological violence against him, but he did not hit her as a form of punishment, as Xu Ling did. Instead, he regarded it as one of the many obstacles he might face in his life and was determined to treat her better in order to win her back:

> She really broke the basic principle that I believe in, but so what? When you find the thing that you love and care about the most, then you … you must give up the principle. I have no other way – I have to regard it as an opportunity that forces me to grow.
>
> (He Rong, M, 23)

Li, Chan and Law's (2012) article, 'Gender Differences in Covert Fidelity Management among Dating Individuals in China,' presents quite interesting findings. The article was designed to explore tactics and behaviors people use to monitor their partners' fidelity. This study found that women were engaged in more covert fidelity management than men. Ironically, covert fidelity management was found not to correlate to women's relationship satisfaction, but was significantly associated with men's negative satisfaction. These findings have interesting implications for understanding romantic partners' behaviors in infidelity-related situations, and especially help us to understand why young women just cannot but help conduct covert fidelity management even when they are satisfied with the relationship and have confidence in themselves – maybe because they are aware that their powerful advantageous position in dating is short and temporary, because they grow up in the midst of sexism and gender inequality, and they are deeply threatened by the 'leftover women' discourse and therefore quite desperate to protect their last piece of paradise and to establish an equal-love utopia. Sometimes violence becomes their voice and aspiration to get hold of what they believe in, to express their discontentment, to assert themselves, and to demand sexual loyalty and achieve gender equality.

Making use of the role of 'victims'

Even in a relatively mutually violent relationship, young women make use of their suffering to present themselves as 'victims,' tending to define the situation as domestic violence, blaming their boyfriends, and defining them as the perpetrators, while at the same time trivializing and ignoring their own violent behavior. Wu Yun (F, 31), a researcher, has cohabitated with her boyfriend for two years. They seemed to have a great time together until one day her boyfriend's parents suddenly showed up and lived with them in a very crowded apartment. Wu Yun felt extremely uncomfortable but did not feel right to complain about it. She started to work late, lived with friends, and tried her best to stay out of the home temporarily. One day she came home and found her boyfriend was browsing a pornography website and chatting online with other girls, and suddenly her unhappiness and anger burst: she grabbed her boyfriend's laptop and showed it to his parents. The parents did not know what to say. The boyfriend surely felt embarrassed and dragged her into the bedroom:

> I accused him never love me. I accused him never considering my feeling to let his parents stay for such a long time ... we suddenly began to fight with each other. His parents kept knocking the door but we did not stop beat each other, and none of us opened the door ... I am quite strong as a woman, and he is quite slim as a man. We both ended up hurt a little: my waist was strained and his nose was bleeding. The next day, I went to the hospital to check the injury and asked for a written report. I consulted my friend who was a lawyer. Then I went to the police station to report the case of domestic violence and demanded that he give me a written apology.
>
> (Wu Yun, F, 31)

Wu Yun was good at mobilizing social resources to defend her rights, such as seeking help from the police, lawyer, hospital services, and the Women's Federation. Wu Yun seems to make use of the stereotypical victim image in domestic violence to blame her boyfriend for the violence and to define him as the perpetrator, while at the same time trivializing her own violent behavior. In current Chinese society, domestic violence has become a symbolic marker that signifies severe wife/girlfriend-battering, involving abusive husbands/boyfriends and battered wives/girlfriends. With women's consciousness of violence highly raised by Chinese feminists, the stereotypical concept of violence makes it easier for them to regard themselves as victims and trivialize their own violence in the context of mutual violence.

Thus, in the context of mutual violence, women's violence or (over-)reaction embodies different kinds of meaning, contrary to conventional perceptions: 1) it is symbolic of how they have gained more power in dating relationships; 2) it reveals that they have many choices of how to deal with intimate violence – by being aggressive perpetrators, or submissive victims, or utilizing

120 *Sassy girl and tender boy*

the identity of victims to fight back; and 3) it reflects the formation of a new image of a more independent, competitive, willful, and proactive woman.

In this study, three of the 29 women had the experience of attempted suicide with the aim of making their boyfriends feel bad, to gain their attention, or to win them back. There is a Chinese phrase that describes how women deal with conflicts in intimate relationships: 'tears, words, suicides.' The phrase puts women in the position of the disadvantaged. The three different forms of behavior are expressions of pain and a strategy to gain power in intimate relationships. Women know that *shiruo* (making use of the position of the disadvantaged) is a useful strategy in a power struggle that can make men give in, albeit temporarily.

Meng Xi, a 27-year-old woman at the time of interview, suffered from child sexual abuse and grew up within quite complicated relationships (Wang and Ho, 2007b). Meng Xi used to appropriate 'words and suicides' tactics before the break-up of a relationship, especially when her boyfriend wanted to break up with her but she did not agree.

'Keep calling' is her preferred tactic with 'words,' but the outcome of this practice is sometimes hurtful and unexpected. When one of her boyfriends wanted to break up with her, she repeatedly called him, to the point of annoyance. One day she called him when he was having dinner with friends. He proceeded to transfer his mobile around the table and asked his friends to humiliate her verbally one by one over the phone. After the call, Meng Xi never called him again, and they finally broke up.

'Self-harm' or 'attempted suicide' is another typical tactic she uses to gain power. Meng Xi talked about the long-delayed breaking-up drama that she performed before the end of her first serious relationship when she was 18:

> I knew that he is warmhearted, when I cannot control him, I would make him upset by harming myself. I know it's bad, but I turned on the gas, tried to jump off a ninth-floor balcony, and cut my wrists. But every time, to be honest, I didn't want [to die]. I was very clear about it, but I could not control my feelings, which were so strong. Maybe I just wanted to upset myself and make myself wake up. I want to know where my limit is. But the people around me cannot endure this behavior.
>
> (Meng Xi, F, 27)

Sometimes women's actions seem quite impulsive and irrational. Wang Fang, a 25-year-old woman, had dropped out of university and did not have a job at the time of her interview. She was cohabiting with a man who was also unemployed. One day the boyfriend cooked a meal but Wang Fang was late to come to the table and the boyfriend was quite unhappy about it. Then they got into an argument and the boyfriend smashed his bowl and stormed out. Ideally, this would be a 'time-out,' and everything would go back to normal. However, several hours later, when the boyfriend got back a little bit drunk, the violence escalated:

I was playing a computer game while eating some dinner; he was a little bit drunk and patted my head. He thought he was just teasing me, but I thought he was hitting me. I smashed my bowl just like he did, he came over and slapped me. We quarreled with each other, threw things at each other, and slapped each other. The fight didn't last a long time, but I was deeply hurt. I could not believe that I had been exposed to domestic violence. After that, I couldn't fall asleep, I was very angry and then I swallowed more than 20 sleeping tablets.

(Wang Fang, F, 25)

In the interview, Wang Fang did not admit that she had tried to kill herself, and spoke in a very easy tone: 'I know that 20 tablets cannot kill me, even 100 maybe do not work.' She told me that she just slept one whole day afterwards and then woke up and everything was fine. However, one of her friends told me that she was sent to the emergency room and had her stomach pumped in order to get better. She may have felt ashamed or embarrassed at the time of the interview and therefore downplayed the seriousness of the incident; however, her narrative captures the situation quite vividly. 'We are devoted to each other, hurt each other, and harming myself is exactly equal to harming him.' In the Chinese context, the happy ending to 'tears, words, suicides' can be manifested in two ways. One is the woman's success through the display of emotional dependence with the intention to control; the other is the man's submission through conceding. Lempert (1994) argued that both words and suicides could be understood as acts of autonomy and to 'wrest control of herself and the power' (p. 433). Wu Fei's (2011) study on suicide in rural China also pointed out that, 'attempting suicide, as extreme as it sounds,' was a:

strategy to win this emotional, micropolitical, and moral game of power. This logic is embedded in passion and sensitivity to what is considered right, but it is still rational: I see it as a moral sensibility. It was their love for each other that won moral capital for both. Nevertheless, love did not decrease their conflicts, but intensified them. It was love that made an otherwise trivial conflict so unbearable as to provoke a suicide attempt.

(p. 219)

The trap of 'one and only' love

Why does violence often occur in situations of jealousy, cheating, and infidelity? In order to tackle this question, I need to dig deeper into the relations between love and violence. According to Lindholm (1988), romantic love has three components: the idealization of the other, its occurrence within an erotic context, and the expectation of it enduring into the future. Jankowiak (1995) thinks that romantic love has the two characteristics of idealization and uncertainty, and has an essential anxiety:

122 *Sassy girl and tender boy*

idealization and uncertainty ... which later substantially contribute to a person's sense of illusion and deprivation. The idealization heightens the expectation and the pitch of intensity ... The uncertainty drives the pitch of emotional intensity from one extreme to another, exaggerating the sense of deprivation or absence. In this sense the essence of romantic love is anxiety.

(p. 168)

When participants in this study were asked to describe their ideal love, 'falling in love at first sight' (*yijianzhongqing*) and 'being loyal and faithful to the one you love from beginning till death' (*congyi'erzhong*) were two common answers, which illustrate their ambition to establish a loyal, exclusive, possessive, faithful, and 'one and only' type of intimate relationship in the midst of uncertainty and anxiety. The concept of 'falling in love at first sight,' influenced by the romantic love discourse from the West, involves physical attraction and sexual arousal at first sight and becomes a fairy tale-like entry point for pursuing the love journey. In contrast, 'being loyal and faithful to the one you love from beginning till death' is a concept with deeper historical and cultural connotations, and is more like a measurement of love with the characteristics of a sociological institution. In China it stems from Confucian ideas, where it was a restriction to discipline women to maintain chastity and submission to their husbands for their whole lives. In the Christian West, where monogamy was the theoretical norm and institutional arrangement, a vow to be loyal and faithful to death is taken by both men and women in the typical wedding ceremony. Here both male and female informants used the word to express the expected happy ending of ideal love, yet their responses also show that the one-way compulsory loyalty of women to men of imperial China has turned into an imagined mutual commitment for couples nowadays. It directly links dating with inevitable marriage, using a spiritual description to commit to a heavy loyalty and constructing a picture of 'happily ever after' as an 'afterimage' of dating. Ironically, this image, narrated by informants, combines an inheritance of Confucian ideas and the Western romantic love discourse, therefore empowering an old-fashioned sexual discipline, within the love utopia, which transcends class, social strata, race, ethnicity, rural–city division, and Beijinger–*wadiren* division, at least on the expressional level.

In China, since the May Fourth Movement, the concept of 'love,' together with those of 'democracy' and 'science,' has become a symbol of a new cultural value system, which contributed to a revolutionary and anti-feudal China (Meng and Dai, 2004). During the time of the May Fourth Movement fighting for romantic love and free dating was a significant representation of women's pursuit of individual subjectivity, with the emphasis on 'free' meaning that it should not be bound by the institutionalized marriage system symbolized as women's one-dimensional submission to men to 'be loyal and faithful to the husband from beginning till death.' However, in current Beijing, this cliché is dug out to represent ideal love, by highlighting the interpersonal dynamics while tactically ignoring the current complex and uncertain situations of the post-socialist society. It also shows that young people's description of ideal love is filled with paradoxical desire for control and domination in the first place. As Wu Yun states:

> The love I expected is so perfect that it turns into an unlimited exaction of loyalty. My feeling for him is absolutely exclusive, and I want him totally to belong to me.
>
> (Wu Yun, F, 31)

By sticking to this ideal perception of love, Wu Yun seems to risk turning love into exclusion and dominance and therefore conflict and violence. Many informants admit that with the 'one and only' pure ideal love in their minds, they enter into a changing and complex dating market and get frustrated with this 'harsh reality,' and they become either enchanted with love or easily lose faith in it. Love suddenly becomes something sacred, like religion, in their lives, saving them from boredom and meaninglessness. For these Beijing young people who live in the commodified cosmopolis, romantic love somehow turns into a spiritual pursuit, sometimes perhaps the only pursuit in their lives. Larson (2000) describe:s

> the lover emerged as a sign of new, exciting, and utopic emotional fullness. A number of stories and novels depicted people in the cities and counties who were overwhelmed by strong emotions of love and who struggled against social restrictions that masqueraded as revolutionary or 'feudal' ideology. The post-Mao lover was dedicated to the loved one and to the emotion of love to the point of death, promoting a self that was unified in thought, emotion, and action.
>
> (pp. 351–352)

Larson argues that the existence of love is always amidst different struggles within the social context. In the May Fourth Era, love was entangled with revolution and was used as a weapon to demonstrate individual subjectivity and opposition to semi-feudalism and semi-colonialism in China. In the Maoist Era, romantic love was criticized as a bourgeois sentiment and personal affection needed to be reconciled with a grand narrative of love, such as love for the party, people and country. The history of the pursuit of free dating is filled with political violence, and the CCP's socio-cultural authority has always violated personal dating lives. Right now, the pursuit of love has become a modernity project to shape the self and its emotions – as Illouz (2007) put it: 'Heterosexual romantic love contains the two most important cultural revolutions of the twentieth century: the individualization of lifestyles and the intensification of emotional life projects' (p. 9). Researching the

124 *Sassy girl and tender boy*

relations between love and violence provides a rather clear understanding of why so much psychological violence happens when infidelity is involved in a dating relationship; moreover, it is central to capturing the individual motives of authenticity, autonomy, equality, freedom, commitment, and self-realization through their gender performances and struggles.

One-child policy and revised parental influence

In understanding young Chinese women's assertiveness and therefore aggression it is important to take note of the impact of China's one-child policy on the family. The target group in this study is that of youths born in the late 1970s and early 1980s, part of the first cohort born under the one-child policy. Among the 43 informants, 17 were only-children and 23 had had the experience of dating only-children. These young adults had grown up in unusual family circumstances, in which their parents treasured them as only-children and hoped they would achieve a great deal in the future.

A series of studies shows that in urban society female only-children get more attention from parents than girls who have siblings, and that they receive equal education to boys. Their parents are very concerned about their academic achievements; they encourage their development and invest a lot in them. Girls score as high as boys in math achievement and have equally high educational aspirations (Tsui and Rich, 2002). Generally, these urban girls are empowered and have a strong sense of gender equality (Chow and Zhao, 1996; Davis and Sensenbrenner, 2000; Deutsch, 2006; Fong, 2002; Tsui and Rich, 2002). Bringing this taken-for-granted equality into dating relationships, young women claim that they will not tolerate violence from their boyfriends and even have the right to exert violence by saying 'my parents haven't laid a hand on me since I was born' (Wang Mei, F, 25). Unlike in the USA, where physical punishment is regarded as serious child abuse, in Chinese tradition physical punishment is more a normal way of disciplining children. There is an old phrase: 'Failing to discipline the son is the fault of the father' (*zi bu jiao, fu zhi guo*). Therefore, parents having not laid a hand on a daughter/son since they were born is definitely a symbolic sign of being treasured.

After a mutually violent event, only-child Xia Bing (F, 20) even stated that: 'If he dares to touch me again, I will perish together with him.' There is a big weight and height disparity between Xia Bing (45 kg) and her boyfriend (100 kg). However, she does not live within the 'ongoing pattern of fear,' as Worcester (2002) suggests, which means that men have an ability to control women and children by creating an ongoing pattern whereby women and children live in fear. She is capable of acting out of anger without considering possible negative consequences: her own aggression can be ignored because her size is small and her boyfriend's behavior is unforgivable.

Deutsch (2006) raises an interesting hypothesis: that 'the one-child policy may help urban daughters in China more than did decades of Maoist slogans

Sassy girl and tender boy 125

about gender equality' (p. 385). Here I agree that the one-child policy does offer space for urban only-child women to be more assertive and willful, and therefore they have more advantages to pursue their love, freedom, and autonomy. On the other hand, we need also to understand that under the one-child family system, the relationship between parents and children became even closer, which meant that parents had to invest more and expect more too. Chu and Ju (1993) argue that in the Post-Mao Era, relations among young couples are less stable than parent-children relations, so that young men and women may share intimacy with their partners but somehow always regard themselves as their parents' children and trust their parents as the most reliable persons in the world, who 'can love you unselfishly with all their heart' (Ding Yi, F, 22). Many informants told me that obtaining parents' approval and blessing is still extremely important in their dating lives, and some participants reported their willingness, though with a certain reluctance, to break up under the pressure of parents' disapproval. As college student He Yi narrates:

> What I really want to do is to show filial piety to my parents. This is why I try so hard ... I keep telling them, I do not want to get married. Marriage is bondage for me. If I finally get married, it must for them.
>
> (He Yi, M, 22)

Many participants expressed their fear of getting married as He Yi did, and the growing number of single men and women in big cities can demonstrate that they are afraid to turn the excitement of love into the everyday routine of marriage. Parents sometimes become the huge external pressure pushing them to set foot on the 'right' and 'only' path – to get a good degree, find a proper mate, buy an apartment, get married, and then have a child or children. Then the parents will feel relieved, and that their overall responsibility for their children has finally been completed. Though some participants complained that 'parents do not have their own lives, so monitoring our lives become their main focus and ambition,' they seem to respect their parents much the way they used to, and to consult them (except on sexuality) and obey them often.

This is why some other studies illustrate that women turning 27 were regarded as 'left over,' even in their own family and were under huge pressure from their parents to get married (Fincher, 2014). In the lesbian and gay community, the pressure from the parents to get married is extremely strong and therefore brings out some unimaginable phenomena. Common Language (2010) published the first report on the experience of violence among Chinese lesbians and found that the participants experienced more violence from parents than they did intimate partner violence, with the critical moment being when the parents found out their sexual orientation and felt disappointed that their daughters might never live the 'normal' life that they expected. Sexologist Liu Dalin and activist Zhang Beichuan estimate that 90% of gay men in China enter into marriages with heterosexual women who are unaware of

126 *Sassy girl and tender boy*

their sexual orientation, and have created a huge group of 16 million to 25 million '*tongqi*' (wives of gay men) (Liu, 2013). Instead of deceiving unaware women, some gay men and lesbians help each other by entering '*xinghun (xingshi hunyin)*,' or formal or fake marriages between a gay man and a lesbian, to cope with parents' pressure, and this is pursued as a way to cope with familial and societal pressure to marry (Liu, 2013).

Based on in-depth interviews with 14 parents who bought or wanted to buy an apartment for their grown-up children in Guangzhou, Zhong Xiaohui and Sik Ying Ho (2014) proposed a 'negotiative intimate relationship' as the ideal parent-children relationship that parents pursue, which integrates three intersectional elements: collective decision making, monetary transfers, and emotional communication. With the current rocketing apartment prices in Beijing and other metropolitan cities in China, parents invest a substantial amount of money to buy an apartment for their adult children. While the general public focuses more on the behavior of '*kenlao*' (using up the parents' money) among the younger generation, I cannot help but notice that when there is monetary transfer from parents to children for their property purchase, parents nowadays attempt to obtain more power and even take very active roles in their adult children's mate selection. In Sun Peidong's (2012) book, *Who is Going to Marry My Daughter?*, based on nine months of fieldwork in a blind date corner in a public park in Shanghai, she describes the recent phenomenon of Shanghainese parents (in reality, parents in many major cities) who gather in a park to arrange blind dates for their children, using advertising posts and pictures. Most of these parents were born in the 1950s – they were 'Children of Mao,' accepted 'incomplete education' because of the Cultural Revolution, and experienced all kinds of opportunities and predicaments that the economic transformation had brought, and finally became the middle class in the city. Their children were the first generation of only-children in the Deng Era, who were fully invested and highly educated, and were bachelor's degree graduates, overseas students, PhD holders, company employees, civil servants, accountants, and even wealthy businessmen, etc. It is interesting to note that many adult children were kept in the dark when their parents were actively taking the responsibility to find suitable partners for them – although the parents' success rate was very low, the parents just never gave up and kept trying. This market is a very realistic, heteronormative, and exclusive one which sets a high bar for selection of potential candidates, where people with lower education or different sexual orientations, or who are migrants or working laborers, etc., are completely excluded. It became an intersectional setting of gender, class, desire, money, and market, in which parents emphasized most the utilitarian and materialistic levels – family background, education, job, and income – of the potential candidates.

Some participants feel that the love of parents is just stressful and unbearable and therefore controlling, and they choose to escape to the big city, cut/decrease communication with parents, and stick with their boyfriends or girlfriends in spite of their parents' disapproval.

Sassy girl and tender boy 127

There is a popular online discussion group on douban.com called 'anti-parents' in English, with a horrific Chinese name: *fumu jie huohai*, which means 'parents are all hurtful and harmful.' The objective of the discussion group is clearly stated: 'we are not "not filial," we just want to lead a better life on our own. Under the condition of filial piety, we resist bondage and harm from parents with decayed and ignorant minds.' It is interesting to note that this critical online discussion group has attracted thousands of young members, and became a private virtual space for young people to complain, share, and discuss with their peers their tensions and conflicts with their parents, even just for the purpose of emotional relief and outlet. This website never facilitates communication and dialogues between parents and young adults, and most of the time parents are kept in the dark, while young adults may perform quite well as filial sons or daughters in front of them.

Anthropologist Yan Yunxiang's (2011) account of children-parent relationships is the most optimistic that I have seen in many years. Yan quotes young urban and rural women and argues that young people's 'happiness in life makes their parents happy and thus their pursuit of pleasure and comfort in life should be viewed as their way of fulfilling the duty of filial piety.' However, what if they have different views on happiness, what if they have different ideas about the ideal life? Yan (2011) does not go further to discuss the potential conflicts and ambivalence, but presents a picture that is too beautiful to be true.

From the parents' side, on the one hand they attempt to play an active role in their adult children's intimate lives and in their mate selection, and regard 'getting married and having (a) child(ren)' as the only option for a promising future. On the other hand, they are reluctant to teach young people about love, sex, and dating, and they fail to provide good role models for establishing intimate relationships for their adult children in the fast-changing society. The young adults thus learn and practice love and dating all by themselves. They attempt to develop a new emotional vocabulary suitable for dating which did not exist previously and so could not be passed down by their parents, and which cannot be directly imported and translated from the West. Sometimes this lack of vocabulary can be expressed in a very non-verbal, reactive and un-nuanced way – through dating violence. This is not the only reason for dating violence, but it seems to be one contributor. The participants seem to be trying to build emotional bridges while at the same time walking over only partially finished bridges as they date.

Women's competition vs. men's expectations

When I asked these young people about their ideal imagined marriage, I found a paradoxical and rather interesting phenomenon: many young men expect their girlfriends to become housewives in their imagined marriages, while young women desire to have a career and somehow regard dating as a never-ending competition with their boyfriends. This shows that in dating relationships, men and women may have different perceptions of gender roles,

128   *Sassy girl and tender boy*

marriage, and family, and they have different strategies and tactics for doing their masculinity and femininity:

Sometimes conflicts and violence arise from the differences. He Yi classifies two types of desirable girlfriend and shows that he has finally chosen the type that totally depends on his own need.

> One is the good insider helper (*xian neizhu*), very intelligent, and helpful with my career; the other type is tender and considerate, and can do chores. Sometimes, I feel that I do not need others to control me, so now I want to find the latter type.
>
> (He Yi, M, 22)

According to my understanding, the categories are not very different: both types of girlfriend are essentially helpers, the difference being that one is helpful with his career, the other is helpful with his life. However, in comparing the two types of girlfriend, he feels that if a woman is very helpful to his career, maybe she will be too competitive and assertive to be controlled. So he expresses his preference for the latter one, emphasizing women's domestic skills, and avoids being controlled. Here what He Yi said is only about finding the type of desirable girlfriend for marriage – but what are these unmarried young women's expectations of gender roles and arrangements in their imagined future marriages? Both Ding Yi and Zheng Xin are female postgraduate students, and both of them express their dissatisfaction with their boyfriends' 'ridiculous' expectation of them becoming housewives after getting married:

> He always boasts that he is a modern man, emphasizing gender equality. At the same time, he always says something like, I never count on you to make money, you can do nothing other than be a housewife. I do not understand what he means, but I definitely do not want to be this. I have a higher degree than he does, I believe I would not make less money than he does now. I don't know why, maybe he just wants to belittle me, get rid of my superiority, and have me stay with him.
>
> (Ding Yi, F, 22)

> I think that I should be independent, and it's safe to rely on myself. He always wants me to be a housewife, but I think that is not suitable for me.
>
> (Zheng Xin, F, 23)

At the time of the interviews, both Ding Yi and Zheng Xin were pursuing a higher level of education (master's degrees) than their boyfriends had achieved (bachelor's degrees). Though they were still students and did not make regular money, as their boyfriends did, they did have more potential to develop their careers. In these two cases, another situation needs to be noticed: neither of their boyfriends were rich or successful according to so-called 'normal' criteria: they did not have houses or cars, or even stable jobs. In this competitive consumer society, it seems much wiser for them to invite their girlfriends to strive together with them for the life they expect. Why would they want to refuse their girlfriends as allies and be solitary heroes? It seems that both women thought that their boyfriends belittled their capabilities, trying to make them more vulnerable and dependent in the relationships, which just shows the boyfriends' insecurity.

Unlike the boyfriends' expectations of their girlfriends becoming house-wives, the girlfriends regard dating as a never-ending competition. The sense of competition makes women put their self-esteem as the first priority in their lives, and in some situations they may even overreact when they feel that the boyfriends challenge their independence and autonomy, no matter whether they mean to or not:

> Once he told me that he would make much more money to *yang* me. I immediately lose my temper, and said how come I will lose my job? I also told him, 'I can earn much more than you, how dare you talk to me like this?'
>
> (Deng Li, F, 33)

Though the boyfriend's intention was just to show his concern about her overt hard work, Deng Li immediately picked up the verb, '*yang*,' which means 'to provide for or take care of,' and is most commonly used to describe parents' care for their children and, later, children's care for their parents in old age (Osburg, 2013). Deng Li even sensitively felt that her identity as a successful businesswoman was challenged by her boyfriend since he might have been implying that she should quit her job to be a housewife. Moreover, the reason she lost her temper was that she might have thought that her boyfriend was even 'downgrading' her to the category of 'mistress' or 'second wife,' since the term '*baoyang*' also has the character of '*yang*,' meaning that young women rely on wealthy businessmen or powerful cadres to provide them with a monthly stipend, apartment, and car, and solve all kinds of dif-ficulties in trade for sex. Deng Li obviously viewed such women with disdain, and was determined to be a financially independent modern woman. The sense of competition also brings a dilemma for modern women like Deng Li in the dating market: on the one hand, they internalize the dating norm of 'women date up' and hope to find somebody that they can 'look up to' and 'rely on,' both emotionally and financially; on the other hand, they are so assertive that they easily put the dating partner into the role of competitor and then feel terrible and stressed. Qin Cui explains:

> I expect that a man should be like a man, who can take charge of many things and have the ability to tell me what to do – but sometimes I think, if I can find the ideal man, maybe I will feel uncomfortable again because he may look down on me and I will feel I am not good enough.
>
> (Qin Cui, F, 31)

130   *Sassy girl and tender boy*

Wu Xiaoying (2010) wrote an article to document a current debate about the identity crisis of young women in the Reform Era on whether to 'work well' (*gan de hao*) or 'marry well' (*jia de hao*) is the better option for them to construct their subjectivity and autonomy. The discourse of 'work well' implies gender equality, independence and autonomy, which emphasizes young women's need to improve their education, professional training, communication and all kinds of skills and capacities in order to thrive in the competitive modern society and achieve self-actualization. The discourse of 'marry well' confines women within traditional gender roles of mother and wife in a patriarchal system, and therefore attractive appearance, sexy body, and feminine features are key elements for achieving this goal. The debate demonstrates competing discourses of state, market, and Confucian traditional gender roles and norms, among which young women may be trapped in the dilemma of making choices, or can filter all kinds of discourse in order to situate themselves in advantageous positions, to solve the identity crisis and construct their own desires and subjectivities.

Women's competition with their boyfriends and determination to be career women are closely related to the state discourse for liberating women in the workplace. Beginning in 1949 Mao Zedong claimed that, 'times have changed, women and men are equal. Whatever men can accomplish, women can as well' (Kristeva, 1986, p. 148). Therefore, the 'low wage but universal employment' social policy coupled with the 'same job, same pay' gender ideology turned both husband and wife into a dual-job couple, and both were financial providers for the family in a subsistence economy (Tan, 1993). In addition, the state discourse modified the meaning of work not only to encompass the fulfillment of personal goals and the achievement of career ambitions and financial prosperity, but also to denote a revolutionary mission every individual had in the course of social construction (Whyte and Parish, 1984). Nurtured under the communist work ethic and dual-job family environment, Qin Cui, Deng Li and many other well-educated women in this study strongly associated work with their identity as modern women. Being career women was a way to expand their womanhood beyond being a daughter, partner, wife, and mother, and brought them a sense of individuality, accomplishment, self-actualization, and economic independence.

Many informants expressed their negative attitudes toward the label of housewife. To them, 'housewife' meant 'jobless, ill-educated, ignorant, narrow-minded, nagging, isolated, chained-to-the-stove, and so forth' (Zuo, 2003, p. 326). However, the negative image of housewives was also formulated in the state discourse. In the early Maoist Era, the class standing of 'housewife,' in the CCP's perception, was dubiously close to 'bourgeois' (Wang, 2005). Hence it was necessary for the state to transform the image of housewife from bourgeois parasite to poor woman of lower class by using Engels's (1972) theory to argue that her work was unpaid and therefore had no significance for social production. Therefore, the negative image of the housewife became especially useful as a comparison to justify how the 'new China' liberated women by offering equal opportunity for them to participate in public labor, and the image of the liberated daughter and the figure of the strong female party leader was celebrated in literature, media, film, and in all kinds of cultural and ideological productions.

Though more and more urban young women are obtaining the opportunity for higher education, their career development in reality still encounters all kinds of glass ceilings, and there is far more work needed to achieve gender fairness and justice in the work setting. The year 2007 was the first time in Chinese history that more girls than boys went to colleges and universities, and ever since then the sex ratio of college admission has been maintained relatively equal, with girls occupying a slight advantage. At this time, educators like Sun Yunxiao (2010) and many others called on society to 'save boys' by reestablishing their masculinity, and refuted the current exam system said to favor girls and exclude boys. According to a study conducted by Media Monitor for the Women Network in China in 2014, 59% of 112 top Chinese universities maintained a practice of discriminative restrictions and exclusions for girls in various majors and disciplines in 2014 – for example, by requiring higher admission scores for girls than boys. Even though girls were successfully accepted into the ivory tower, they encountered much more discrimination in the process of job seeking. Tong and Su (2010) found that since many female bachelor's degree graduates could not find ideal job positions in the market, they had to go on to study for master's or PhD degrees if they hoped to earn incomes similar to those of regular male college graduates. Society still places a huge stigma on women with academic ambition, mocking women with PhDs as 'the third category,' having divided human beings into three categories: 'men, women, and women with a PhD.' Shoads and Gu (2012) conducted a study of the challenges of women academics to show that a virtual glass ceiling confronted women, as well as showing that organizational structures and processes reflected male-dominated norms and practices.

Zhang Yuping and her colleagues (2008) argue that gender gaps in employment and earnings are strongly related to family status, and that married women and mothers face more significant disadvantages. The early retirement policy is another huge barrier for women's career development, especially in the upper ranks, given that Chinese women must retire five years earlier than men. The challenges and obstacles are embedded in all the dimensions of women's career lives: education, employment, promotion, and retirement. Young women like my participants are determined to secure decent jobs, obtain recognition, and even fulfill their career ambitions; they have to be more assertive, competitive, and ambitious to survive and thrive.

Men's expectation may relate to the Confucian division of work between a couple as 'men work outside and women do chores inside' (*nan zhuwai, nü zhunei*), which has formulated fundamental gender roles for men and women for thousands of years, when China was an autarkic agricultural society. This form of agricultural life, with food production as its basis, meant that the

132 *Sassy girl and tender boy*

sexual difference in the social division of labor – that men plow and women weave (*nan'gengnüzhi*) – carried a certain significance of dominance and subordination (Rofel, 1999). When the opening market brought the meaning of work as 'fulfilling personal goals, career ambitions, or financial prosperity,' rather than 'revolutionary career,' young men combined it with gendered roles in their imagined marriages and assigned themselves to be breadwinners; it was important to conceive of this as a family responsibility as well as a privilege.

However, their expectation that 'women do chores inside' to be 'virtuous wives and wise mothers' sometimes was just too difficult to be true. Wen Jie is a postgraduate student and her boyfriend is her peer classmate. She illustrates how she successfully uses a 'break-up' as a strategy to transform her boyfriend from a 'male chauvinist' to a tender lover:

> His personality looks open, but in essence he is very conservative, even a male chauvinist ... Sometimes I cooked for him but he just sat there and did nothing ... Once I just asked him to put something back in its place, he glared at me, angrily. In his mind, how could I 'order' him to do anything? He thought that all trivial things should be done by women, not men. I was extremely angry, and I could not accept this typical male chauvinism. So I told him that in my family, my father not only worked hard outside (*zhuwai*) but also did chores inside (*zhunei*), and a good man should be like this. If he couldn't change, I would insist on breaking up with him. Because I believe that no man is too good to be lost ... Insisting on breaking up is lethal for him, and an effective tool for me to pursue equality.
>
> (Wen Jie, F, 26)

According to a cross-cultural study, Chinese are less egalitarian than Americans in work-related gender attitudes, while in regard to domestic gender roles Chinese and Americans are not very different overall. Chinese women are more egalitarian than their American counterparts in Florida (Chang, 1999). Existing studies argue that women's egalitarianism is associated with increasing violence reported, and the more modern and liberal a woman is, the more likely she is to report being abused and the less time she is likely to remain in a violent dating relationship (Follingstad et al., 1988). In this study, I also find that women's egalitarianism is associated with conflict and violence, especially when men and women have different views on gender roles and gender equality. When Wen Jie uses breaking up to fight for equality, the tension concerning egalitarianism between men and women is so obvious. Wen Jie achieves her goal because she is very determined and has a strong belief in herself, and sticks to her own criteria of selecting a good man: *work hard outside and do chores inside*, which is a pragmatic way to ask men to share the double burden with women and indeed revise the Confucian division of work within a family, and even between members of a couple.

Sassy girl and tender boy 133

The double burden is the term used by Li Xiaojiang and other second-wave Chinese feminists, which refers to the double workload of women who work to earn money, but also have responsibility for unpaid domestic labor. The dual-job couple is the most common arrangement in Chinese families; however, the woman often spends significantly more time on household chores and care work, such as child rearing and care for the sick and the aging, than the male partner. Yu and Xie (2011–12) conducted a comparative study of Mainland China and Taiwan and raise a hypothesis of 'gender display,' which means that women who out-earn their husbands tend to do more household work than women whose earnings are similar to those of their husbands, in order to compensate for their deviation from gender norms. Their results show that the evidence for gender display is more pronounced in Taiwan, while it does not exist in urban China. This finding may echo Chang's (1999) argument that men and women are more egalitarian at home, which shows that the young women's everyday struggle for gender equality may gradually change the imbalanced gender dynamics and patriarchal system at home.

The conflicting perceptions of gender roles within intimate relationships between men and women in this study are also a lived response to the debate on 'whether women should go home to be housewives.' The debate started in the early 1980s, under the new social context of economic reforms, when some scholars raised the issue to reevaluate the gain and loss of women taking part in social labor, and argued that to 'let women go home' was a way to alleviate the pressure of housework within the dual-job couples. Throughout the 1980s, the debate did not produce two opposite camps, but by 1994 it had, when a big debate was launched in the top Chinese journal of sociology, *Sociological Research*, by two young male rising stars in Chinese sociology who took the initiative to publish articles and to argue that women should go back home to be housewives. Later, feminists reacted to this and fiercely critiqued the argument. Chow et al. (2004) have a detailed description of the events:

> Using a functionalist perspective, Zheng Yefu (1994) argued that the quest for equality promoted by the state disrupted the traditional gendered division of labor, resulting in a bizarre form of inequality – 'the robbery by the weak from the strong.' Sun Liping (1994) proposed women going home as a way to solve the labor surplus problem and to restore traditional gender relations. These young male rising stars in Chinese sociology received strong criticism from women scholars, who argued that differences in basic value systems and sexist ideology prevented the two men from seeing women's interests as valid and as valuable to society and subjected women to the 'societal interest' of economic growth and efficiency.
>
> (p. 169)

134 *Sassy girl and tender boy*

Li Xiaojiang (1994a), as a leader of Chinese women's studies in the 1990s, critiqued how during the May Fourth Movement many male thinkers dedicated their work to women's liberation, but that during the Reform Era there were none. From 1994 until today, 'asking women to go home' (*rang nüren huijia qu*) has been a disputed topic in the public discourse, and has been raised by different people in different settings from time to time. Ever since the 2000s, 'let women go home' has been raised as a proposal at the national committee level of the Chinese People's Political Consultative Conference. Two male congress representatives raised the issue in 2001 and 2005, respectively, with little feedback, while in 2011 a congresswoman, Zhang Xiaomei, raised the issue again using the phrase 'encouraging some women back home, improving the social happiness index,' and obtained a lot of attention. Among thousands of proposals raised every year in the conference, this proposal was immediately picked up by the media, maybe because this 'woman against women' case could draw a lot of attention. It is difficult to decode whether the media wants to stimulate a real debate on women's rights and labor, or whether they want to use this case to divide women's groups, create a backlash against the women's movement, and justify the rationale of 'let women go home.' The *Women's Voice Newsletter* published a series of articles to refute Zhang Xiaomei's arguments in 2011 and brought about a new round of discussion among the feminist groups.

Ironically, those proposals to 'let women go home' not only emphasized letting the 'more suitable men' keep their jobs and solve the labor surplus, but also made use of the feminist complaint of women's 'double burden' to suggest that women going home was the best way to alleviate women's burden and allow them to become better caregivers to their children, husband, parents, and families. Female scholars criticized these male scholars and politicians for depriving women of an active choice for their own lives. Here the dislocation of Confucianism emerges again: these male elite intellectuals argue that modern society disrupts the values of Chinese cultural traditions and pretend to save and reconstruct women's femininity by imposing their own ideas for women's lives. The male elites wear two masks: with one they use the traditional ideal to interfere in women's free choice for their lives; with the other they borrow the power of the state to interfere in people's family lives and emphasize the sexist ideology. While the one-child policy successfully and directly controls women's autonomy of reproduction, this appeal even attempts to deprive women of their choice of self-development, which is a total regression, even abolishing the only 'achievement' of gender equality – that in the workplace, which began during the Maoist Era. Under the impact of the market, women seek the 'lost femininity' of past years; however, they also emphasize a 'feminine' appearance and a 'masculine' inside, and turn virtuousness into a performance. In contrast, men recollect the 'virtuous wife and good mother' as their imagined ideal of women, although in everyday life they have to be tender to accommodate their aggressive girlfriends and their expectation is difficult to realize, therefore influencing their perception of marriage and family.

Conclusion

The dating stories of these young men and women have helped us see more clearly the changing gender norms and how men and women have appropriated socio-cultural discourses to express themselves and to be the kind of dating partners they want to become. It is striking that psychological violence is predominant in young dating couples' lives, 'breaking up' and 'infidelity' being the two situations in which all kinds of violence are focally embedded, which diverts the focus of physical violence in current violence studies in China. Their violent dating stories are constructed and performed within the transformation of femininities and masculinities in China. Rofel (1999) argues:

> I contend that gender serves as one of the central modalities through which modernity is imagined and desired. Gender differentiation – the knowledge, relations, meanings, and identities of masculinity and femininity – operates at the heart of modernity power.
>
> (p. 20)

This chapter demonstrates the gender hegemony that young people resist in four ways. First, the analysis deconstructs an image of 'proper' girls who were supposed to be submissive, attentive to their looks, family oriented, professionally unambitious and compliant (Aapola et al., 2005, p. 6), and establishes a new image of sassy girls who are aggressive, willful, assertive, competitive, and professionally ambitious. This also problematizes the gender-stereotypical discourse that violent women are *mad* or *bad*. Women's aggression, as an ignored image other than the victimized-woman image of the studies on violence against women in China, is now calling for attention. This has theoretical implications for updating Chinese feminist scholarship concerning violence against women.

Second, this chapter deconstructs the stereotypical couple image of 'abusive men and abused women' in the existing violence research by illustrating the new dating mode of the sassy girl and tender boy. Although this dating mode is predominant in the dating practices of such couples, it also needs to be mentioned that there are some men who still cling to women's submission as a sign of their femininity, and I argue that this disparity of perception on gender equality between men and women often stirs up conflict and leads to dating violence. Pimentel (2006) has a similar finding in her study of gender ideology and household behavior in urban China:

> Contemporary China may be experiencing a form of 'backlash' not unlike that described in the West. Younger women appear to take earlier gains for granted, to be used as their starting point for even further movement. Meanwhile, younger men may resent the increasing demands

136   *Sassy girl and tender boy*

of their partners to participate in labor they consider beneath them and end up even less egalitarian.

(p. 361)

Third, this chapter gives a description of the transformation of femininity and masculinity from the Maoist Era to the Post-socialist Era. The data challenge a common cross-cultural finding about 'masculinity' and 'femininity': that manhood is deemed to be something achieved through acts of competition with other men, whether physical or mental, whereas womanhood is linked to considerations of erotic attractiveness, reproductive success, and other related domestic achievements (Jankowiak, 2002). In this chapter, the changing image, from female Red Guard to sassy girl, shows that the latter not only has the feminine appearance but also inherits the former's guts and changes the battlefield from the public to the private for personal interests and intimacy rather than class struggle. On the global level, the rise of women's aggression is a response associated with 'girl power' in both the West (Aapola et al., 2005) and in China, and even in Chinese rural areas (Yan, 2003). The tenderness of young men in this study resists the 'hegemonic masculinity' that portrays Chinese men as feminine in comparison to Western men by arguing that tenderness is an inevitable component of Chinese masculinity (Louie, 2002). On the practical level, as these men may not achieve success while they are young, tenderness becomes even more significant for them to win the hearts of women and maintain intimate relationships. In some ways, this is an element in the market that provides alternative opportunities for these men to use other qualities to redefine 'success.'

Fourth, unlike Gilbert (2002), who argues that gender stereotypes continue to permeate our society and criticizes violent women, this chapter shows that the intersectionality of competition, and multilayered discourses on gender, state, and market, leave some space for young adults to justify women's aggression as socially acceptable and to redefine the cultural meaning of 'virtuous wife and good mother.' The one-child policy empowers urban girls, who are treasured by their parents, to make them intolerant of violence from their boyfriends, and encourages them to take for granted the state discourse on gender equality. Meanwhile, although young men work very hard on everyday gender equality, at the same time they wish to win back the glory of being breadwinner and reorganize the gender roles in their intimate relationships, as the market resets the meaning of work as the pursuit of individual achievement. For women, 'virtuous wife and good mother' is more like a gender performance rather than everyday practice: they are finally succeeding in making 'virtuous transactions' which profit their own well-being. For men, 'virtuous wife and good mother' is their imagined ideal woman who is unattainable in daily life. The contradiction of the gender roles in the imagined marriage intensely characterizes the gender tension within them.

Here 'tradition' is a label, a mask, an imagined narrative that focuses not on the past, but on the present and imagined future, and symbolizes the impotence and vulnerability of masculinity in the free market. The meaning of imagined tradition is interpreted as a reestablishment of traditional values on the surface, but deep down it is a revision and a revised discourse of sexist ideology, presented as a sexual double standard. Therefore, in addition to the state discourse and women's own struggles under the market regime, the revised sexist ideology as fabricated tradition becomes the other most dangerous enemy in the way of women's pursuit of autonomy and subjectivity, and the way is never easy.

Notes

1 Neveu, 2001, www.kfccinema.com/reviews/comedy/sassy/sassy.html..
2 Minor physical violence is defined as throwing something that could hurt, twisting, pushing or shoving, grabbing and slapping, probably without physical injury; while severe physical violence includes using a knife or gun, punching or hitting, choking, slamming, beating up, burning or scalding, and kicking (Straus et al., 1996).
3 In this phrase, the popular translation using 'bitch' rather than 'willful' to translate '*renxing*.' The buzzword originates from a real event: in April, Mr. Liu spent 1,760 yuan online buying a health care product. Soon after, he received calls from a stranger who persuaded him to buy other, complementary medicines. In the following four months, Mr. Liu remitted a total of 540,000 yuan to the swindler. He said that he had already realized that he had been cheated when he was fooled out of 70,000 yuan. 'I just wanted to see how much could they take from me!' See: yingyu.xdf.cn/201412/10177270.html..
4 Three obediences and four virtues were a set of basic moral principles specifically for women in Confucianism. The two terms ('three obediences' and 'four virtues') first appeared in the *Book of Etiquette and Ceremonials* and in the *Rites of Zhou*, respectively. The three obediences for a woman were to obey: her father, as a daughter; her husband, as a wife; and her sons in widowhood. The four feminine virtues were: morality; proper speech; modest manner/appearance; and diligent work.
5 The statistics can be found on the official website of National Bureau of Statistics of the People's Republic of China, www.stats.gov.cn.
6 Sadomasochism is the giving or receiving of pleasure – sometimes sexual – from acts involving the infliction or reception of pain or humiliation.

5 Virginity loss, sexual coercion, and the unfinished sexual revolution

This chapter looks at the meaning of sexual coercion in dating relationships through exploring the critical moment of virginity loss and, later, exploring the sexual lives of young Beijing women. While the previous chapter focused on women's aggression and physical, verbal, and psychological violence in dating relationships, this chapter extends the examination to their sexual lives, including unwanted sexual experiences. In Chapter 4, I argued that a new dating mode was emerging: girls who are assertive, willful, and aggressive; and boys who are loving, tender, and even fragile. In this mode, 'tender' boys go very far to accommodate their 'spoiled sassy' girls, and the traditional pattern of 'men being superior to and dominant of women' has somehow shifted. However, this is not the whole picture. I came across a contradictory phenomenon described in the interviews that puzzled me very much: young women were aggressive in their everyday lives but seemed to be quite submissive when it came to sex.

There were 17 cases involving sexual coercion in this study. Thirteen women expressed that they had experienced 'unwanted' sexual advances or sexual coercion, while three men mentioned that they had employed certain coercive behaviors to initiate sex or to perform sex. Two women reported that they had experienced date rape and/or attempted date rape, and had suffered severe physical violence. The majority of young women informants' narrations involved cases of sexual coercion related to their first experiences of sex, most of which were described as 'minor,' 'trivial,' and without clear physical force. They did not employ language that clearly articulates this, but they retained unhappy memories of virginity loss.

Why are young women aggressive in their daily dating relationships but seem relatively submissive when it comes to sex? How is the 'everyday aggression vs. contextualized submission' reflected in a larger cultural context, and how is the formation of their individual sexual subjectivity related to the wave of 'sexual revolution'?

I find that although many women experience virginity loss submissively, in the stages 'before' and 'after' their virginity loss they develop different ways to establish their subjectivity. By paying attention to the 'minor,' 'trivial' sexual coercion in dating relationships, I argue that women's virginity loss is often

Virginity loss, sexual coercion, sexual revolution 139

associated with sexual coercion and that the 'female virginity complex' is just a convenient discourse used to explain their unhappiness at being sexually coerced. The moment of virginity loss becomes a moment for rethinking one's self, status, and strategy in the competitive dating and marriage market in metropolitan China.

In this chapter, I first tell a 'typical' story of date rape, pointing out that both date rape and marital rape have not been fully recognized by the judicial system or by the general public. I then continue with a description of women's time-based and stage-based subjectivity in their sexual lives, and in addition the concept of 'gender-asymmetric modes of mutual violence' is raised as a way to understand the contradiction between women's everyday aggression and contextualized sexual submission. Finally, I attempt to link individual sexual subjectivity to the discussion of sexual revolution, and I argue that the existence of various sexual behaviors and activities does not necessarily lead to sexual revolution – unless gender equality becomes the core of all kinds of sexual practices, the sexual revolution is by no means finished.

A 'typical' story of date rape

Huang Mei was a nurse, a single, divorced woman. At the time of the interview, she was dating and cohabitating with a man who was between jobs. She had been physically abused by him, sometimes even in public settings. Her experience of sexual coercion often occurred immediately after being physically and verbally abused:

> Last time, after he punched me heavily three times [she was injured and needed to see a doctor], he acted like a monster trapped in a small space. He kept walking to and fro in the living room nonstop, and at the same time verbally abused me. Suddenly, he just jumped on me. I didn't want this. I pushed him but couldn't succeed in avoiding *it* [sex]. He did *it* anyway, while at the same time scolding me. I felt I was raped. Afterwards, he did not show any guilt or remorse, and fell asleep immediately. I couldn't sleep and crouched at the corner of the bed, crying. At midnight he woke up, seemed surprised, said, 'What are you crying for?'
>
> (Huang Mei, F, 33)

Huang Mei emphasizes the feeling of 'being raped' rather than experiencing a real rape, which brings up the question of whether young women can voice their negative experiences of sexuality openly or whether they can only express their painful emotions. Existing studies show that this case is a 'typical' account of date rape. The event takes place after physical abuse and combines all types of violence: sexual, physical, verbal, and psychological. Throughout the whole process, Huang Mei's boyfriend was continually violent in action: even when he was inside her, he did not stop rebuking her. It has been found that an abusive situation is more serious if a woman

140 *Virginity loss, sexual coercion, sexual revolution*

experiences sexual aggression and physical abuse at the same time rather than only experiencing physical violence (Black et al., 2001; Kuffel and Katz, 2002; Monson and Langhinrichsen Rohling, 2002; Ryan, 1998).

Huang Mei actively sought help by calling a hotline, seeing counselors and attending all kinds of seminars on love and marriage. She tried very hard to understand what had happened, and attempted to prevent the physical and sexual violence from happening to her again. She was the only one in this project who seriously associated sexual coercion with rape, a word denoting a crime in the understanding of the general public. However, such an accusation of rape is interpreted only as an emotional expression – the emphasis being on the '*feeling* of being raped' – which ironically shows that, even facing the serious situation of sexual coercion, women cannot express their negative experiences of sexuality in a more powerful way.

Based on their nationwide random sampling survey among teenagers aged from 14 to 17, Pan and Huang (2013) found that among teenagers who had had sexual experience, 24.4% of boys and 40.7% of girls reported that they had experienced sexual coercion. Date rape in China is usually considered the most serious type of sexual violence. The term has been popularized in China due to the case of Huang Jing. Huang Jing was a 21-year-old female teacher in Xiangtan City, Hunan Province, who died in February 2003, in her dormitory, naked, with bruises and her boyfriend's sperm all over her body. Huang Jing's mother and supporting feminist activists believed that her death was due to date rape by her 26-year-old boyfriend. The local court made use of the general public's concept that 'only rape by strangers counts as rape' and found her boyfriend 'not guilty,' since they used to be romantically involved, while ignoring injuries that were found all over her body and sperm that was found on her belly, and neglected her unwillingness to participate in sex. Criticizing the unjust judgment and revealing the patriarchal and sexist ideology associated with this case, Chinese feminist activists Ai Xiaoming and her colleagues supported Huang Jing's mother's appeal and launched a movement to fight against date rape and sexual violence. Their actions involved writing articles (Ai, 2004a, 2004b, 2004c), organizing symposia, establishing a memorial website, filming the documentary *Heaven Garden* (*tiantang huayuan*) about the case, and so on. All these actions sparked off a social movement against date rape, and Huang Jing has become a symbol for mobilization against date rape and sexual violence, making it more visible in public discourse.

Although marital rape and date rape have gradually gained scholarly attention in recent years, the influence is limited and the focus has been, and still is, on serious physical violence closely associated with sexual violence, as in Huang Mei's case. At the time of interview, if I had not taken the initiative to probe into the issue of sexual violence, Huang Mei would never have mentioned it to me. Afterwards she told me that this was a 'secret' shared with me, and she was too ashamed to tell anyone else, including the counselor she was seeing. Most rape survivors keep silent under the pressure

Virginity loss, sexual coercion, sexual revolution 141

to protect their face and that of their families, and the public perception and stigma of rape always involves victim-blaming.

Some participants in this study (for example, Ding Yi) even doubt whether rape can actually 'occur between couples.' When the concept of sexual coercion (including date rape, marital rape) has not been widely accepted in academia, and therefore the general public know even less about this, young women have no clear understanding of sexual coercion, and there remain huge barriers for them to acknowledge their pain and suffering that have stemmed from it. Wang, Fang and Li (2013) conducted quantitative research among 1,103 women and 1,017 men aged 18–49 years, and they found that one in ten women who had had sexual partners reported having experienced rape by male partners. Among men who had had sexual partners, 14% reported having perpetrated rape against female partners. Pan and Huang's (2013) nationwide survey shows a set of contrasting figures: among the population aged from 18 to 61, more than 25% of women had suffered the experience of rape, and 71.1% of those women claimed that the perpetrators were their husbands; however, every year only a little more than 30,000 rape cases have been reported to police stations and thus are dealt with by the judicial system. While the existence of marital rape has already became an undeniable fact, the general public still lack enough awareness, and the education system, the media, and the law are still busy constructing the myth that 'rape is synonymous with rape by a stranger.' In the newly released Anti-Domestic Violence Law in 2014, intimate partner violence in dating relationships and cohabitation was not included, sexual violence was vaguely defined, and there was no clear definition of marital rape.

Compared to the account of date rape that Huang Mei experienced, in which there is at least a rather clear classification of 'perpetrator' and 'victim,' the majority of accounts of sexual coercion that I came across in this study were more complicated and ambivalent. The interviewees had more difficulty in defining their unpleasant sexual experiences as rape because no clear physical violence was involved and the men would often use 'soft' techniques of persuasion to obtain sex. These types of sexual coercion are common in young people's everyday lives and are often regarded as 'ordinary,' 'minor,' 'non-violent' (Hird and Jackson, 2001), and therefore 'unimportant' and ignored.

Performing the traditional: active 'gatekeepers'

A number of women were pressured by their boyfriends to have sex and resisted by acting as gatekeepers, and during this process, they felt conflicted. Qiu Ye, an office worker, struggled a lot over whether to have sex or not with her ex-boyfriend, whom she had finally broken up with one year before the interview. During the three years that they had gone out, they had had a lot of conflicts about having or not having sex:

142 *Virginity loss, sexual coercion, sexual revolution*

He asked me many times, and I refused every time. It was unpleasant, every time he lost his temper – although I liked going out with him, I was still very traditional.

(Qiu Ye, F, 23)

Even when faced with her ex-boyfriend's persistence and anger, Qiu Ye was good at making all kinds of excuses for not having sex with him. However, sometimes her ex-boyfriend just could not take it and shouted, 'Who are you going to marry if not me?' and then Qiu Ye felt she needed to 'protect herself.' Qiu Ye narrated the following scenario:

That day, we were out hiking. The weather was nice, and the mountain was beautiful. We sat on a big rock for a break. Nobody was there, so he hugged me and kissed me quite naturally. Later, he tried to take off my clothes. At that point, my level-headedness came back and I wouldn't let him. However, he insisted on doing it, and he forced off my T-shirt. I used all my strength to hit him in the chest with my elbow – He stopped, stared at me for a few seconds, and then let go of my T-shirt and left. I just stood there, thinking, 'Even if I let you see it, I will never let you get *it!*'

(Qiu Ye, F, 23)

Existing studies often describe the role that Qiu Ye plays in the above scenario as that of a gatekeeper (Baumeister, 2004). Besides feeling it unacceptable and uncomfortable that the ex-boyfriend attempted to have sex with her without her consent for the first time outdoors, Qiu Ye explained her consistent resistance as related to the protection of her virginity, because she stated that it was her responsibility as a 'traditional girl' to avoid engaging in premarital sex. She was not sure if she would marry this man and so did not want to run the risk of losing her virginity to him. Though premarital sex has become more and more common, young people learn to justify it through love and engagement (Farrer, 2002). While the future of the relationship is still uncertain for Qiu Ye, choosing not to do it seems a rational choice for her. I remember that during one focus group I conducted with six female college students, when I asked about virginity loss and premarital sex, one of the participants was very dominant and responded immediately and adamantly, 'I will stay virgin till marriage, won't you?' She looked around seeking for confirmation. Under the pressure of 'won't you,' I noticed that four of the others expressed their agreement, strongly or carelessly, while one of them kept silent and even blushed when the others talked. I could sense the tension and uneasiness brought on by the topic among the group, and I guessed that she maybe had already had sexual experience. I might be wrong, but I dared not invite her to break the ice, because I knew that it would be huge pressure on a college girl to confront her classmates and share her own sexual experience, especially when others emphasized their 'purity' as virgins.

Virginity loss, sexual coercion, sexual revolution   143

Aside from fighting back physically to protect themselves, as Qiu Ye did, women participants have adopted many other tactics, such as thinking of good excuses for postponing sex – for example, 'I'm not feeling well,' 'I'm having my period,' or 'let's wait for a better time,' 'after we are engaged or are married,' or negotiating a date for their first experience of sex and thus buying time. Yu Ling was a sophomore at the time of interview. She used to date a senior fellow student, and one of the reasons why they broke up was because they could not come to an agreement about the date of their first sex. Yu Ling narrated:

> He said that it's okay for me ask him to wait, but I should give him a deadline. So I offered a deadline, which is after my college graduation. But he disagreed. He said it should be before his graduation.
>
> (Yu Ling, F, 21)

Another key strategy is for women to use masturbation or oral sex as a way of keeping their 'virginity' and postponing intercourse. Xia Bing was a college student at the time of interview. Once she had a male friend with whom she had been intimate, but she was hesitating to identify him as a boyfriend and move the relationship forward. She described a little sexual game between them: 'We did not have sex. We just slept there; used our hands or mouths to satisfy each other, which was good (Xia Bing, F, 20).

In Xia Bing's narrative, sex only refers to vaginal-penile intercourse, and masturbation or oral sex should not be counted as sex. By appropriating 'proper sex' (Holland et al., 1996) only as vaginal-penile intercourse, she argues that as long as a woman's hymen is intact, she can keep the identity of being a virgin and at the same time enjoy the pleasure that masturbation or oral sex can bring. Pei and Ho's (2009) study on masturbation shows that young women in Shanghai understand masturbation as a way to 'make love to oneself,' 'fulfill the physical needs of a virgin,' and 'enhance the sexual relationship' (p. 515), which is also true in Xia Bing's story, except that she draws a clear line between intercourse and other types of sex. The case further illustrates a woman's negotiation between performing the traditional and being modern. The paradox is that if Xia Bing were as traditional as she labeled herself, she might not have actively explored alternative ways of seeking pleasure and satisfying desire. Clearly, she has redefined the meaning of 'proper sex' (Holland et al., 1996) so as to establish herself as a 'powerful' and 'perfect' woman by putting on a performance of traditional womanhood, yet at the same time has shifted the boundaries of 'traditional' and maintained a 'modern' image.

It was interesting to notice that sometimes during the interview informants used the words 'traditional' and 'feudal' interchangeably to describe their unwillingness to participate in sex, which shows clearly their ambivalent feelings about premarital sex. 'Traditional' is a neutral description of how women treasure their virginity and femininity and hold on to certain values, while

144 *Virginity loss, sexual coercion, sexual revolution*

'feudal' is a negative word and refers to something outdated needing to be discarded. When they call themselves 'traditional,' it does not mean that they are really conservative or that they really care about chastity very much. Very often, they are just not certain about timing in their relationships and the nature of love, and have just not made up their minds on whether to have sex or not, or with whom. In the previous chapter, I adopted Rey Chow's concept of 'virtuous transaction' to show that women's performance of the traditional is related to getting what they want; in this situation, it is related to rejecting something they do not want – one strategy that can be used for different purposes. Moskowitz (2008) conducted fieldwork in the most famous foreign pick-up club in Taipei and found that the Taiwanese female regulars often pretended that they were new to the place and often agreed to be picked up by giving a foreigner a phone number instead of walking out directly with him, in order to maintain a 'good, pure' girl image. I argue that representing oneself as a 'traditional' woman becomes a flexible tactic of 'performing the traditional,' which involves a symbolic fluidity with which one may travel from being a passive sexual object of patriarchy to being an active subject, and involves saying no to unwanted premarital sex.

Virginity loss: uncomfortable, unpleasant, and unwanted

Although both men and women could lose their virginity with a same-sex partner, through fellatio, cunnilingus, or anal intercourse, this chapter focuses on the context of heterosexual dating relationships and on women's virginity loss as 'the first time she engages in vaginal-penile intercourse' (Carpenter, 2002, p. 348), because this is still a dominant understanding of virginity loss among young Chinese people. Many of the women who had lost their virginity through coercive sex suffered from feelings of guilt, remorse, and shame; especially when they started a new relationship with another man, they often feared their non-virginity would wreck the new relationship. For example, Ding Dang, a college student, was in the middle of breaking up with her old boyfriend, Bao, with whom she had had intercourse, and was dating a new guy, Lin. She said good-bye to her old boyfriend Bao and told Lin 'I have feelings for you' on the same day. Within the first month of beginning to date Lin, she threatened to break up more than five times, even though she believed that she was deeply in love with him, as she just could not cope with the guilt feelings of having to hide her sexual history from Lin. She told me that sometimes she 'played innocent' whenever Lin and she discussed sex, but every time afterwards she felt her behavior was fake and disgusting. She also pondered whether getting back together with her ex-boyfriend Bao would be a better choice, though she stated that she did not love him anymore:

> The first time was the day before I started college. Bao asked me to go to his place to hang out, and then things happened. He coerced (*qiangpo*) – just did it. I cried all the time. I felt that he should not do that: he should

Virginity loss, sexual coercion, sexual revolution 145

respect my choice – I really had already said 'No,' but he continued to do it. After that, we kept quarreling but stayed together.

(Ding Dang, F, 22)

Ding Dang's narration is a representative account of the female virginity complex in China: the woman's first experience of sex is coerced. Loss of virginity at such a young age made her ashamed of what she had been through and even made her feel 'inferior to other girls.' When she finally made the decision to break up with Bao, another self-struggle problem was raised: should she tell her new boyfriend of her past sexual experience?

I won't tell him. No one knows. I just pretend that I don't know anything [about sex]. Sometimes he talks about sex and feels that I am so naive. But I feel terrible. I feel that I am lying to him … Yesterday, he said that if two people really love each other, the guy should not care whether the girl has had any past sexual experience. But I doubt [he really believes this].

(Ding Dang, F, 22)

All these struggles have made it difficult for Ding Dang to go further in her new relationship; in contrast, reconciling with her ex-boyfriend turns into an easy way out, since she has 'lost [her] virginity to him anyway.' Such narratives revolve around how virginity loss brings young women much emotional uncertainty: the young women are worried about whether their new boyfriends will learn about their past sexual experiences and end up despising them. In China, 'female virginity complex' (*chunü qingjie*) is a popular term used to describe how people's 'fetish of female virginity' remains strong for both men and women (Buitelaar, 2002). *Complex*, as directly translated from the Chinese characters *qingjie*, literally means 'a related group of emotionally significant ideas that are completely or partly repressed and that cause psychic conflict leading to abnormal mental states or behavior,' and 'a disproportionate concern or anxiety about something.'[1]

For men, the complex means that they still emphasize women's virginity as an important criterion for dating and marriage selection; however, paradoxically, they are eager for premarital sex with their virgin girlfriends. The complex for women is at least twofold: under the pressure of men searching for virgins as girlfriends, they feel they are responsible for maintaining their chastity and purity; and yet under the pressure from their boyfriends and their own desires to maintain relationships, they try to act as gatekeepers but sometimes give in. According to Buitelaar (2002), the core value of virginity is part of a wider symbolic complex, in which the chastity of women is the key concept. An undamaged hymen and women's bleeding during their first experience of sex are often used as the proof of this state, although this is unscientific (Buitelaar, 2002; Holtzman and Kulish, 1997; Schlegel, 1991). Many medical investigations show that when the hymen is penetrated, only

146 *Virginity loss, sexual coercion, sexual revolution*

around two-thirds of women will bleed. However, Chinese men often look for bleeding the first time they have sex with their girlfriends or wives, as a way of testing whether they are virgins or not. In Chinese, this is called '*jian hong*' (seeing the red blood), which is an unscientific practice, but which has a long tradition. Xiao (1989) connects power with virginity and argues that:

> Women generally have more decisive power in courtship than men. A woman's power resource comes from her virginity and her resistance to early marriage. She loses this position of power the moment she loses virginity.
>
> (p. 287)

Xiao's (1989) study recounts the stereotypical story that men want to find a virgin girlfriend or wife, and women's virginity loss means a loss of everything. It shows how conventional discourses of female chastity and sexual vulnerability, even danger, are still very powerful in discussions of young women's sexuality, creating sexual double standards (Jackson and Cram, 2003) and producing binary images of good/bad girl, virgin/slut, or warrior/victim. As Brown (1993) describes in her literary criticism of Lu Xun's *Soap*, good women are cast as filial daughters and dutiful mothers and bad women are disdained as dangerous seducers; therefore sexuality was an especially important trope to measure women's value and morality in imperial China:

> The good woman's sexuality is defined according to her role in continuing the family line, with all its implications for submission to the patriarchy; the evil woman is defined by her sexuality, according to her ability to give, to withhold, and to manipulate the male's sexual gratification. The good woman preserves the family order, the bad woman disrupts it.
>
> (p. 79)

Moreover, in addition to limiting women's sexuality to the function of reproduction (Fei, 1984), imperial scholars devoted much time to lecturing on women's chastity, preaching that 'losing chastity is even worse than dying of starvation' (*e si shi xiao, shi jie shi da*). Thus women's bodies were turned into a site for gendered tropes for configuring social morality and social immorality (chaste widows/dangerous whores), and women were traditionally credited as being symbols of either the saving or the destruction of the country. For example, reformer intellectuals Kang Youwei and Liang Qichao established a clear teleology: good women = good family = good nation (Edwards, 2000). In his path-breaking 1918 essay 'My View on Chastity,' the well-known writer Lu Xun decried the custom of making women responsible for national salvation and criticized the Kang-Liang reform argument that the backwardness of China was due to the backwardness of its women (Edwards, 2000). Although chastity is no longer an institutionalized form of repression of women, it remains a pressure of consensus gender politics.

Virginity loss, sexual coercion, sexual revolution 147

For some male participants, whether a woman is a virgin or not is still an important factor in deciding whether the man will date her or not. He Yi, a college student, had just broken up with his ex-girlfriend and had begun to go out with another girl at the time of interview. He clearly described his requirement for dating selection:

HE YI: (M, 22): I want to find a pure girl.
R: What's your definition of purity? A virgin?
HE YI: Of course, including this.
R: You mean that if you find a girlfriend, she must be a virgin.
HE YI: If I love her, I will care about her past. Suppose I make love with her, if I don't love her, it's okay. If I do love her, I will think, how has she done this thing with other men? I will feel terrible.

Because he had already told me that he had had sex with his ex-girlfriend, I asked him further:

R: If your ex-girlfriend finds a new boyfriend, and the new boyfriend, just like you, cares about her past, then – ?
HE YI: [Hesitates] I know, I am a traditional man, what I said is just my own idea, it cannot represent others.

Here He Yi clearly articulates a sexual double standard: on one hand, he expects his girlfriend to be a virgin until she meets him; on the other hand, he wants his virgin girlfriend to have sex with him. In his logic, virginity is not only a criterion of date selection, but also a 'sign of a woman's value' (Xiao, 1989), and he uses 'love' and 'being traditional' to justify his own criteria. For him, virginity symbolizes that a woman is pure, loyal, and worthy of trust – put simply, a good woman. If a woman has lost her virginity without serious consideration she will be thought of as an easy, irresponsible 'slut.' The sexual double standard imposed by the unjust male sexual privilege easily traps young women in the dilemma that anything they might do would be wrong.

The dilemma that Ding Dang faced was common among other women (such as Shen Juan, Ding Yi, and Zhong Qing) in this study, who also described their experiences of virginity loss as being coercive. According to previous studies, men's first experience of sex is generally empowering, while women's experience of it is more complicated (Carpenter, 2001, 2002; Holland et al., 1996, 2000; Sprecher et al., 1995). This argument is represented and reflected in this study, and it can be said that sexual coercion is one of the many factors that complicate women's experience of virginity loss. Among all the complaints of being coerced into sex, 'not being respected' was put much higher than maintaining 'chastity' and was the major reason why they felt bad about their experience of virginity loss.

Zhong Qing felt that she had lost her virginity too easily and expected to emphasize to her future children the significance of feeling emotionally ready:

148 *Virginity loss, sexual coercion, sexual revolution*

'If I have a daughter, I will tell her that *the thing* [virginity] is really important for a girl. Whether she wants to do it or not, I hope she can think about it more carefully before she decides to have sex.' Women in this study desired to have the first sex in a relationship with long–term prospects, in which there is love and trust, and in which they are respected and taken seriously. They might not be prepared for the pain the first time they have sex and they hope they will be treasured and treated with tenderness. They also desired to have sex for the first time in a romantic and private environment, though this is perhaps not possible, especially if they are college students without their own apartments and are living in dormitories.

However, their boyfriends develop some powerful methods to gain domination in sexual encounters, such as indirect persuasion ('If you loved me, you would have sex with me' – Ding Yi, F, 22), immediate intimidation ('I didn't want to, and then he lost his temper' – Ding Yi, F, 22), emotional blackmail ('If you do not have sex with me, we are finished' – Wen Xin, F, 31), persistent harassment ('He just kept asking me and bugging me' – Zhong Qing, F, 21), and authoritative force ('He just did it' – Ding Dang, F, 22). These women claimed that their boyfriends' strategies were too powerful to resist, and they felt powerless in the face of verbal manipulation, threats to terminate a relationship, and sexual advances with little or no tenderness, even though they thought that the sexual experience had been 'uncomfortable,' 'unpleasant,' and 'unwanted'.

Pain, pregnancy, and abortion

In the current study, none of young women spoke about sexual pleasure when describing their idealized fantasies of virginity loss and no one mentioned that they reached orgasm during their first sex. This does not necessarily mean that they had no sexual desire or that they did not want to experience orgasm, but rather that they were more concerned about their 'loss of value' and the moral judgment of their boyfriends and potential future husbands, which then overwhelmed and detracted from their desire. Besides, achieving orgasm often is a process of learning and practice, and female sexual desire is often gradually aroused and awakened. Based on a nationwide survey in 2010, Pan and Huang (2013) found that more than 20% of married women never or seldom had orgasm during sex.

For young women who lack sexual experience, sometimes the negative outcomes of virginity loss are physically unexpected and undesirable – namely pain, pregnancy, and abortion. Shen Juan is a college student, and her boyfriend is a senior college student at another university. She acknowledged that she was willing to have sex with him at first and then changed her mind because of the unexpected physical pain. However, her boyfriend insisted on doing it in spite of her pain, making her feel miserable and regretful:

Virginity loss, sexual coercion, sexual revolution 149

At the beginning, I was willing, because I was happy to be with him and felt that it's our fate to be together. First time, I bled a lot and it hurt very much and then he gave up without satisfaction. The second time, we were in his dormitory, nobody else was there, he wanted to do *it* again, but I was scared, it was really painful. I bled again and he couldn't fully get in again. He wanted to keep on doing *it* and I pushed him back off and dressed up immediately. Maybe it's so hard for him to hold it back, and I heard a low 'Fuck' coming from his mouth. He scolded me: 'It's such a trouble to be with a virgin'; and his facial expression was so ferocious. At that moment, I began to regret it. He stormed out and I cried.

(Shen Juan, F, 21)

This story is not only about unexpected pain but women's desire to be treasured and treated with tenderness during sex. It also illustrates how they are berated for having the pain – men both want their partners to be virgins and yet find this to be problematic; the value of virginity suddenly drops from 'something valuable' to 'something stigmatized.' Shen Juan felt that being criticized as a troublesome virgin was something that she could live with, but she was furious that her boyfriend compared her sexual performance with that of his ex-girlfriend, who, in his description, 'had a better body shape and better skills'. The obvious male sexual privilege and sexual double standard made Shen Juan feel ambivalent about her right to stop 'it' whenever she did not want it. She often felt that she was used and trapped in the sexual relationship and she had quite a few complaints: first, since the boyfriend could not 'get in' because of her pain, he required her to give him oral sex all the time but was never willing to provide oral sex for her; second, she thought that he bragged too much about his sexual ability, while she never felt it was enjoyable, not to mention the achievement of orgasm; third and finally, the boyfriend was not willing to pay the hotel charge, which she thought he should do since the major purpose was to fulfill his sexual needs.

Most women in the current study also reported that they did not use contraception the first time they had sex. Contraceptive use is highly dependent on whether women are able to make decisions about their own fertility and whether the relations between men and women are equal (Xu et al., 2011). Since most of the first sexual encounters occur in situations where women are not emotionally prepared, most of the time the couples never discuss the issue of contraception face to face beforehand. Some informants complained of the shame of buying condoms in the supermarket and of the inaccessibility of condoms on campus. A few female participants stated that since their boyfriends were keener to have sex, therefore they should shoulder the responsibility of buying condoms. Other female participants shared their concern with me that if they bought condoms beforehand, they would worry that their boyfriends would think them 'experienced,' 'sluts,' and 'not innocent at all.' Sometimes maintaining the image of an 'innocent, pure, good girl' was just too important for them to demand reliable contraception. Many sexually active

150 *Virginity loss, sexual coercion, sexual revolution*

participants told me that they used emergency contraception pills as their regular contraceptive methods without being fully aware of the potential health risks. Meng Xi (F, 27) had undergone two abortions at a young age, and each time her boyfriend had made excuses for not accompanying her to the hospital. This later became one of the major reasons for their break-up:

> I was 18 at that time, and he was my first real love. For a certain period of time, we were on and off, quarreled a lot. One day, after a huge fight, he went out to drink with others and called me when he was drunk. He was a shy person and never said anything passionate. Over the phone, he said a lot of passionate sweet words and promised to love me forever. I was worried about him, and went out to bring him back to his home. Then I got pregnant that night. He said that he could not accompany me to the hospital because of guilt, shame, and face, and he also said that he could not bear the looks from the doctors and nurses. But I had no choice. I had to bear all those. A female friend went to the hospital with me and I stayed at her house for a few days afterwards. Several months later, I was pregnant again, this time it was very tricky, because I took an emergency contraception pill but vomited afterwards. I thought that would be fine, but I was pregnant again. This time he did even worse, he went out of town to travel with his friends.
>
> (Meng Xi, F, 27)

When the boyfriends are not ready to shoulder the responsibility for contraception during sex, the girlfriends are the ones to bear the consequences. Avoiding the judgment of friends and classmates and afraid of bumping into acquaintances in the nearby hospitals, Ding Dang went to another city alone by train to have an abortion on the International Labor Day holiday and came back immediately after the operation. However, due to the holiday season, the train was overcrowded, so that she was unable to buy a seat ticket and had to stand for the duration of the five-hour journey back. As Carpenter (2001) has argued, the quality of the experience of virginity loss can be affected by the quality of the contraceptive used. In the case of Meng Xi and Ding Dang, all the corporal and spiritual suffering of pain and abortion intensified their antipathy to having unwanted sex.

Among their complicated feelings about 'unwanted' and 'unpleasant' sex, some women articulated their complaint more explicitly, as 'not being respected.' As Yu Ling put it, respect means that 'there should be love and trust in an equal relationship, as well as long-term prospects.' Despite the explicit social goals of pursuing gender equality, the 'female virginity complex' is an established discourse that most of the participants could conveniently appropriate to articulate women's unpleasant experiences of their first act of sexual intercourse. *Female virginity complex* is an imprecise term that can express women's frustration over not being respected as well as the disappointment they experience the first time they have sex. It is not completely clear

Virginity loss, sexual coercion, sexual revolution   151

whether 'virginity loss,' and its attendant social risks, is the main concern of female participants, or whether it is the sexual coercion that they experience, or both. Therefore it can be convenient to resort to the 'virginity complex,' where the tension is framed as having to alter their mindset, which can lead to worry about being seen as 'immoral,' 'casual,' or 'cheap,' but where 'performing the traditional' can cause the break-up of their current relationship.

Gender-asymmetric modes of mutual violence

One engrossing phenomenon that can help to solve the puzzle that I raised at the beginning of this chapter is that although these women experience sexual coercion, they do not perceive themselves as 'victims' at all, because they are aggressive in their everyday lives and their boyfriends have spoiled them a great deal. In Ding Dang's narrative above, her ex-boyfriend comes across as a 'villain,' but elsewhere she makes it clear that he has a good side:

> He loves me very much, and always puts me first. He is the kind of person who treats me unbelievably well. He does everything that I ask, and puts up with my temper all the time.
>
> (Ding Dang, F, 22)

Postgraduate student Xiao Hong described a similar scenario. He had dated Hui for more than three years, during which time he insisted on having sex with her on many occasions, but he was unsuccessful because she resisted furiously. In his own words, 'I cannot bear her stubborn resistance.' However, in everyday life the picture was reversed – he treated her very well, and Hui was physically aggressive with him, especially after she found out he was cheating on her:

> Every time we quarreled with each other, no matter who was at fault, I was the one to apologize. I bought her food and took hot water to her dormitory everyday. I even washed her underwear [by hand]. You know, it was embarrassing to wash your girlfriend's clothes in the public male bathroom. My classmates often teased me, 'How can you wash women's underwear?'
>
> (Xiao Hong, M, 26)

Chan (2012) conducted quantitative research on dating violence among 3,388 college students in Beijing, Shanghai, and Hong Kong, and found a similar research outcome to that of this qualitative study. He found significant gender differences in the rates of all types of perpetration of dating violence. Specifically, a greater proportion of females (54.3%/73.8%) than males (34.2%/67.3%) reported perpetration of physical and psychological violence, respectively, in intimate relationships. In contrast, a greater proportion of males (14.7%) than females (4.7%) admitted to perpetration of sexual violence. To explain this phenomenon, I develop the term 'gender-asymmetric

152 *Virginity loss, sexual coercion, sexual revolution*

modes of mutual violence' to draw attention to the complexity of power struggles and the nature of violence involved in dating relationships.

Many studies have shown that dating violence has a distinguishing characteristic: 'reciprocal' or 'mutual' violence is more common (Crawford, 1997; Gray and Foshee, 1997; Molidor and Tolman, 1998; Straus, 1997). Although Gray and Foshee (1997) define mutual violence as both sustaining violence and initiating violence within a dating relationship without specifying which types of violence are involved, most of the aforementioned studies focus only on mutual physical violence, which means that they examine the situation where the man hits the woman and the woman fights back. This study, however, describes a gender-asymmetric mode of mutual violence: women are physically aggressive toward men, while men are sexually coercive toward women and may treat women very well in other aspects of their lives; meanwhile, they may or may not be verbally or psychologically violent towards each other. This mode of mutual violence contributes a new perspective to understanding the escalation of violence in dating relationships. This concept illustrates the intersectional self explicitly at the moment of self-fashioning and negotiation, when women are caught between public behavior and the private, everyday aggression and contextualized sexual submission.

On the one side, boyfriends' tolerance in daily life gives an impression to women that they are entitled to hit, lose their tempers, and keep threatening to break up, and those acts provide them with channels through which they can vent their anger and expel the subordinate oppressive emotions that they experience in their sexual lives. Furthermore, because their boyfriends treat them well in daily life, it seems 'acceptable' for them to endure some unhappy sexual experiences as a tradeoff, so that they tend not to define such experiences as rape or sexual coercion, but rather as normal but unhappy dating experiences. Different from polarized relations of male domination and female subordination between the perpetrator and victim, the ambiguity and paradox of women's aggression in their daily lives and submission in their sex lives make it even more difficult for them to find their own voices to express their discontent at being sexually coerced.

On the other side, a similar question needs to be asked concerning men: Why are they 'gentlemen' with tenderness in the day and 'monsters' with sexual privilege at night? It is interesting to notice that men also use 'tradition' to justify their sexual privilege and conservatism. It seems that both men and women perform the 'traditional' with different purposes – women do so to resist the sex they do not want, while men's emphasis of the traditional is more strategy oriented and benefits their own personal interests. Moreover, men's emphasis of the traditional is a metamorphosis of a discourse of men's sex drive, which describes the sexual aggression of men as 'biologically driven' (Hird and Jackson, 2001; Jackson and Cram, 2003), and almost implies that women should give in when facing men's sexual desire. It is predicated on a masculinity conceptualized as active, persistent, and powerful, and femininity as passive, receptive, and responsive to male sexuality.

Virginity loss, sexual coercion, sexual revolution 153

Xiao Hong raised 'women's fantasy of being raped' (*qiangjian huanxiang*) to justify his idea that 'sometimes coercive sex makes them feel better.' This is based on the male chauvinist imagination that since 'being raped' is women's secretly desired fantasy, then man is entitled to grab the fantasy and make it come true. This perception deprives women of the right to sexual fantasy and regards them as masochists, with the corollary idea that women desire men regardless of the circumstance in which sex is proffered. As I mentioned before, Xiao Hong had had a girlfriend, Hui, for three years who was determined to keep her virginity before marriage; at the same time, he developed several occasional affairs with other women. He narrated a story with a young woman in Nanjing, and attempted to use this experience to testify his own 'theory':

> I had this experience with a girl in Nanjing. That day I took the train from Beijing to Nanjing to visit her. She picked me up at the station and sent me to the hotel. I naturally wanted to have sex with her as soon as we reached the hotel, but she said that she had to go to work immediately. But I grabbed her, hugged her tightly, kissed her passionately, just did not let her go. Then we had sex. It was a little bit rough and coercive. Later she called me back from work and said that the feeling was so great. I think that many women may have the fantasy of being raped.
>
> (Xiao Hong, M, 26)

Here the girl expressed her satisfaction over the phone, perhaps because sexual appeal, passionate love, the pleasure of cheating, and the sense of being needed were fulfilled. However, Xiao Hong jumps away from all possible reasoning, connects it instantly with 'women's fantasy of being raped,' and assumes the 'rapist' as a perfect lover in his imagination. For him, coercion has become integral to male sexuality, 'performed rape' may even be sexual to the degree that is irresistible. Wang, Fang and Li (2013) conducted a quantitative study on masculinity and gender-based violence, and they found that 52% of male respondents believed that men need more sex than women, and that most women (71%) agreed with this, showing that many women have internalized the idea of men having stronger sexual desire than women. They argue that the wide acceptance of men's sexual privilege partly legitimates the practice of perpetrating rape and sexual violence against women. This reminds us that in the Chinese history of sexuality, men and women's voicing's of their sexuality are entangled with all kinds of ambiguities and paradoxes: desire and guilt, pain and pleasure, and love and violence. However, this story connects all these ambiguities to entertainment, which deconstructs the historical heaviness of sexuality and formulates a sexual double standard.

Lacking voice, lacking space

The 'female virginity complex' is an established discourse that many women can conveniently appropriate to articulate the unpleasant experience of their

154 *Virginity loss, sexual coercion, sexual revolution*

first act of sexual intercourse, but it is not a precise term that can express the frustration over not being respected and the disappointment they experience in their first experience of sex. It is not completely clear that 'virginity loss' is the main concern of these women, and sexual coercion may bother them more. They have a limited vocabulary with which to voice their unpleasant sexual experiences – for example, 'uncomfortable,' 'unpleasant,' and 'being coerced' (*bei qiangpo*).

The difficulty the women have in speaking about their unhappy sexual experiences may be related to how they understand the boundary between public and private. Usually these women are well treated in public places, such as in the canteen or dormitory, and they may act willfully in these places, while their boyfriends' acts of sexual coercion are usually carried out only in private places, so that people who see these couples together may have the impression that the boyfriends are 'tender' and the girls are kind of 'sassy.' Surrounded by admiration and envy, these women are thus isolated and even more unable to articulate their unhappy sexual experiences because they may also want to preserve their good image of proper women or beloved girl-friends. Ding Dang's comment, 'I don't know, it's just annoying [*fan*],' clearly depicts the situation in which the woman wants to talk about her discomfort about sex but does not know how to do so. According to Zhang (2005):

> The discussion surrounding the vulnerability of young women and girls in heterosexual relationships can be seen as related not only to the issue of sexual violence against women, but also to another old debate regarding the kind of sexual knowledge girls and young women should have.
>
> (p. 9)

In a way, the isolation that women experience is not only social and emotional but also involves discursive challenges to articulating their experiences and practical difficulties in seeking help. The dating culture is diverse and complex in society at large – the media, Internet and society are filled with all kinds of sex information; the dating show 'If You Are the One' (*fei cheng wu rao*) has become one of the most popular programs on TV; Internet dating websites and companies make fortunes from the business of matchmaking. However, the education system adopts a purified, sanitized, and moralistic discourse about dating and premarital sex, and no proper sex education is offered to young people.

Peking University Institute of Population Research (2010) conducted a nationwide survey among 22,288 youth aged from 15 to 24 and found that 40% reported that they had received some sort of sex education – the study defined sex education to include classes on puberty, lectures on the prevention of HIV and other sexually transmitted diseases (STDs), and lectures on pregnancy and contraception. Pan and Huang (2013) also found that 73.5% of teenagers aged from 14 to 17 think that they seldom receive any sex education at school. The current limited sex education often focuses on

Virginity loss, sexual coercion, sexual revolution 155

abstinence and prevention of STDs, and a comprehensive gender-based sex education program is desperately needed to help youths establish healthy, mutually respectful, and responsible intimate relationships (Wang and Wang, 2012). Studies have shown that 50.4% of boys and 34.9% of girls aged from 14 to 17, and 70% of college students, are actively involved in dating relationships (Pan and Yang, 2004; Pan and Huang, 2013). In spite of dating becoming an inseparable part of growing up in youths' lives, the *zaolian* discourse still widely exists and is promoted in middle schools and high schools. This discourse argues that students in middle and high schools are too young to date, and that their love is puppy love, which is not real and is a distraction from their studies. 'No advocacy, no opposition' (*bu tichang, bu fandui*), just like 'don't ask, don't tell' in the US military, is the predominant attitude toward dating in universities. Under this suppressive school environment, dating has not been totally accepted and sex has been seen as a forbidden fruit, so that it is difficult for girls who have had unwanted sexual experiences to seek formal help from the school, and they feel that they can only keep to themselves or discuss their problems with very close friends, so that hiding things seems like a much better strategy than speaking out.

At the same time, there is almost no family sex education in China. Pan and Huang's (2013) nationwide survey shows that 86.6% of teenagers aged from 14 to 17 thought that they almost never received any sex education from their parents. On the one hand, parents prefer to treat their daughters as 'pure children' rather than as sexually mature adults; on the other hand, parents lack knowledge and communication skills to discuss sex with their teenager children, and studies show that they hope the schools will shoulder the responsibility of sex education and let them off the hook (Wang and Wang, 2012). As Ding Dang says, 'my parents cannot imagine that I have done this [had sex]. If they knew it, I am sure that they would strangle me.' Ding Dang may exaggerate her parents' reaction, but her words show clearly that when young women encounter difficulties in their sex lives, their parents are the last persons that they would like to tell and ask for help. Qin Cui complained that:

> during all the school years, my parents told me to focus on studying and not be distracted from *zaolian*, and then suddenly, when I graduated from the college, they said that I should get married soon. I feel angry that they never taught me anything useful about dating, love, and sex. How are we supposed to know about love and dating since we lack practice? How are we supposed to get married since we have no experience of dating?
>
> (Qin Cui, F, 31)

The desire of women in contemporary Chinese society is closely connected to the policy of opening up, and the development of the economy, the modernization of China, and the globalization of the world (Wang and Ho,

156 *Virginity loss, sexual coercion, sexual revolution*

2007a). Young women's lack of voice about sex and the lack of family and school sex education are closely related to the ignorance of sexuality in Chinese cultural tradition and political discourse, and yet they are increasingly exposed to global discourses about sexuality.

In the May Fourth period, interest in what constitutes a modern sexuality increased rapidly in intellectual circles, and sexual reformers such as Zhang Jingsheng (known as Dr. Sex) conducted surveys, published articles and books, and generally popularized thinking about sex as an integral aspect of modern change (Larson, 1999). However, the split between dating and sex also started at that time. On the one hand, pursuing romantic love and free dating became an act of resistance to the old society, and for the pursuit of humanity, subjectivity, and individuality, and therefore national modernity. On the other hand, sexual angst is the most significant emotion in the lives of the protagonists in several well-known stories. In both Larson's (1999) and Meng and Dai's (2004) respective literary criticism of Ding Ling and Feng Yuanjun, dating was closely related to revolution, while sexuality was repressed and confused and still attached to Confucian ideas on chastity. Therefore, the avoidance of sexuality turned into a way to testify to the purity of love – by ignoring women's pleasure and desire, and thus neglecting women's sexual subjectivity.

In the Maoist Era, the Zhang Jingsheng legacy of the idea of the sexualized modern person was virtually demolished, and the split between dating and sexuality was expanded into every corner of the general public's lives. Modern sexuality was harshly criticized as bourgeois, and therefore sexual repression became a part of state domination through two methods. One was that of putting nation and class over gender and sexuality. As I have demonstrated, the state discourse turned Xier's experience of acquaintance rape in *The White-Haired Girl* into a class struggle between a landholder and a peasant, so that the abused woman's body and sexuality completely faded out of the story (Meng, 1993). As Zhang Yuehong (2005) argues, '[t]he state's sovereign claim on the body in the Maoist period differs from indirect regulation of the body in capitalist society, and features a combination of the fever of sacrifice among the masses for collectivism with direct control of body' (pp. 6–7). '*Re'ai* (enthusiastic love) can only be directed toward the greater leader, the party, or the revolutionary classes and their cause. *Aiqing*, a phrase exclusively referring to romantic love since the Republic period, disappeared altogether from public discourse during the cultural revolution' (Zhang, 2011, p. 132).

The other method was that of only legitimating marriage-oriented dating and institutionalizing sex within marriage, with sexuality reduced to its function of reproducing successors (*jiebanren*) for communist careers. Polygamy, adultery, pandering, seeing prostitutes, having sexual pleasure-centered entertainment, having adventures in erotica, watching pornography – all these practices were sharply condemned and legally prohibited by the state discourse. The state sexuality discourse served to marginalize and stigmatize

Virginity loss, sexual coercion, sexual revolution 157

practices that fell outside 'reproductive citizenship.' After the Maoist Era, in the New Era the state still maintained the core policy on sexuality, and the CCP launched political campaigns in 1981, 1983, 1987, and 1989 to eradicate foreign 'spiritual pollution' (*jingshen wuran*), a noxious byproduct of 'bourgeois liberalization' (*zichanjiejie ziyouhua*) (Pickowicz, 1991). It has been politically expedient to blame China's problems with sexuality on the influence of pernicious foreign culture, and on the culture of the capitalist West in particular. To this day, the government is concerned about exposure to outside influence, such as that of Internet pornography and the LGBT movement. The establishment of the 'Great Firewall' on the Internet, and the blocking of Western social media such as Facebook, Twitter and YouTube, serve pretty much this purpose. In this sense, sexual coercion exists not just at the micro level of dating relationships, but also at the state level, where young men and women are actors trying to negotiate their sexuality and prescribed social roles. On the one hand, the state's political discourse has been translated, through women, into the private context of desire, love, marriage, divorce, and familial relations; and on the other hand, it has turned woman into agents who politicize desire, love, and family relations by delimiting and repressing sexuality, self, and all private emotions (Rofel, 1999). Michel Foucault's (1997) critique of the repressive hypothesis in Victorian Europe is a reference for understanding the state repression of sexuality from the Maoist Era to the New Era:

> It is not a question of denying the existence of repression. It is one of showing that repression is always a part of a much more complex political strategy regarding sexuality. Things are not merely repressed – The way in which sexuality in the nineteenth century was not repressed but also put in [the] light, underlined, analyzed through techniques like psychology and psychiatry shows very well that it was not simply a question of repression.
>
> (p. 126)

Some studies, such as Larson's (1999) and Honig's (2003) articles on sexuality in the Cultural Revolution and Zhang's (2005) paper on sexuality at the transition from the Maoist Era to the post-Mao period, have demonstrated the negotiation between the repressive power of the state discourse as it punished people who transgressed sexual norms, engaged in premarital sex, or had extra-marital affairs; and the resistant force of the general public as it did precisely those prohibited things in order to entice and construct sexual desire. Thinking about repression as a way to provoke sexual desire instead of as total repression is inspiring only if we keep from losing sight of the existing sovereignty (Zhang, 2005). Ironically, here the state discourse again maintains consistency with Confucian ideas on women's chastity and purity. This also shows that the state discourse is still powerful now in silencing women's discussion about sexuality and turning the external repression into women's

158   *Virginity loss, sexual coercion, sexual revolution*

unconscious sense of guilt, frustration, embarrassment, and hurt. The state cannot prevent women from engaging in sexuality and starting their sexual adventures, as they 'feel lonely and have needs too' and 'are curious'; however, at the same time, all of their ambivalent and negative feelings, as illustrated by the current study, are reinforced because public repression is internalized as a private problem.

Happy to be non-virgins

If the experience of virginity loss is that of submission, after the first time, how do the women face the stigma of being a 'slut' and accommodate the identity of no longer being a virgin? Can they take the initiative in their timing of having sex? Can they deal with the hurt and worry that they get from the early sexual experience and become happy non-virgins?

As Farrer (2002) argues, the age of young people is a more important determinant of their decision about whether to engage in sex for the first time or not, than those of gender or social class. The young Chinese women in this study generally considered that being under 20 was too young to have sex, and for many female college students, graduation seemed an appropriate time to begin being sexually active. Wen Jie, a postgraduate student, had dated a guy for more than five years, but they did not have sex with each other. When she turned 25, she decided it was the right time:

> I feel that deciding whether to do it or not [have sex] is related to one's age. At that time I was just 19. Looking back, the thing that bothered me most was that I didn't know whether we would have a future. I should keep it till later. Things have changed because my idea has changed. I'm 25. I am a mature woman, physically and psychologically. I think that I can accept it.
>
> (Wen Jie, F, 26)

This case illustrates how a woman can change her views on virginity loss as she grows older. Six years ago she was 'too uncertain to have sex,' but now she has taken the initiative to have sex for the first time and she is happy about it. It is worth noting that all the women in this study who claimed that their experience of virginity loss was unpleasant had sex for the first time below the age of 20. In the USA, many adolescents have had sexual intercourse by the age of 17, and by the age of 19 the majority (75% or more) of males and females are sexually active (Brooks-Gunn and Paikoff, 1993). In contrast, Chinese young adults have sex much later than their American peers.

According to a national survey among adults aged 18 to 61 carried out by Pan and Huang (2013), men have first intercourse, on average, at 22.50 years old, and women are later, at the age of 22.75. In Pan and Yang's (2004) national survey on college students' sexuality, only 16.9% of undergraduate students (they are 18 to 22, mostly) were found to have had sex at least once.

Virginity loss, sexual coercion, sexual revolution   159

Pan and Huang's (2013) survey among teenagers from 14 to 17 finds that 12.6% of boys and 8.3% of girls had had intercourse; the results are higher than similar studies because their study included those teenagers not in the school system. Chi, Yu and Winter (2012) conducted a questionnaire survey among 1,403 college students and found that 12.6% (15.4% of males versus 8.6% of females) reported having had heterosexual intercourse, 10.8% (10.5% of males versus 11.2% of females) had had oral sex, and 2.7% (3.4% of males versus 1.7% of females) reported same-sex activities. All the available figures show that Chinese teenagers and young adults do start being sexually active at a rather later age. For men, having sex at an early age is something worth boasting about, while for women it is something that is always accompanied by anxiety and pressure.

I agree with Farrer's argument that age is an important determinant of women's decisions about whether to engage in sex for the first time or not. I further offer a more in-depth understanding of the timing these young Chinese women have in mind regarding sex: below 20 is considered too young to have sex, and they prefer to have sex later, when they have a better sense of control over their own lives and less uncertainty and insecurity about their future. For many female college students, graduation seems to be the most appropriate time to start their sexual lives. Women like Wen Jie and those who are older than 25 may take the initiative to change from being gatekeepers to becoming active participants in sex. When women reach 30, virginity may become a burden to get rid of rather than a treasure. Farrer (2002) argues that young people in Shanghai are inclined to invoke moral purity to justify premarital sex, which means that they justify having sex on the grounds that they love their partners or that they will marry them. Farrer's argument is validated in this study, and 'sex is a sublimation of love' is often quoted by participants in legitimate premarital sex, who justify their 'purity of purpose' (p. 223). Therefore, the clear-cut standard of the purity of the body of the Maoist Era becomes relative, ambiguous, and never absolute in the Reform Era.

I believe that age may bring women different perspectives for understanding the meaning of virginity loss. Two years after the first interview, I followed up with Ding Dang, when she was not in any relationship. She told me clearly that though the experience of virginity loss remained as an unhappy memory, it no longer bothered her that much, and she no longer worried whether her future partner would find out about her past sexual experience and thus despise her. Through personal experience, friends' stories and all kinds of information, such women gradually convinced themselves that virginity loss is not that big a deal:

> One close friend of mine broke up with an ex-boyfriend and then found a new one who treats her even better. I read in the paper that, in Beijing, every year more than 1,000 couples get married, and more than 500 couples get divorced.
>
> (Zheng Xin, F, 23)

160 *Virginity loss, sexual coercion, sexual revolution*

I have a teacher who majored in women's studies. She said: 'Men want to date virgins. If none of you are virgins, how can men insist on finding them?'

(Ding Yi, F, 22)

When their experience tells them that even if they have lost their virginity they can still find good partners, they really feel that virginity loss is not something so terrible. Zheng Xin refers to Beijing divorce statistics to argue that if divorced women can get married again, maybe it is much easier for a single non-virgin to find another boyfriend who can accept her past sexual experience and will marry her. While Zheng Xin argues that virginity loss is only a personal issue, Ding Yi, quoting her teacher, turns the personal into the political and makes an unusual remark that implies that a social movement can liberate women from being suffocated by the discourse of the 'female virginity complex.'

Young women often run into problems in trying to present themselves as sexual beings without being objectified, because the discourses of the 'female virginity complex' seem to offer little space for discussing women's desire and agency. Being self-determined is one of the most important qualities for them to face the state of not being a virgin, to shake off the influence of the repressive power of the virginity complex, and to pursue the happiness that they desire. As Zheng Xin says, '[i]f you don't worry, then nothing bothers you'; as Ding Yi says, 'I cannot discard my happiness for my whole life just because I am not a virgin.' These perceptions make clear that virginity loss should/would not block the path to happiness and 'true love,' which represents a rising awareness of women's desire that brings women's sexuality to a public forum.

Carpenter (2002) uses three metaphors to describe virginity: virginity as a gift, which means that the first experience of sex is an act of gift-giving to another; virginity as a stigma, which means that the first experience of sex is a casual act to shed the stigma of being a virgin; and virginity as a process, which means that the first experience of sex is a desirable and essentially positive transition to adulthood. These Chinese young women have more difficulties dealing with virginity loss than their Western peers. For them, virginity loss is more like a 'loss' than a 'gift'; turning it into 'a process' takes different stages. As Ding Yi says, 'young' Chinese women 'learn to accept the situation of virginity loss slowly.' Eventually, the transition to womanhood will be complete, sex will be desirable, and they will be independent and autonomous, but it takes time.

According to Schlegel (1991), one way to assess a woman's autonomy is to ask her whether she controls her own sexuality. It seems that virginity loss was a turning point, and that the group of non-virgins in this study was more independent and assertive and seems to have had more freedom and autonomy to do whatever they wanted. Qi Mei was a 29-year-old new Beijinger working as a manager in a foreign company at the time of the interview. She

Virginity loss, sexual coercion, sexual revolution   161

went to a teaching college and became an English teacher in a high school after graduation. She was a woman originally from another city who really did not like the job, but took it mainly to secure a Beijing *hukou*. She used to live alone in the school dormitory and felt terribly lonely because most of her colleagues were local Beijingers. She was soon matched up with a Beijinger physical education teacher from the same school through the matchmaking of an older teacher. She moved into a very crowded local courtyard home (*siheyuan*) where her husband's family occupied two rooms. She never felt that she was passionately in love with her husband and she never got along with her parents-in-law, who lived next door. She originally thought that the marriage could save her from loneliness, but she became even more desperate and miserable than before. The marriage did not last long and she quit her job when the relationship ended. She said: 'After the divorce, I suddenly realized that I did not know what love is and how to love.' She was also surprised to find that she was not as devastated as she expected to be, but rather enjoyed the freedom after a short period of gloom. The regained single life seemed quite carefree and pleasurable in comparison to the obligations of married life. With the secured Beijing *hukou*, she found an office job in an international company rather easily, and soon she was promoted to manager because of her excellent English skills. She felt as if she lived in another world with all kinds of opportunities and new love and sexual adventures. Once she went out of town on business with a male Chinese colleague, and they ended up sleeping together under the influence of alcohol. However, after a few more sexual encounters with her colleague, she decided to end the affair, though her colleague wanted to continue. She said:

> The desires of the body should be respected, so I didn't reject one-night stands because of the needs of the body. But I could not stand the sex without love. After a few times, I just felt bored. I had to end with him.
>
> (Qi Mei, F, 29)

Qi Mei had also been involved with a married man for more than one year. At the beginning, he was a client of the business and she took the initiative to call him for a date. She knew that he was two years younger than she was and it never occurred to her that he might be married. She soon found that he was married but did not care that much since she 'admired his charm and the love was quite passionate.' They met each other regularly once per week or biweekly, usually in different hotels. However, soon things got even more complicated: she found that he was involved with another, much younger woman, whom she knew:

> Usually I want to keep distance from married men. But he looks very simple, sincere, and authentic. He is a high achiever among his peers and I admire him very much. I feel that a woman should be independent, and love sometimes only belongs to yourself. I chose him, this was my choice

162 *Virginity loss, sexual coercion, sexual revolution*

and decision, and I am never going to change who he is. I never asked him to divorce and never discussed the future with him. I was always adjusting. I hoped that we could enjoy the moment. I enjoyed the sex with him and especially turn on when I take the initiative during sex. I want to get rid of the sense of possessive love. I tried to be appreciative of what he gave me and what we could share. But sometimes what he did was unimaginable. Once we were in a hotel, and he started to text to someone at dinnertime. I knew it was his other girlfriend, but I did not say anything. Till almost 12 o'clock, he was still there texting. I finally lost it, said, 'You are such a lousy lover,' and then stormed out.

(Qi Mei, F, 29)

Though dating a high achiever is on the old track of 'women date up,' Qi Mei's love affairs have had many anti-traditional features – she has taken the initiative and chosen somebody younger than herself and, most importantly, her understanding of love is unusual. Unlike the emphasis on the 'one and only,' 'happily ever after' type of romantic love, Qi Mei thinks that love is a woman's personal matter and individual drama, and that it is inclusive and a matter of 'enjoying the moment.' Her understanding of love echoes Giddens's (1992) concept of 'confluent love' and 'pure relationship,' which does not value the 'forever' and 'one and only' quality of romantic love, as the finding of a 'special relationship' becomes more important than pledging oneself to a 'special person.' Confluent love also relies on reciprocal sexual pleasure as a core element of a relationship, and in doing so presumes the disappearance of the 'respectable' woman (Giddens, 1992; Hooff, 2013).

By emphasizing 'enjoying the moment' and inclusive love, 'appreciating the gives and takes' and playing an active role during sex, Qi Mei's attitudes to love and sexuality capture the major spirit of a 'pure relationship'; however, her partner may not share the same spirit, and this became the reason for her final break-up with the lover. I never got the chance to meet or interview Qi Mei's partner, and I can only guess his perceptions through Qi Mei's description. Qi Mei told me that the thing she was fed up with most was that 'we only had such a limited time, but he just could not focus and commit to me.' She did not complain about his marriage, his wife, or even his other girlfriend, but told herself that a 'special' person is more valuable than a possessive monogamous relationship. However, she was 'deeply hurt' when she realized that she was not being fairly and equally treated and valued. She felt that 'love without dignity' is not something she wanted, and decided to let it go. A recurring theme in Giddens's (1992) work is female equality as a necessary precondition for the pure relationship to exist, in which partners who are 'in principle' equal negotiate their wishes and desires. In Qi Mei's case, we can argue that one-sided confluent love cannot constitute a pure relationship, and the only possible solution is the ending of the relationship.

The other distinguished feature of Qi Mei's story is that she candidly talked about her bodily sexual desires, which disrupted the stereotypical sexual

Virginity loss, sexual coercion, sexual revolution 163

pattern of 'active men and passive women.' She stated that she enjoyed playing the active rather than the passive role in sex. Women writers have taken the lead in demystifying sex and acknowledging bodily desire in contemporary China. Not until the 1980s did some women writers begin to write about the body and acknowledge the bodily desires and sexuality of women. Renowned writer Wang Anyi began to experiment with eroticism, subjectivity, and socially transgressive themes in the early 1980s. She explored sexuality and female subjectivity as a means of testing the limits of reality and the boundaries of human consciousness (Liu, 1993). In the 1990s more and more women writers, most of whom were born in the 1970s, such as Weihui and Mianmian, adopted an avant-garde mode of writing. Their writing does not just lay bare 'women's real experiences,' their youth, or their gender, but also their unabashed sexuality (Ferry, 2003b). Just like the 'New Woman' or 'Modern Girl' writers of the 1920s and 1930s, a group of new women writers has emerged in contemporary China as a force for social and cultural change (Ferry, 2003b) in the new millennium. The publication of *The Left Behind Love Letters* (*yiqing shu*) on the Internet in 2003 definitely created the sensation of an open expression of women's desire:

> *The Left Behind Love Letters* began as a blog written by Muzi Mei, a magazine staff writer in her mid-twenties living in the city of Guangzhou. Muzi Mei used the blog to chronicle her sexual encounters with numerous male partners – both acquaintances whose telephone numbers she chose from the long list in her address book, as well as men she picked up in bars or other public settings. In her blog entries, Muzi Mei describes in detail the bodily sensations she felt during her exploratory sexual experiences, in an equally experimental writing style. For a time, *The Left Behind Love Letters* generated such a high volume of online traffic that Muzi Mei's website temporarily crashed. *The Left Behind Love Letters*, notorious for its positive depiction of the pursuit of sexual gratification, which critics condemned as unethical, nevertheless promoted strongly Muzi Mei's alternative ethical position: that seeking sexual pleasure is not shameful but a celebration of life, so long as the persons involved were willing participants in the encounter.
>
> (Zhang, 2011, pp. 111–112)

Though Muzi Mei's original blog, *The Left Behind Love Letters*, was banned by the government, she still managed to maintain a new blog on Sina. com with nearly 400,000 fans, and she published several books without using the name Muzi Mei. It is interesting to note that direct candid sexual description is no longer the major content of her current blog, and that the blog basically includes very trivial aspects and details of her life. She started to play the role of an online sex and relationship counselor, since a lot of fans wrote to her to discuss their confusion on love and sex, and asked for her suggestions and opinions. She successfully turned the online questions and

164 *Virginity loss, sexual coercion, sexual revolution*

answers into a business by posting her candid replies, retaining her positive depictions of sexual adventure and gratification. Readers can pay her through online banking if they like the articles.

Women's desire and sexuality have been tied to larger issues of cultural identity and modernity (Farrer, 2002; Ferry, 2003a, 2003b; Larson, 2000), and the positive, individualistic, and self-deterministic sexuality among women is closely connected to the policy of opening up, the one-child policy, the development of the market economy, the modernization of China, and globalization. These conditions seem to have created a public space for Chinese women to construct their own identities, create complex and diverse images of women, pursue individual subjectivity and bodily desire, and produce new dating and sexual lifestyles.

In this chapter, both men and women talk about tradition. When women do not want sex they call themselves 'traditional'; when men want sex and virgin wives they also label themselves as 'traditional.' Here, 'tradition' is a label, a mask, a narrative that focuses not on the past, but on the present and imagined future, which symbolizes the impotence and vulnerability of masculinity in the free market. Happy non-virgins are the only ones who do not talk about tradition, and they are more willing to express their desires and embrace their sexuality. The meaning of tradition is interpreted as a reestablishment of traditional values on the surface, but deep down it is a revision and a re-emergent discourse of phallocentrism, presented as a sexual double standard. Therefore, in addition to the state discourse and women's own struggles under the market regime, the re-emergence of phallocentrism as fabricated 'tradition' has become the sworn foe standing in the way of women's pursuit of desire and subjectivity, and the way is never easy.

Unfinished sexual revolution

Sexual liberation and sexual revolution are buzzwords used by scholars both in China and abroad to capture the transformation of individual choice in love and dating, couple interaction and relationship, and family life and arrangement in China today. Over the course of the twentieth century in China, romance, sex and marriage became prime sites of social contestation, where positive and negative aspects of tradition and modernity were defined and assessed, and the promise of sexual liberation was offered (Dikötter, 1995; Farquhar, 2002; Hershatter, 2007, 2012). Evans (1995) stated that 'China has witnessed a sexual liberation in recent years. Sex – in some form or other – has emerged from obscurity to occupy a position of unprecedented prominence in public life in the People's Republic' (p. 357). Evans (2008) further argues:

> Sex occupies a privileged place in China's postmillennial ideology of private opportunity, commercial competition, and individual expression. After decades during which sex was almost totally obscured from the

Virginity loss, sexual coercion, sexual revolution   165

public eye, it now pervades public space as one of the dominant markers and metaphors of consumerist modernity.

(p. 361)

Based on the five indicators of: 1) the extent of openness of public knowledge of sex, 2) the nature of sexual conduct, 3) the nature of sexual relationships, 4) the sexuality of women, and 5) the status of sex in mainstream society, Pan Suiming (2006) states that Chinese society has gone through the shift from 'sex for reproduction' to 'sex for pleasure,' and the untying of sex from reproduction and marriage. He further argues that a sexual revolution, rather than a gradual evolution in sexual behaviors and relationships, is taking place in present-day China and has almost already successfully finished (p. 22). Other scholars are relatively reserved about Pan's statement – for example, sociologist Li Yinhe, in an interview in 2008, said that China definitely had begun the sexual revolution, but it was just at the very beginning stage. Zhang Yuehong (2011) adopted the term 'sexual revolution' mainly because she could not find another expression that would be more accurate in capturing the enormity of the changes in sexuality over the past decades, and proposed to use 'China's sexual revolution' in order to differentiate it from the sexual revolution in the USA in the 1960s and 1970s (p. 107). I argue that the so-called sexual revolution in China is an unfinished project, because the revolution in sexual behavior is not equal to a real sexual revolution based on human rights, sexual autonomy, and gender equality. Zhang (2011) argues that China's sexual revolution has advanced through three stages:

It started with the reemergence of 'love' shortly after the Cultural Revolution in the late 1970s and early 1980s. At the same time, the implementation of the one-child policy opened the door, unintentionally, for the official justification of sexual pleasure in the 1980s. Then the rapid rise of a consumer society that began after 1992 enhanced individual desire, to which sexual desire is integral, thereby integrating deepening social, economic, technological, and cultural developments, as well as the continued commercialization of China's economy in the new millennium have coalesced so as to decouple sexual desire from reproduction, and even sexual pleasure from love.

(p. 132)

Zhang (2011) attempts to link the transformation of sexuality in China with the reemergence of romantic love discourse and free dating practices, state discourse like the one-child policy, consumer culture, and marketization. Farrer (2006) had made a similar endeavor to describe romance as the centerpiece of Chinese youth's sexual storytelling, and pointed out that 'the sexual public sphere is a rhizomatic space in which private narratives and mass media stories are shared, compared and retold, avoiding state-imposed restrictions while using state-owned resources' (p. 121). Though the state

166 *Virginity loss, sexual coercion, sexual revolution*

withdraws its direct intervention in the private lives of the general public in the Reform Era, it remains a powerful force that impacts people's everyday lives, and has become one of the biggest barriers to the final achievement of a sexual revolution. Zhou (2012) vividly describes the ambivalent situation of sexuality between the private sphere and public sphere:

> The complex relationships between the private sphere (such as sexual desire and pleasure) and the public sphere (such as social norms and public policies) of sexuality have also contributed to the ambiguity and contestations inherent in its public discourses and policies in China.
>
> (p. 88)

The separation of sex from reproduction and the increasing emphasis on sexual love and sexual pleasure are usually regarded as the results of modernization and therefore as representative of sexual liberation in terms of making possible the acceptance of non-reproductive sexual love, and thus non-heterosexual relationships, in the West (Giddens, 1992). However, in China, the unusual phenomenon is that the introduction of the one-child policy interrupted the traditional link between sex and reproduction. Pan Suiming (2006) argues that 'sexuality in China cannot be conceptualized as an autonomous entity or something that is individualized in the body of the person' (p. 22). He has raised the concept of the 'primary life cycle' to describe sexuality in China as embedded in the network of marriage, sex, reproduction, child-rearing, love and other aspects of most basic human activities and relationships (Pan, 2006; Zhou, 2012). Under the one-child policy, the primary life cycle of Chinese people has gone through rapid change. When a couple is only allowed to have one child, most sex throughout a lifetime has to have the purposes of mutual affection and sexual pleasure. With the wide accessibility of contraception and abortion, the separation of sex and reproduction is further validated. 'The one child policy transformed both the demographic profile of the vast Chinese population, and also the sexual desire, expectations, and practices of its constituents' (Zhang, 2011, pp. 136–137). When sex is no longer deeply tied to reproduction, sexual behaviors and practices that were once considered to be 'abnormal,' 'illegal,' and 'immoral' flourish – premarital sex, masturbation, oral sex, anal sex, multiple sex, one-night stands, extra-marital sex, cyber sex, commercial sex, couple swapping, homosexual sex, STD/HIV prevalence, and divorce – as numerous studies show (Farrer, 2006; Osburg, 2013; Pan, 2006; Pan and Huang, 2013; Pei and Ho, 2009; Parish et al., 2007; Zhou, 2012; Zhang et al., 2010).

Sigley (2006) argues that China's central authorities continue to intervene in the sexual arena due to the historical twinning of concepts of moral virtue with signs of national progress in China (pp. 6–7). Besides the one-child policy, other state policies also play a huge role to make the issue of sexuality more ambivalent, sometimes with unpredictable consequences. The institutionalized 'sweeping the erotic and cracking the illegal' (*sao huang da fei*) campaign has never stopped, and it continues to exert all kinds of efforts to combat 'spiritual pollution.' For example, the state has maintained a consistent line toward pornography and commercial sex, and both remain officially illegal; meanwhile both are widely sought and practiced, at least by state officials and businessmen, as many studies have demonstrated (Zheng, 2009; Osburg, 2013). However, Parish et al.'s (2007) research findings show that Chinese youth consume just as much pornographic material as do American youth, and the prevalence of commercial sex in China is higher than in many countries in East and Southeast Asia, with the exception of Thailand.

The censorship of sexual issues and LGBT issues is everywhere, and the government is reticent about openly addressing sexual subjects. Cui Zi'en (2010) claimed that the system for censoring films on LGBT issues in China is much stricter than the censorship of printed materials and TV, since all films have to be sent to the Beijing Film Bureau for inspection in order to decide whether to grant them public release permits or not. Numerous queer independent films and documentaries have been produced but have been censored and therefore are not accessible to the general public. Ang Lee's Oscar-winning (for Best Director) movie *Brokeback Mountain* was banned because of its homosexual content, and another of his movies, *Lust, Caution*, had seven minutes of sex scenes cut in order to obtain permission for public release.

I have mentioned that the blog *The Left Behind Love Letters* by Muzi Mei was banned, as was the novel *Shanghai Baby* by Weihui. Even the publication of academic books on sexuality can be difficult: the leading researcher Pan Suiming published many of his academic books in Taiwan and Hong Kong, and it took young rising scholar Pei Yuxin (2013) five years of going through many rejections from numerous publishing houses before she could finally publish her book on Shanghai young women's sexuality.

Ho (2007) argues that the growing commercialization of 'gay space' became a major survival strategy in the paradoxical context of state control, a degree of freedom of speech, and self-censorship. 'Don't ask, don't tell' has become a most accurate description of, and the common situation in, Chinese people's sexual lives. It seems that everyone has the imaginary freedom to do whatever they what, as long as they keep it quiet. Zhou's (2012) study interestingly points out that higher-educated Chinese immigrants in Canada change their sexual behavior but continue to keep silent about sex, and I wonder if this group of people had gone wild even when they were still in China. The boundary between private and public is never clear, and under the pressure of state censorship and the 'sweeping the erotic and cracking the illegal' campaign, people think that they have freedom and autonomy, at least in their private lives, but they may not be fully aware that sometimes even private activities can be problematic. For example, in 2010, a professor in Nanjing was detained at the police station for organizing couple-swapping activities at home. In almost every recent anti-corruption case, one alleged accusation against corrupt officers is adultery. Moreover, many ethnographies

168 *Virginity loss, sexual coercion, sexual revolution*

vividly document the triangular relationship between businessmen, sex workers, and officials in night clubs, where businessmen build relationships with government officials through the entertainment, fantasy, and sexuality provided by sex workers (Zheng, 2009; Osburg, 2013).

The current 'sexual revolution' is embedded in the social structure of the primary life cycle, which makes it extremely difficult to challenge the traditional moral and gender norms and makes it vulnerable to the intrusion of state power to discipline and intervene in matters concerning individuals' bodies and sexuality. A real revolution usually needs a core new value system and leadership to bring a rapid change to society and push things forward. For example, 'the U.S. sexual revolution was intertwined with contemporaneous social movement (the civil rights movement, the anti war movement, the gay and lesbian movement, the feminist movement) and became a manifestation of the overall challenges to the established values and practices. It was a way to call for open, diversified sexual practices, which translated into sexual rights through due process of civil liberty' (Zhang, 2011, p. 139). However, the so-called 'sexual revolution' in China is more a matter of numerous spontaneous sexual behaviors emerging from the change of the society, with neither a clear value system nor a core leadership. The preacher of sexual revolution Pan Suiming is no doubt the leading scholar in sexuality studies, and he has been radical in promoting sexual human rights. Unfortunately, most of his study lacks clear gender awareness and sensitivity. Many sex educators at the forefront are concerned about how to adapt his radical thoughts for everyday sexual education of children and teenagers in the rather conservative school environment. The feminist movement and the LGBT movement have gone through huge developments in the past two decades; however, sexual rights and sexual autonomy have never been put into the center of the movement.

The worst part of the current 'sexual revolution' is that it has not granted sexual autonomy equally to men and to women, to people from different backgrounds, education levels, and social strata. Instead it makes the existing sexual double standard even more intense and refashions patriarchy in a different mode. Existing studies (Pei, 2013; Pei and Ho, 2009) show that many Chinese women in their twenties and thirties equate sexual liberation with gender equality and being modern women. However, in the current situation, sexual capital and resources are unequally distributed to men and women, youth and the aged, the urban and the rural. Pan and Huang's (2013) study shows that more educated men engage in more sexual practices and activities, and many ethnographies show that men with money and power have more opportunities to have *ernai* (second wives) and *xiaosan* (mistresses), and to visit sex workers. These practices find their most favorable soil in patriarchal societies with a sexual double standard: chastity and fidelity are expected of women, combined with acceptance and tolerance of men's pursuit of multiple sexual partners (Parish et al., 2007).

Virginity loss, sexual coercion, sexual revolution 169

In contrast, a lot of rural and poor men have trouble finding wives, which makes sex trafficking in certain remote areas a serious problem. Young educated women in their twenties are most popular in the dating market, while they may face the test of being pure, good girls, as some young men are still obsessed with the purity of their girlfriends and at the same time expect their girlfriends to lose their virginity to them. When young, educated girls finally bypass the dilemma of virginity to pursue their individual freedom and sexual autonomy, they may face much more criticism and pressure from friends, family, and society than men who behave in a similar way. The discourse of 'leftover women' is so profound that women in their late twenties feel they cannot escape facing the pressure to get married, as if marriage were the only right path. Large numbers of under-educated girls migrate to the cities, where their choices can be very limited to becoming a factory worker, working in the service industry, marry a city man, or enter the commercial sex industry, and sexual capital becomes their most valuable asset for achieving upward mobility.

The traditional family structure still plays a huge role in individual sexual desires and lives. In the LGBT world, the formality marriage between gays and lesbians is, in a way, a modern arrangement with the spirit of a contract, employed to cope with the traditional pressure to marry and have children. At least 16 million gays have married unaware heterosexual women, who become '*tongqi*' and may face the unexpected risk of STDs/HIV. In the current institutional marriage system, single women cannot enjoy the same health and reproductive rights as married women, since the state still grants reproduction permits only to married women.

Parish et al. (2007) found an interesting puzzle that they could not solve in their study: in China, 'the increasing willingness of women to engage in premarital sex is occurring alongside increasing use of commercial sex among men. This contrasts with post-1960s West, where declining use of commercial sex occurred in the context of increasing mainstream acceptability of women engaging in premarital sex' (pp. 750–751). I think that this phenomenon is due precisely to the unequal distribution of sexual capital and recourse among different groups, and even emphasizes the sexual double standard in the Reform Era.

Conclusion

Before embarking on fieldwork, I had never thought that women's experience of virginity loss had any necessary relation to sexual coercion, but the interviews changed my perceptions as I came to notice how these young women, my informants, talked a lot about their unpleasant sexual experiences and how they felt that they had actually been coerced into sex, especially during their first experiences of sex. I notice that many young Chinese women's first experiences of sex contain elements of sexual coercion, most of which are 'minor' and occur without the use of physical force, and thus are ignored by

170 *Virginity loss, sexual coercion, sexual revolution*

the general public and in academia. By paying attention to women's experiences of 'minor' and 'trivial' sexual coercion in their dating relationships, I argue that women's virginity loss is often articulated by using the discourse of the 'female virginity complex,' a convenient phrase women use to explain their disappointment that their first sexual experiences were not ideal and so highlight their frustration and ambivalence about their relationships. The 'female virginity complex' is also a discourse that has emerged in the context of rapid social changes, in which female sexual autonomy and assertiveness have become possible options for young Chinese women, and the dilemmas they, as modern subjects and actors, encounter cause tensions between their needs and social constraints.

Virginity loss becomes the critical moment for self-fashioning and negotiation in order to construct an intersectional time-based and stage-based subjectivity. Age seems more directly interconnected with sexuality, and this chapter has given details of the timing of women's first engagement in sex. I compare how women use their different roles as gatekeepers, 'victims,' and sexual agents to demonstrate their resistance and agency at different stages: before, at the moment of, and after their virginity loss. Before their virginity loss it is found that women often play the card of 'performing the traditional' to reject sex that they do not want, therefore putting themselves in a relatively advantageous position in the dating market and in their relationships with their boyfriends. After their virginity loss, women are more willing to accept and celebrate their own desire, and identify themselves as sexual agents when they are more ready to interpret themselves as being modern, sometimes even liberal, non-virgins.

The moment of virginity loss becomes a moment for rethinking one's self, status, and strategy in the competitive dating and marriage market in urban China. Although expressions of unhappiness at being sexually coerced could be taken as evidence of the pervasiveness of sexual exploitation or violence, I think that there is a need to examine women's ambivalence about their virginity loss more critically. Virginity operates as a platform for these women to assess how far they have approximated their romantic and marriage ideals, and their visions of prosperity and stability in a heterosexual family. In their narratives, I have observed that women's demand for respect is not simply a demand for respect of their bodily integrity, but also respect for their autonomy to decide when to 'give' the valuable asset of their virginity (according to the normative gender ideals), and to do so in a way that is to their benefit and not only in response to the coercive demands of their partners. The concept of 'gender-asymmetric modes of mutual violence' is proposed to help us understand the escalation of violence in dating relationships and the ambivalence of women's and men's different experiences in their daily and sexual lives. This discourse is simultaneously rooted both in the liberal discourse of individual autonomy in a post-socialist state, and in the traditional Chinese gender ideals of sexuality which imply that women should be gatekeepers of their virginity and be 'givers' only when conditions are ideal, whereas men should wait and qualify themselves as 'takers.'

This chapter shows how the different discourses of state, market, culture, age, and education compete with one another to influence young people's sexual lives, and how the young women strategically situate themselves in a relatively advantageous situation to resist sexual hegemony and embrace sexual liberation to pursue their individuality, subjectivity, and desire. Their personal stories of happiness and sadness in their sexual lives also shed light on the social transformation of sexuality from the sexual repression of the Maoist Era to the pursuit of individual desire in post-socialist China. However, I have to point out that the so-called 'sexual revolution' is unfinished, since it neglects gender equality, strengthens the sexual double standard, and refashions the patriarchy. Giddens (1992) argues that during the transformation of intimacy, sexuality has become an autonomous entity or 'plastic sexuality,' which is freed from its intrinsic relation to reproduction and other obligations and is embedded in individual freedom and equality. This 'plastic sexuality' has been far less established in current China than in the West, though it has become many liberated women's ideal version of sexuality. How to push forward the current 'sexual revolution' in China to make people happier, freer, more equal, and more autonomous in fulfilling their human potential remains a question to be explored.

Note

1 *New Oxford American Dictionary*, third edition, Oxford University Press, 2010, p. 355.

6 Remapping the landscape of dating, gender, and violence

This qualitative feminist study examines dating violence in the context of Beijing, the cosmopolitan and rapidly changing capital city of China with a high degree of culture hybridity. I have explored how young men and women of Beijing interpret the meaning of dating, love, gender and sexuality, and how they make sense of their violent dating experience. I have considered dating violence as an important area of study in its own right, at the same time investigating its connection to the larger subject of gender-based violence, departing from the standpoint of existing studies, which regard dating violence as a matter of interpersonal and psychological problems. Instead, the exploration has been linking interpersonal and psychological problems with socio-cultural perspectives, focusing on the interconnection between the micro-politics of dating violence and the macro-politics of a changing state, market, and culture in the context of China's modernization and globalization. Inspired by the feminist intersectionality theory, I have attempted to establish the multiple layers of Chinese intersectionality, with the intersectional self as the core; the various factors as mediating situational and institutional mechanisms; and the state, market, and culture as macro socio-cultural forces.

The contributions of this book are mainly threefold: first, in establishing dialogues with existing violence research and therefore contributing to the area of gender-based violence; second, in dialoguing with feminist scholarship and Chinese women's studies to establish a new theoretical framework of Chinese intersectionality, especially in terms of contributions to gender and sexuality studies; and third, in engaging in reviews and dialogue with numerous China studies in the areas of sociology, anthropology, cultural and literary critiques, etc., and therefore contributing to China studies by providing thick descriptions of young people's intimate lives and violent experiences and capturing the transformation of dating, gender, and sexuality from the Maoist Era to present-day China.

Remapping dating violence

When claiming that dating violence is an important area of study in its own right, it is necessary to draw a line between domestic violence and dating

The landscape of dating, gender, and violence 173

violence; especially intimate partner violence has traditionally been framed as domestic violence insofar as it was assumed that intimate relationships are located in the domestic sphere, between a married couple, within a nuclear family, etc. Most existing studies of domestic violence exclusively focus on severe physical violence, while I have found 'minor' and 'trivial' violence to extensively predominate in the dating relationship.

Only eight of my 43 participants reported having experienced severe violence. The popular concepts stemming from domestic violence studies, such as 'cycle of violence' (Walker, 1979, 2000) and the 'power and control' circle (Kelly, 1996; Kurz, 1993), etc., are useful to help us understand the power struggle and interactive dynamic within severe violence. 'Breaking up' is an easier way to escape from violence in dating relationships than divorce is in a situation of marital domestic violence. However, several women reported that it took them months or years and all kinds of struggles and countless break-ups and reconciliations finally to break up with their abusive boyfriends. One woman reported that she married an abusive boyfriend, later on experienced domestic violence and finally divorced him several years later.

I attempt to convey some strong messages to both young people and helping professionals. On one hand, both need to be more sensitive to the existence of dating violence, including 'minor' and 'trivial' violence, and to be more aware of the potential danger of escalation from minor violence to severe violence. On the other hand, since most young people in this study managed to stop violence by ending their toxic abusive relationship themselves, it is important for helping professionals to recognize the agency and strength of young people temporarily trapped in violent dating relationships, and to remind them that there are always choices and ways to disrupt an ongoing, escalating cycle of violence. For young men and women, especially young women, they need to learn to disrupt those predominant beliefs and myths of dating violence, including 'only serious violence counts as violence,' 'violence always involves abusive men and abused women,' 'the perpetrators of sexual violence and rape are mainly strangers,' etc., and become fully aware of their right to reject any kind of violence, no matter how trivial it is, in the name of love.

I have portrayed dating violence as a multi-dimensional concept in which the roles of 'perpetrators' and 'victims' are sometimes flexible and fluid, with the boundaries of physical, verbal, psychological, and sexual violence blurred. The typical dichotomy of 'abusive men and abused women' in existing violence research has sometimes not captured the whole dynamics of violent dating couples, while the 'sassy girl and tender boy' may be seen as a new trope for dating patterns at present. With the major feminist mission of promoting gender equality and eradicating gender-based violence, this book has jumped out of the dichotomy of 'abusive men and abused women,' and taken an adventurous step in not ignoring, but instead exploring, women's aggression in dating relationships. I find that the disparity of perceptions on gender equality and gender roles between men and women sometimes stirs up conflict

174 *The landscape of dating, gender, and violence*

and leads to dating violence: in most situations, the women have a strong sense of gender equality and cannot stand their boyfriends' sexist attitudes and behaviors, and this causes conflict and violence. I find that women are not always the, or not the only, victims of dating violence, but are quite aggressive in their everyday lives, especially in situations of minor and mutual violence, in order to defend their rights or obtain more power – yet in most cases of serious dating violence, women remain vulnerable and easily victimized. It is interesting to note that both men and women think that women's aggressive behaviors are more acceptable when they are in situations of mutual violence. Some women are good at using the victim image to accuse their partners of violent behavior, thus ignoring their own behavior, and when their partners are found guilty of infidelity, they think it is legitimate to use violence to punish them.

However, the image of the aggressive girls in their daily lives is never the complete three-dimensional image of being modern women, since they are quite submissive when it comes to sex, which shows that their behaviors may or may not be consistent with rigid social identities. This book links the concepts of 'sexual coercion' and 'virginity loss,' and finds that many young women have the 'unwanted' and 'unpleasant' experience of first sex, but cannot find space and voice to articulate it as 'sexual coercion.' Instead, the 'female virginity complex' is the convenient discourse for them to identify their experiences and to blame themselves. The concept of 'gender-asymmetric modes of mutual violence' is proposed as a way to explore the ambivalence and elaborate the paradox. While most existing studies that have focused primarily on mutual physical violence as a situation in which men hit women and women hit them back, this concept of asymmetry presents men and women as using different modes of violence (such as women's physical aggression toward men and men's sexual coercion of women) as weapons and strategies to gain power, sometimes leading to an escalation of violence in dating relationships.

Since the boundaries of physical, verbal, psychological, and sexual violence are blurred, and since minor violence is the most prominent form in dating relationships, this book vividly illustrates how psychological violence, as the most prevailing form of violence, plays out in dating relationships. Money (or lack of money) and infidelity (or jealousy leading to doubts of fidelity) become two important sites of power struggles as, filled with obstacles and frustrations, they are the most common causes of violence. The drama of a 'break-up' is often the critical moment in the occurrence of violence, involving psychological violence that may be a prelude to more serious physical and sexual violence. Young men and women are masters of emotional control and emotional blackmail. They use cold war, cyber-stalking, spreading rumors, phone harassment, attempted suicide, etc., as their rigorous and relentless strategies. Sometimes I just could not help but wonder why young men and women were so desperate to use all kinds of means to protect the love they believed in. How does this kind of love facilitate violence as an

The landscape of dating, gender, and violence 175

undesirable consequence? When their belief in love is of a delusional 'one and only' variety, involving living 'happily ever after,' and legitimatizes jealousy, possessiveness, and exclusivity, they are not prepared to prevent conflict, tensions, and violence within their intimate relationships. On the one hand, the 'delusional' view seems very rational, in the sense that an 'intimate relationship' is an imagined mandatory responsibility for young people in fulfilling social expectations and obligations concerning the age at which they should date, the age at which age they should 'be in love' and marry, and the age at which they should have children. However, their relationships are always intertwined with the patriarchal system and with certain structures promoting violence embedded within it. In such a situation, their love sometimes is doomed to be twisted with violence, and so they learn to be very good at using love to justify their violence, and using violence in order to maintain their love.

Transformation of dating, gender, and sexuality

I have mapped out the dating landscape and geography in Beijing today, and described the imagined paradise of the dating market as filled with all kinds of dating practices, including casual dating and longer-term, committed courtship. The various dating phenomena of long-distance relationships, transnational relationships, the uncle–Lolita complex, peacock girls and phoenix boys, one-night stands, premarital sex, etc., have been discussed through the intersectional lenses of gender, sexuality, class, age, and migration within the big matrix of state, market, and culture in the era of globalization. Power struggles, either within couples, or between young people and society, are tense. Young people are involved in struggles to obtain social status and upward mobility, and they are keen to pursue desire and enjoy life. On one hand, dating becomes an important self-transformative experience for every young adult, and therefore pursuing love with free will, expressing love, affection and sexuality, and demonstrating agency and autonomy in choosing their ideal love and happiness have become undeniable rights and choices. On the other hand, when dating in this imagined paradise, they encounter all kinds of visible and hidden norms and rules interfering with their free choices, sometimes aware of them and resisting them, and sometimes unconsciously conforming to norms and reinforcing dating hierarchies. Most of the time, however, these dating norms and rules are ambiguous and contradictory, and cause considerable tension and uncertainty for young people. I argue that there is no dominant, unidirectional hegemony affecting young people's dating lives, gender construction, and sexual identity, but rather a set of competing and complex hegemonies offering young people space to penetrate dichotomies and express individual subjectivities and desires. I have depicted the ways in which young people develop diverse strategies to establish their agency, subjectivity, and autonomy in the process of conforming to and resisting dating, gender, and sexual hegemony.

176 *The landscape of dating, gender, and violence*

All the participants in the study were eager to embrace the ideal of a 'desiring self' (Rofel, 2007; Yan, 2010), and to pursue ideals of love, romance, and autonomous partner choice; however, their choices were often enmeshed in material, rational, and family concerns. There are some policies – for example, the *hukou* system and the quota for entering Beijing (though these have been loosened in the current period) – that are still effective in creating inclusion in and exclusion from the dating market. Other policies, such as the house purchase regulations that limit the opportunities of migrants to buy an apartment in Beijing, also indirectly intensify inclusion and exclusion. Therefore, Beijingers and *waidiren* (college students, new Beijingers, and migrant laborers), urbanites and smalltowners, 'peacock girls' and 'phoenix boys' have different dating experiences because of differences in social status, family background, and *hukou* status.

Other tacit rules of date selection also function to reinforce dating hierarchies. Women prefer dating up, desiring taller, richer, older, and better-educated men; conversely, men prefer dating down, desiring shorter, younger, prettier, and less well-educated women. The phrase *gao fu shuai* (tall, rich, and handsome) characterizes the best choice for dating men, and the phrase *bai fu mei* (rich and pretty with a white complexion) designates the best choice in dating women. These two idiomatic expressions both have *fu* (rich) as a desirable quality for both men and women, as the market force driving economic status complicates the original simple rule of 'dating up and dating down,' which endows beautiful women and successful men with the power to obtain more chances and possibilities to penetrate the existing dating hierarchy and engage in upward mobility.

Among the tacit rules of dating selection, age is a tricky factor, as it creates a sexist double standard for men and women, especially those who are approaching their thirties but have remained single. The idiomatic expression of 'golden bachelor' implies that older economically successful men are desirable for single women. However, single women approaching 30 are labeled 'leftover women' (*sheng nü*), which means that nobody wants them; however, this label does not conform with the reality since statistics show that there are many more single men available than single women among people born in the 1980s and 1970s.

Another tacit rule, since the arranged marriage has become a matter of history, is that 'free love and dating' and 'romantic revolution of courtship' (Yan, 2003) are now predominant ambitions and practices, although the criteria for selecting a date from a similar family background (*mendanghudui*) remains a hidden rule, requiring similar or balanced conditions in terms of couples' family backgrounds, educational and occupational categories, economic and social status, and so on. 'Choosing the one I like' now seems to be becoming the golden principle of mate selection for many young people; however, 'choosing the one we all like' is, in fact, quite a common practice. Here the 'we' refers to young people and their parents, as the emotional ties between parents and young adult children are quite strong among many

The landscape of dating, gender, and violence 177

participants who are only children. Many participants often emphasize that obtaining parents' approval and blessing is always a critical moment, and sometimes a precondition, for moving a casual dating relationship towards a longer-term, more committed courtship. A few participants have shared the ways in which their parents or partners' parents intervened in their relationships and finally caused break-ups, and other participants have stated that they would choose to break up if they encountered their parents' disapproval. As more and more young people in Beijing cannot afford the rising prices of apartments without parents' financial support and investment, it seems that parents may play an even more powerful role than before in the choice of who will be 'the one.' It is ironic that young Chinese have been trying to escape this influence from the parents and yet it has become stronger.

There are many dating practices that have long existed, but now their connotative meanings have changed. For example, long-distance dating used to be caused by 'assigned jobs' and 'the need for revolutionary work,' and once carried the meaning of 'eating bitterness for future happiness.' Now, though, 'enjoying life in the present' has become a much more legitimate reason for long-distance arrangements, which are mostly engaged in as a matter of 'personal choice' and the 'pursuit of sexual desire.' Though long-distance relationships are still quite common practice, some participants complain that they are difficult to maintain, since people find it terrible to deal with loneliness, and so they let other relationships flourish – a few male participants clearly stated that they enjoyed the arrangement of the co-existence of a long-distance stable girlfriend with their other lovers in the same city. Long-distance relationships thus usually involve wrestling with jealousy, cheating, conflict, and violence, and lead to break-ups.

This book is focused on dating violence rather than on dating relationships in general, but some dating practices have only been mentioned briefly – for example, interracial dating and dating among migrant laborers. Though three working laborers were recruited, and though their stories do offer some insights for us to understand their dating lives, there is not enough to present a comprehensive and vivid picture of migrant working laborers' dating violence. Only three women mentioned romantic relationships with foreigners, and this information is not rich enough to allow a deep discussion of the complicated situations of international dating in China. Some other dating practices have been omitted from this book – for example, dating in the LGBT circles, cyber-dating, pick-up dating in bars and nightclubs, new technology-facilitated casual hook-up dating, dating arranged by matchmaking companies or by determined parents in parks, etc. All these new dating practices are beyond the scope of this slender book and need to be further explored.

Through depicting a contradictory picture of the 'sassy girl' in daily dating interaction and the quite submissive girl during sexual encounters, this book sheds light on the gender and sexuality transformation from the Maoist Era to the Reform Era. I have articulated a new dating mode of 'sassy girl and

178 *The landscape of dating, gender, and violence*

tender boy,' describing the changes of images of aggressive women from those of 'the lion roars' and the 'female Red Guard' to that of 'sassy girl' and the emergence of 'tender boy.' Tenderness has become one of the important qualities for young men in establishing intimacy and doing their masculinity.

In discussing virginity loss and sexual coercion, I have adopted a timeframe consisting of the periods before, during and after virginity loss, and have illustrated women's actions and sexuality at these different stages, to shed light on the social transformation of sexuality from the sexual repression of the Maoist Era to the pursuit of individual pleasure and desire in post-socialist China, mirroring the political transformation in the country. I point out that the current sexual revolution is unfinished, and consider that the basic principles of this sexual revolution should be gender equality and equal sexual auton-omy for men and women. Without these principles, the so-called sexual revolution would merely amount to multiple sexual behaviors and unequal sexual capital distribution between advantaged and disadvantaged groups.

Though the social transformation of gender and sexuality from the Maoist Era to the Post-socialist Era is depicted in this book, the process of social development is never linear, and its implications for gender roles and sexuality constructions are filled with all kinds of setbacks, contradictions, and uncer-tainties. The participants' personal lives are enmeshed in the intertwining factors of gender, class, sexuality, *hukou* status, age, migration, family back-ground, religion, and education – all within the matrix of discourses of state, market, and culture. Over the past seven decades, gender roles and sex rela-tions in China have undergone moments of deep crisis and realignment throughout the various stages of the socialist transformation of Chinese society and its subsequent turn to state-led capitalism. These moments of crisis and realignment have been unsettling and transformative: in some ways they have challenged patriarchy in China without uprooting it, and in other ways they have reinforced sexism and patriarchy and created a 'resurgence of gender inequality' (Fincher, 2014). Progress towards gender equality therefore has been an important aspect of political projects, socio-economic develop-ment, public discourse, and individuals' experiences of personal life. At the same time, though, young women's and men's personal lives continue to be molded by deep gendered inequalities in values, beliefs and practices. In their everyday lives, this contradiction frequently manifests itself in various forms of violence.

This generation is trapped between the modern and the traditional. The society changes so quickly that young dating couples do not have role models from prior generations for things that are important to them – how to express their feelings (violence being one way when other emotional vocabularies are lacking), how to be intimate, and what it means to be a man or a woman. Many of the new generation of women, especially urban daughters, are only-children, who have been treasured and invested in by their parents. They are doing well at school, they are ambitious and competitive, and they take 'gender equality' and 'being respected' for granted – although, at a certain point, especially when facing gender segregation in college admissions and job applications, their good academic credentials cannot bring them fair and equal treatment and opportunities, as they would for their male peers. They can be sassy girls for a while, but this leverage cannot last forever, since women's value is often judged according to age and marital status in China.

On the other hand, the new generation of young men is growing up with all kinds of expectations, and sometimes these expectations are too high, and therefore bring on a lot of frustration. At school they have been challenged by outstanding girls with excellent academic achievements. In the dating market, they have been intimidated by older, successful men whose eyes are always on young pretty women. They may be willing to be tender and may regard 'tenderness' and 'kindness' as important qualities for being modern men, but at the same time they have nostalgic aspirations for patriarchal power and to be homeowners. For young women, femininity means a feminine appearance, great ambition, virtuous performance, as well as an expected future of a balanced family and work. However, for young men, success with money and power becomes almost the only means of establishing masculinity, and tenderness is only a temporary alternative supplement to success. Thus when young men and women escape the chaotic reality and try to find comfort and support in 'real love,' they have different needs, desires, and expectations.

Sexual double standards are still pervasive in dating relationships, and sexual coercion and violence were less recognized than other forms of violence. Many participants reported that the experience of losing their virginity involved coercive elements, but were reluctant to label this as sexual coercion. The 'female virginity complex' was a perfect discourse for women to justify their role as gatekeeper and make excuses for their tolerance of sexual aggression. It is also a convenient discourse for men to justify their sexual privilege and coercive behavior. None of the young men or women had had any training in establishing a healthy and mutually respectful relationship, and they were not a generation good at tolerance and compromise. Their last romantic resort of love could be disappointed, with violence becoming their language because of their incompetence in emotional expression and communication. Some liberated women attempted sexual autonomy in their experiments with love, dating, and sexuality, and established the 'confluent love' and 'pure relationship' that Giddens (1992) has described; however, these concepts were not widely accepted, and so they were liable to face enormous challenges and 'slut-shaming.' Fulfilling the promise of gender equality thus has a long way to go: the so-called sexual revolution remains unfinished.

Construction of Chinese intersectionality

Dating violence is never only about a conflictive young couple, but always about the tension between youth and society as well. In an age of rising individualization in society, dating violence becomes a perfect site for

180 *The landscape of dating, gender, and violence*

analyzing the tensions between individual and society, and this calls for an intersectional approach that reflects social flexibility and individual fluidity. In the development of intersectionality theory, the gender analysis matrix has gradually included more and more factors – 'class' and 'race' were added thanks to black feminism, and 'state/nation' has been added by post-colonial feminism. However, the developed gender matrix still seems not to capture the complexity, instability and uncertainty within the current Chinese context. I argue that the self is always missing in existing intersectionality theory, and therefore the intersectional self becomes the core of my map of Chinese intersectionality. Present-day China is so unique in the scale of its social transformation that it needs this rather comprehensive framework of intersectionality on three different levels: the micro-politics of the intersectional self; the meso-politics of multiple oppression and interlocking institutional systems; and the macro-politics of state, market, and culture.

The concepts of the 'enterprising self' (Rose, 2007) and 'desiring self' (Rofel, 2007) focus on the strategy of achieving certain goals and constructing the inner self, and the 'divided self' (Kleinman, 2011) describes an emotionally fragmented state between past and present, public and private, moral and immoral, and so on. The intersectional self is a rather comprehensive concept, emphasizing how the individualized self resists, conforms to, and rises from the intersectional institutional socio-cultural structure, which emphasizes the personal emotional state, individual agency and strategy, and the institutional social structure. However, I have to admit that I put many institutional factors on the meso level. Under different situations, different factors may interconnect with gender and sexuality and have intersectional effects. Not all of the listed factors spontaneously function at the same time, and the factors of religion and ethnicity were not useful for this study since most participants were of Han nationality and did not mention religion.

The contrast of the aggressive girl in daily life and the submissive girl in sexual life presents an example of the 'intersectional self,' especially when young women deal with their experiences of first sex. The other example of the intersectional self includes age, which often makes a difference to women's sexuality, as most women have their own timeframe for the ideal first sex, and some women learn to grow out of the unhappy experience of virginity loss to embrace their own desire and autonomy and emphasize their own sexual choice in their more mature adulthood.

The symbolic race issue, too, is reflected in international dating, as more foreigners are choosing to live in Beijing and transnational dating and marriage among young professionals is becoming a fashionable symbol for living a 'Western' middle-class life. The migration issue always works together with the *hukou* system and education, as urban daughters under the one-child policy have been treasured and invested in by their parents and have acquired good education, thereby acquiring more space for willfulness and assertiveness and taking gender equality for granted, resisting unequal treatment within the intimate relationships and institutional sex discrimination;

The landscape of dating, gender, and violence   181

however, rural daughters may not be as lucky as urban daughters, and many of them migrate to the city after secondary school with limited education and fewer choices in selecting jobs and partners.

Education plays a huge long-term role in promoting individual upward mobility, and the story of the 'phoenix boy' perfectly demonstrates how higher education helps rurally born young people bypass the obstacles of *hukou* and settle as new Beijingers. As young people prefer to locate themselves within a global world, the global media, such as the Korean movie *My Sassy Girl* and the Taiwanese music video 'Xiao Wei,' make an impact on young people's lives. Young people interact with these images and make their own interpretations of and justifications for the violence they encounter in their daily lives. Most young people cannot afford to pay rising prices for apartments without their parents' help, thus parents once again obtain lost bargaining power in their adult children's mate selections, so that young people sometimes have to make hard choices between being filial and forming their own modern, intimate relationships.

The tensions between young men and women, and between relatively disadvantaged youths and modern society, echo the concept of 'incomplete modernity' raised by Wu Fei (2011). For young people living in a society of 'incomplete modernity,' the major challenge is how to deal with tradition and modernity at the same time. Most of the time they become trapped 'in between'; they try to be modern Chinese couples, but with no existing role models to follow, and sometimes end up in confusion, conflict, and violence. Wu Fei (2011) defines 'incomplete modernity' as follows:

> On the one hand, China has become quite modernized; on the other hand, Chinese modernization is accompanied by profound moral conflicts and emotional struggles, which make people in modern China unable to feel at home or content. The more modernized China is – in technological, institutional, and economic ways – the sharper such conflicts become. China needs to complete modernization at the level of relationships, subjectivity, and moral experience. As long as the process of modernization in this sense is unfinished for ordinary Chinese people, it is an 'incomplete modernity.'
>
> (p. 215)

The macro-politics of state, market, and culture demonstrates the characteristics of an 'incomplete modernity': the still-powerful state, the hyperactive market, and the revival and reconstruction of Confucian ideas. I disagree with the conclusion reached in many recent studies of Chinese gender and sexuality which focus too much on the retreat of the state and the growth of the market and argue that the market constitutes a much more powerful discourse than the state in China. On the contrary, I argue that it is still important to examine the interconnection between state and gender, and not over-emphasize the role of the market. The state discourse, including law,

182 *The landscape of dating, gender, and violence*

policy, and regulations, often seems invisible, but it is inescapable in young people's everyday lives. For example, I have illustrated how the household registration system and *hukou* quota for entering Beijing creates a dating hierarchy and produces the class of desirability in the dating market. Higher education allows the group of new Beijinger young men to bypass the rural–urban distinction and to achieve greater upward mobility and possibilities of reaching the social standard of success – to become 'phoenix boys.' However, the regulations for buying apartments in Beijing increase the difficulty for *waidiren* finally to become Beijingers. This contradiction between the freedom of migration and the rural–urban division created by the *hukou* system gives *waidiren* who are working laborers the least desirability and far fewer choices in the dating market. The gender analysis interacts with the *hukou* to produce a dating map for ordinary young people in Beijing, although the influence of the *hukou* system has been decreasing since the expansion of market reform and now allows much more fluid mobility and migration. Then too, the structural obstacles may not be faced by young people from privileged families who have extreme wealth and power, even if they are from outside Beijing. In the book, I have mentioned different state discourses of law, regulations, and policy here and there – for example, the *hukou* system, the one-child policy, the regulation of housing purchases, the 'sweeping the erotic and cracking the illegal' (*sao huang da fei*) campaign, etc. – but I have no intention of digging deeper into the particular content or policymaking process of each particular state discourse. Instead, I have mainly focused on how the individual negotiates with these state discourses and how sometimes these state discourses act as an 'invisible force' on young people's navigation of intimate life.

The hypercompetitive market sets new criteria for date selection, brings a new lifestyle ideal, creates diverse dating modes and sexual activities, and changes young people's perceptions and practices of gender, love, sex and marriage. The new phrases for the ideal date choices among men (*gao fu shuai* – tall rich and handsome) and women (*bai fu mei* – white, rich and beautiful) highlight wealth and appearance as two important desirable qualities in the dating market, emphasizing men's success and women's beauty. The market also establishes new styles for doing masculinity and femininity. Tenderness becomes an important quality for a modern man, especially for one without other capital. The market has a tendency to objectify women, so that young women learn to establish both a feminine appearance and a 'masculine' ambition. The fast-changing market stimulates the existence of all kinds of sexual activities, intensifies sexual double standards and unequal distribution of sexual capital among different groups, and in this process women claim that their sexual desire and autonomy often face unwelcome stigma and challenges. The speedy market sets up a simplistic universal definition of success – to have a car and an apartment, to obtain a good job as a young professional, and to get married – so that most young people are bound to a solitary idea of success and do not pursue diversified dreams. Faced with gradually intense competition for upward mobility, young people are desperate to become 'successful,' and so must face great stress and deal with disadvantages and unfairness.

The interaction of local–global feminism leads Chinese feminists to seek their own positions from which to understand violence against women. Many scholars, in their accounts of gender roles involved in 'violence against women,' often resort to 'Confucian ideas regarding men as dominant and superior, with emphasis on women as virtuous and inferior' (Hester, 2004, p. 1432), and explain how Chinese women are tolerant of abuse because of their internalization of such beliefs. Through such analysis, they hope to establish an indigenous way of understanding violence against women. However, I argue that using Confucian ideas in existing violence research represents a cultural dislocation, which is just too simple to capture the cultural complexity of individualism, cosmopolitanism, and consumerism in the current society. Wu Fei (2011) argues that:

> It is an incomplete modernity at the same time that it is also an incomplete tradition. Modernity had destroyed many traditional institutions and endangered traditional moralities in China. While people still identify with some ideas in traditional Confucianism, such ideas are not sufficient to provide a good life for them.
>
> (p. 235)

This book thus has documented how young people extol Confucian ideas as internal maps for behavior on the one hand, while on the other they are actively revising and reconstructing Confucian ideas. Rey Chow (1993) uses the term 'virtuous transaction' to describe how Chinese women learned to give up their own desire in exchange for their social place in the Maoist Era; however, the young women in this study have emphasized a 'feminine' appearance and a 'masculine' inside, and have turned virtuousness into a performance. I term their new strategy 'performing the traditional.'

Both young men and women are using this strategy for different purposes and with different understandings of 'tradition.' By performing the traditional, women justify their aggressive behavior, pursue their desires, and reject the sex that they do not want; men express their nostalgic desire to marry virgin brides who will be 'virtuous wives and good mothers.' When 'tradition' becomes a label, a mask, and a performance, the struggle between tradition and modernity actually turns into a war between the promotion of gender equality and the reestablishment of the patriarchal sexist ideology. Despite all of the challenges and changes that they are facing, young people are hanging on to their hope for, and belief in, love, and they are determined to reconfigure dating practices for themselves.

Methods: Researching a sensitive topic

This is an exploratory feminist qualitative study, with the purpose to explore how Beijing young men and women interpret the meaning of dating, love, gender and sexuality, and how they make sense of their violent dating experiences. The objective is to map out the interests, motivations, attitudes, feelings, and experiences that shape young people's intimate lives as they are situated in complex and sometimes competing sociocultural discourses. The study does not intend to find cause-effect relationships between variables and violence or to generalize the results for a larger population. In-depth interviews and focus groups were the two major methods for collecting data. The process of data collection can be divided into three phases over the last decade.

Pilot study

As soon as I selected dating violence as my research topic, I started to conduct some pilot interviews in 2003. I interviewed my seven friends (six females and one male), all born in the early to mid-1970s, each interview lasting 30 minutes to one hour. I also conducted a focus group among seven female postgraduate students, all single and aged from 24 to 27 years old at the time. Not all the participants had necessarily had experience of intimate partner violence – the major function of the pilot interviews was to make me familiar with the topic; to know what they did in, and what they thought about, dating relationships; and to help me raise research questions and develop a further research plan. The focus group was an explorative attempt to have a discussion with young people on their perceptions of love and marriage (including perceptions of the gender image of the Korean movie *My Sassy Girl*), on gender roles and gender equality in dating relationships, on what constitutes violence, and on how to cope with it, etc. Two sentences emerged from the discussion: 'The different perceptions of gender equality between men and women may be a cause for violence' (Li Ping, F, 25); and 'I like *My Sassy Girl* because sometimes I am violent too' (Chen Lin, F, 24). These helped me to shape my ideas on dating violence and to articulate research questions for this study. *My Sassy Girl* presents an aggressive female image, and this image was raised by the participants themselves and used as stimulus material in later focus groups.

Major data collection

43 in-depth interviews (29 female and 14 male) and three focus groups were conducted from May to July 2004, and these have contributed the major data for this book. The rhetoric of interviewing 'in depth' involves listening very carefully to informants' experience and stories, while 'semi-structured' means the interview has clear guidance. If the main purpose of the interviews was to explore the individuals' experiences and stories of dating violence, the purpose of focus groups was to provide a space for young people to express their attitudes, opinions, and thinking on violent dating relationships.

Identifying participants

Since dating violence is a rather sensitive topic, and there is no particular existing institution dealing with the problem in Beijing, I had to develop multiple resources to identify individual informants. I used the following four major methods:[1] 1) introductions by my friends (most being journalists, teachers, or researchers) and through my social networks (15); 2) introductions from the university counseling center and the Psychological Counseling Hotline (nine); 3) contacts made through online chat and discussion platforms, BBS in particular (seven); and 4) questionnaires sent out to students at the universities (six).

Using an online discussion platform was a rather new method to identify informants at that time. Tsinghua BBS[2] was the website that I used most. It has two popular hot columns, entitled *Love* and *Family Lives*, respectively. During my fieldwork period, I browsed these two columns every day. As soon as I noticed that someone had posted personal stories related to conflicts and violence in her/his dating life, I would send the person a private email[3] through the platform and invite him/her to accept an interview. This was quite a successful strategy for identifying informants on sensitive topics, and is a good practice for other sensitive research, especially in the present era of social media.

During the fieldwork, I often felt that the problem of dating violence was everywhere, and yet nowhere at the same time, somehow remaining hidden, and I was determined to find a method to invite it to emerge by itself. Using questionnaires to identify informants is a special strategy designed to invite relevant people in a category to come out and be included in a potential group. I designed a very simple questionnaire concerning dating violence, with 11 questions, and at the end of the questionnaire I put down a simple sentence: If you would like to take part in an in-depth interview, please leave your contact information, including telephone number. I sent out 114 questionnaires to students in two universities, and 24 college students responded

186　*Methods: Researching a sensitive topic*

by leaving their telephone numbers. After calling to follow up with the 24 students, six came to individual interviews – some of them had misunderstood that leaving their telephone number was to check the validity of the questionnaires, and some of them were intrigued by this topic but had not had violent dating experience. I think that there were several reasons for participants to come for the interviews: on the one hand, I had been introduced by their professors when I came to distribute the questionnaires and therefore it was rather easy for them to trust me; on the other hand, I was an absolute stranger to the students, and so they may have felt safer talking to me, especially when they encountered dating problems and had few chances to be listened to.

When I asked friends, hotlines, and counseling centers to refer respondents to me, I always explained my definition of dating violence to them and let them to decide whether their recommended choices were suitable for the study. Usually I told participants that my study was about young dating couples' conflicts, including violence, and avoided using the term 'dating violence' directly, in order not to scare off potential informants. I also noticed that it was relatively easy to develop friendly and trusting relationships with those participants who were introduced to me by friends, hotlines, counselors, and their teachers, while I needed to make extra efforts to establish trust relationships with participants whom I found through BBS, including giving them my business card, showing my ID, introducing myself and my project more thoroughly, and by devoting more time to an informal chat.

Purposive sampling

Purposive sampling enabled probing a diversity of dating experiences across social sectors of Beijing society, sociological variables: age, dating history, sexual experience, employment, education, *hukou* status, and only-child or not, were listed as sampling criteria. The 43 participants (14 male and 29 female) ranged in age from 16 to 33, with a mean of 24.5 and a median of 23.

Of the 43 participants, 41 were single, two were married women, and three had divorced once. There were two pairs of dating couples,[4] one of which had already broken up before the interviews; the other couple broke up later on. 28 of the 43 participants were known to have had sexual experience at the time of interview; 11 had not had sex, and the other four were unknown. 18 of the 43 had experienced cohabitation at the time of the study.

All had had dating experiences, and most were dating at the time of interview. There were heterogeneous dating modes among the participants: 15 participants had had only one dating relationship, 19 had had two to four different dating relationships, and seven had had five or more different dating relationships with different persons. 22 had had monogamous dating relationships at the time of interviews and 19 were either actively (11) or passively (eight) involved in multiple dating relationships, including triangular dating. There were many other dating practices: two participants had experience of one-sided relationship (*danlian*); four had established dating relationships through the Internet (*wanglian*); eight had maintained long-distance dating; four had broken up because of long-distance dating; seven had experienced one-night stands (*yiyeqing*), three of whom had been involved in extra-marital affairs as the third party; two women were dating men ten years older than themselves (*wangnianlian*); and three had had international dates with white and/or black men.

Among the 43 participants, 39 had experienced dating violence of some sort (such as physical assault, verbal aggression, psychological aggression, and sexual coercion), either having inflicted it or received it, whether minor or serious. The other four participants had not experienced dating violence, perhaps because they only had had a few dating experiences.

At the time of interviews, all participants resided in Beijing. Their education level was quite high, with 33 of them either pursuing or having completed at least a bachelor's degree. More than half of the informants were students: undergraduates (14), postgraduates (eight), and a high school student (one). The other 20 participants worked in various kinds of jobs, as journalists, teachers, researchers, in office work, individual industrialists, individuals in commerce (*getihu*), laborers (*dagongzai*), nurses, accountants, etc.

Most were born in the late 1970s or early 1980s, and thus are members of the first generation affected by the one-child policy. The study included 17 only-children and 26 children with siblings. Fifteen of the 17 only-children had had experiences of dating another only-children, while eight of the 26 children with siblings were dating, or had dated, only-children. The generation to which these well-educated young people belong will gradually become the foundation of society, inevitably bringing their own values, behavior modes and objectives into social life and influencing all the dimensions of society, including the social norms, social relations and social psychology. Like the 'baby boom' generation in the USA, the generation of only-children will definitely influence Chinese society and culture, and the intimate relationships constructed by them will inevitably influence the dating culture in China.

In-depth interviews

Interviews were conducted in Chinese and most of them lasted around two hours, although one interview lasted nearly eight hours.[5] The interviews were conducted in coffee shops, on campuses, at the interviewees' offices, and at their and my living places – generally, whenever and wherever informants felt it to be convenient and comfortable. Usually, the interview began with an explanation of procedures, assuring confidentiality, and the receipt of informed consent, in order to establish rapport.

Most informants were only interviewed once or twice at most, but I interviewed two informants, Zheng Xin (F, 23) and Huang Mei (F, 33), four times and three times, respectively. Both of them were involved in serious

188 *Methods: Researching a sensitive topic*

girlfriend-battering cases of the research and had struggled with whether they should break up their relationships or not. Both first interviews were conducted just a few days after serious violent incidents, and the second interviews were arranged a few weeks later. I also conducted follow-up interviews with them a few years later. The multiple interviews gave me a better idea about how people had changed under different conditions.

'Please tell me your dating story' was often used as an initial open-ended probe, which allowed informants to construct their narratives in their own terms and logic. Different informants had different personalities and thus their reactions were different. Some were very talkative, and this simple question could lead to two hours' talk, during which I just let them lead the interview. Some just talked a little bit and then waited for another question. Most informants' stories are complex and their dating practices are diverse. Their stories capture a wide diversity of salient features of the dating lives of Chinese urban youth.

Focus groups

The first focus group consisted of six undergraduate female students whom I had recruited through the questionnaires I sent out at one university. The second focus group consisted of five postgraduate male students. The discussion focused on their views of *My Sassy Girl*; their understanding of dating violence; their perception of love, dating, sex, and marriage; their criteria for mate (date) selection; the conflicts and power struggles among dating couples; and on virginity loss, virginity complex, and sexual coercion. Focus groups can be used to explore persons in context and the interaction among group members (Wilkinson, 1998). The interaction not only gave me a feeling of the process of collective meaning making, but also offered participants a chance to learn from each other. The third group consisted of more than 20 volunteer counselors for the Youth Hotline, so the function of this group was different from that of the other two, because the participants were a group of people who best knew about young people's dating and the problems associated with it. The function of this focus group was to help me gain some background information on young people's needs and problems, solicit the support of the participants in identifying potential informants, and to discuss the problems that I had encountered in the interviews.

Follow-up interviews and observations

After the major round of interviews in 2004, I kept in touch with one-third of the 43 informants, mostly by phone calls and emails over the next two to three years. Some of them shared their diaries, blogs, and love letters with me, while others wrote to me when they encountered 'love problems' in their intimate relationships. Whenever I received their emails, I always answered them right away.

Methods: Researching a sensitive topic 189

In April 2006, I had the opportunity to go back to the field for ten days and attempted to further interview 15 of the aforementioned 43 informants whose stories contributed significantly to this study; however, I only managed to find seven of them. The purpose of the follow-up was to update their dating stories, learn how the time transition had reframed their opinions on dating violence, and to present some findings and ask for their feedback. In addition to limited time and budget, there were several reasons for the difficulties in finding them. First, I could not get in touch with some of them since their contact information had changed. Second, some of them were not willing to be interviewed again, for whatever reason. Third, some informants had graduated from school, changed job, and left the city. The searching process per se once again emphasizes that Beijing is a city of mobility and fluidity. All seven of those I managed to contact claimed to have stopped their dating violence, and six of them had used the strategy of breaking up. Among the six break-ups, three participants had kept searching for dating partners; among the other three, one expressed her disappointment in love and said that she just wanted to be alone for a while, one stated that he was just sick of 'normal' dating and one-night stands were all he wanted, and the third had just left a relationship filled with conflict and was leading a happy life with another guy. It was engrossing to notice that the same person could have both sweet relationships and dating nightmares at different times and places, and with different partners.

I have studied, lived, and worked in Beijing for most of my adult life (1996–2002; 2007 until now), and sometimes I feel that everyday lives are my field of participatory observation. As an empathetic listener, I have always been the one with whom colleagues, friends, and students share their personal stories. Since 2007, I have conducted several related research projects on domestic violence, sex education, transnational dating and marriage, and women living with HIV/AIDS. Though the stories and data were not used in this book, these listening and research experiences have expanded my understanding of gender-based violence, intimate relationships, and gender and sexuality.

In 2010, I suddenly received an email from one informant, Zheng Xin, requesting a meeting with me. Zheng Xin was the only one in the follow-up round of interviews in 2006 who told me that she did not break up, but got married to her 'once abusive boyfriend' because they managed to halt the violence and improve the relationship, at least for a while. She told me that her partner became a Christian and they learned to improve their communication skills. I remember the sunny afternoon in 2010 when she came to my office and sat on my comfortable purple couch. She started with the sentence, 'I want to come here to have closure,' then she told me that she had just divorced her abusive husband. For her, and for many other participants, I have thus been an observer of, and a witness and listener to, their stories and experiences. It has been such an honor to have kept them company even for a little while during their lives, and what I aim to do is document their stories and narratives as truthfully as possible.

190　*Methods: Researching a sensitive topic*

Data analysis

All the interviews and focus groups were audio-taped and transcribed verbatim in Chinese. Data emerging from the two methods are complementary and were analyzed using the same method. I made use of an inductive process of coding and data analysis. I coded in Chinese and translated extracts into English. Through the coding process, I inductively generated the analytical themes and concepts. Composing the arguments, I documented the significance of these themes and concepts through the participants' narratives. My analysis here is not meant to offer empirical generalizations about the distribution of attitudes and practices (Gomm et al., 2000); I rather seek to offer in-depth insights into the complexities of everyday dating relationships among young people. I document in depth the various cultural dynamics and institutional conditions that shape their intimate lives. I have highlighted the importance of the participants' experiences by tying them to broader public issues and debates on state, market and culture, as well as relevant themes in the academic literature. In order to protect the participants' privacy, all names in this book are pseudonyms.

Reflexivity

In qualitative research, researchers become the instruments of their research, and to be reflexive means that the study is 'accomplished through detachment, internal dialogue, and constant (and intensive) scrutiny of "what I know" and "how I know it"' (Hertz, 1997, p. ix). According to Helen Callaway (1992), reflexivity becomes a continuing mode of self-analysis and political awareness, and the practice of reflexivity is to embrace 'a more radical consciousness of self in facing the political dimensions of fieldwork and constructing knowledge' and to be aware that 'factors intersecting with gender – such as nationality, race, ethnicity, class, and age – also affect the anthropologist's field interactions and textual strategies' (p. 33).

A feminist approach to fieldwork includes an awareness of the issues of 'power and control' in the research process and argues for self-reflexive practices (Reinharz, 1992). Generally, researchers are described as either equal to or more powerful than their participants (Harding and Norberg, 2005). Grenz (2005) has an interesting comment on the different power that researchers and participants have: the only actual power the participants have is to disguise, and the only actual power the researchers have is related to the way they interpret their stories. The gender issue was always entangled with power during the interviews, and it became more obvious when interviewing men than when interviewing women. For example, I found that it is extremely difficult to talk about sex with men, especially as Han Chinese culture is more limiting than some others concerning frank discussion, especially between men and women, of sex, as well as of intimacy generally (Jankowiak, 1993). Almost every single interviewee talked about sex only after I asked him or her directly. For most female interviewees, after I brought the issue out, they might have hesitated a little, but then talked about their sexual lives in a candid way. Some male participants directly rejected my questions using sentences including, 'Does it relate to the topic?' or 'I think that your question strays from the point,' while others just offered very simple answers like 'good,' 'not bad.' I remember that one man had been talkative during the whole interview but immediately blushed after I raised questions related to his sexual life. I have to admit that it was also challenging for me to ask them further when I felt their embarrassment or rejection. On the one hand I felt I needed to respect their own choices, but it was also true that I had not had much experience and training in probing men's sexuality and sometimes felt embarrassed and could not carry the topic on. I found that some participants wanted to talk to me because they hoped that I could help them stop the violence or help them improve their intimate relationships. In this sense, they wanted to talk to a counselor rather than a researcher. Facing this kind of requirement, I usually emphasized that this was an interview rather than counseling, and at the same time, I also told them I would be a good listener and hoped that the dialogue would give them some space to reflect on their relationships. Some participants did regard the interview as a therapeutic session, and hence were willing to open up emotionally. Some participants cried during the interviews – most of the time I just sat with them and waited quietly, sometimes with tears in my eyes. Sometimes I shared recent research findings on violence against women with them, and I also shared one informant's story anonymously with another if I found they were in similar situations while adopting different coping strategies. I always had some information at hand, such as telephone numbers of hotlines and legal services centers, and when I thought the participant's situation was quite serious I would give her/him those numbers. I think that I established trusting, friendly, and mutually respectful relationships with almost all the participants.

Through systematic documenting of the research process, I hope to offer to other scholars a sense of conducting research on sociologically sensitive topics in urban China. Using BBS and questionnaires seems an innovative method to identify informants. In the complex relationship between researcher and research subjects, in terms of different positions, identities, and standpoints, the researcher needs to be aware and to take into account the impacts of these factors on the research.

192   *Methods: Researching a sensitive topic*

Table A.1 List of participants

Name	Gender	Age	Data description
Ai Ling	F	24	A migrant worker originally from Anhui Province who used to be a domestic helper, and then was in sales. She dated and cohabitated with her *tongxiang* but did not want her family to know
Bai He	F	18	The youngest interviewee of the project, a high school student, who vividly narrated her love life in her high school
Chen Bing	M	29	A university teacher, originally from Heilongjiang Province, who had a girlfriend in another city and had a few lovers in Beijing
Chu Yu	F	22	A woman in work, originally from Anhui Province, who was involved with one of her high school classmates
Dan Fei	F	22	A college student who had one brief relationship with her classmate
Deng Li	F	33	Deng Li ran a small media company. She had several serious relationships, each time with lots of conflicts and tensions
Deng Wen	F	21	A college student, originally from Beijing. She had only a brief dating experience
Ding Ling	F	22	A college student, originally from Henan Province. She experienced sexual violence and abortion during a dating relationship. She did not like her boyfriend anymore, but still maintained a relationship with him for a while
Ding Yi	F	22	A college student who had many conflicts and tensions with her ex-boyfriend
He Rong	M	23	A college student, originally from Jiangsu Province. He had been in a relationship with a woman for four years, and he found that she had cheated on him with her colleague
He Yi	M	22	A college student who was born in Xinjiang as an only-child. He had dated two different women at college, and regretted that he had hacked his ex-girlfriend's computer
Honey	F	22	A postgraduate student who had had several romantic relationships
Huang Mei	F	33	A nurse who suffered from serious physical and sexual violence from her boyfriend
Li Qiang	M	18	A college student, originally from Xinjiang Province. He had a very brief crush on his high school classmate
Lin Zhao	M	23	A college student, originally from Zhejiang Province. He was involved in a triangular relationship at the time of interview

Name	Gender	Age	Data description
Ling Liang	M	26	A postgraduate student. He had a long-distance relationship and thought that he had experienced psychological violence from it
Liu Ming	M	21	A college student who had to break up with his girlfriend since his parents did not approve of their relationship
Long Qun	M	22	A security guard who had a few brief relationships
Lu Man	F	30	A married interviewee who talked a lot about the conflicts within marriage
Luo Xi	M	21	A college student who had a huge crush on one of his classmates
Mei Gui	F	27	A housewife who narrated at length her experience of psychological violence in her past dating relationships
Meng Xi	F	27	Meng Xi ran a small business in Beijing. She had had a very complicated dating experience, had experienced all kinds of violence in dating relationships, and was dating an African-American at the time of the interview
Nan Yue	F	22	A college student, originally from Jiangsu Province. She had had a few brief relationships
Ou Qiang	M	22	Ou Qiang had just graduated from college and had become a junior copywriter for an advertising agency. He had just broken up with his ex-girlfriend. Their relationship was filled with all kinds of conflicts
Qin Cui	F	31	Qin Cui was divorced and dated around to find the pure relationship she believed in
Qiu Ye	F	23	Qiu Ye was unemployed. She broke up with her boyfriend because she could not stand his sexist attitude and non-stop sexual advances
Sei	M	20	A college student who had a few brief romantic relationships
Shen Juan	F	21	A college student and a Beijinger. She dated a boy from another university, and experienced unwanted sex
Wang Fang	F	25	Originally a Beijinger, unemployed at the time of the interview. She was dating and cohabitating with a man ten years old than herself. They had lots of conflict, and once, after an incident of physical violence, she had attempted suicide by swallowing sleeping pills
Wang Mei	F	25	An accountant with a master's degree from a prestigious university in Beijing. She had to break up with her boyfriend since he could not stay in Beijing and find a good job with his rather limited qualifications

194 *Methods: Researching a sensitive topic*

Name	Gender	Age	Data description
Wen Jie	F	26	A postgraduate student, originally from Wuhan. She spoke a lot about how to fight for gender equality in a dating relationship
Wu Yun	F	31	A researcher, originally from Sichuan Province. She experienced severe physical violence during her relationship with her previous boyfriend. She was very active in seeking all kinds of help
Xia Bing	F	20	A college student who dated and cohabitated with a businessman ten years older than herself and had lots of conflicts and violence within the relationship
Xia Yu	F	29	An editor of a fashion magazine who had had quite complex dating experiences, including one-night stands and dating two people at the same time. At the time of the interview, she was romantically involved with a married man
Xiao Hong	M	26	A postgraduate student, originally from Hubei Province. He had a lot of dating and sexual experience, including Internet dating, long-distance dating, one-night stands, and was occasionally romantically involved with married women
Xiao Wei	M	22	A postgraduate student who had a long-distance relationship with a college student in Tianjin. Xiao Wei was jealous and controlling, and always suspected that his girlfriend might cheat on him. Once, when he saw his girlfriend having dinner with another boy, he lost control and beat her up
Xu Ling	F	25	An office worker who had had several romantic relationships. At the time of the interview, she was cohabiting with her boyfriend
Yi Mei	F	25	An office worker who had been romantically involved with her colleague
Yu Ling	F	21	A college student, originally from Beijing, and an only-child. She had twice had rather non-serious relationships in college
Yue Feng	M	24	A postgraduate student at a prestigious university who had experienced heart-breaking break-ups and had started not to take love or dating seriously
Zhang Fan	F	27	An office worker who had a crush on her colleague
Zheng Xin	F	23	A postgraduate student who suffered from severe physical abuse from her cohabitating boyfriend
Zhong Qing	F	21	A college student who had had many unwanted sexual experiences with her boyfriend

Notes

1 There were some other ways to identify informants: I met three interviewees by chance, two interviewees were introduced by other informants, and one interviewee approached me after reading an article about dating violence that I published in the *China Youth Daily* (a famous newspaper in China that mainly serves adolescents and young adults).

2 A bulletin board system, or BBS, is a computer server running custom software that allows users to connect to the system using a terminal program. Once logged in, the user can perform functions such as uploading and downloading software and data, reading news and bulletins, and exchanging messages with other users through email, public message boards, and sometimes via direct chat. The one I used was run by Tsinghua University students, but it was very popular not only among Tsinghua University students but among ordinary young Beijing people as well.

3 In Tsinghua BBS, when I clicked the Internet ID, the inner email box of the BBS would appear. Then I would write an email to briefly introduce the project and myself, leave my contact information, and invite the person to accept being interviewed.

4 The original research design was to interview pairs of dating couples, because I wanted to understand the interaction and dynamics of violent incidents, but my fieldwork told me that dating in contemporary Beijing is much more changeable, flexible, and chaotic than I had imagined. Some participants led long-distance relationships, so that it was impossible for me to interview their partners; some were willing to be interviewed, but their partners refused; some had multiple relationships and did not want me to interview any of their partners; and some simply had had too many experiences of breaking up, and no romance lasted for a long time, and so were reluctant to introduce their 'ex-partners' to me, etc. The interview experiences had already told me that dating per se was apparently much more unstable than marriage, and thus interviewing individual women and men was a practical choice.

5 I interviewed Meng Xi (F, 27) in a branch of Starbucks in the district of Chaoyang in Beijing. I met her at 7:00 pm and we talked until midnight (when Starbucks closed). She had thought that her boyfriend would come to pick her up after the interview, but he did not show up. She did not know where to go because her home was far away, so I invited her to come to stay overnight at my place. We ate snacks, ice cream and continued the interview until 4:00 am the next day. I wrote up her story into a journal article (Wang and Ho, 2007b).

Glossary

Ah, Shanghainese Men 啊,上海男人
ai cuo qiong 矮挫穷
aiqing 爱情
bai fu mei 白富美
baihe 百合
baimaonü 白毛女
banbiantian 半边天
bang dakuan 傍大款
Baoshi 褒姒
baoyang 包养
bei qiangpo 被强迫
bentu 本土
bentuhua 本土化
bu tichang, bu fandui 不提倡,不反对
butinghua 不听话
caizi jiaren 才子佳人
changgong 长工
Chang Hen Ge 长恨歌
chaoji nüsheng 超级女声
chezi 车子
China Youth Daily 中国青年报
chi qingchun fan 吃青春饭
chunü qingjie 处女情结
cuowei 错位
dagong 打工
dagongmei 打工妹
dagongzai 打工仔
Daji 妲己
dalaopo/aida 打老婆/挨打
dang de nüer 党的女儿
danlian 单恋
danwei 单位
dashu kong 大叔控

dashu luoli kong　大叔洛丽控

diaosi　屌丝

Dong Shanshan　董姗姗

dongya bingfu　东亚病夫

ernai　二奶

e si shi xiao, shi jie shi da　饿死事小,失节事大

fan　烦

fangnu　房奴

fangzi　房子

fei cheng wu rao　非诚勿扰

Fenghuangnan　凤凰男

fulian　妇联

fumu jie huohai　父母皆祸害

funüxue　妇女学

funüyanjiu　妇女研究

gan de hao　干得好

gao fu shuai　高富帅

getihu　个体户

gui　跪

hanxu　含蓄

haola　好了

he　和

hedong shihou　河东狮吼

hexie shehui　和谐社会

hongweibin　红卫兵

Hua Mulan　花木兰

huanghunlian　黄昏恋

Huang Jing　黄静

Hu Jintao　胡锦涛

hukou　户口

hunyin jieshaosuo　婚姻介绍所

jia de hao　嫁得好

jian hong　见红

jianren　坚韧

jiating baoli　家庭暴力

jiawu shi　家务事

jiebanren　接班人

jiegui　接轨

jingjishiyongfang　经济适用房

jingshen wuran　精神污染

jinjing zhibiao　进京指标

Kang-Liang reform　康梁变法

keju kaoshi　科举考试

kenlao　啃老

kezhi　克制

198　*Glossary*

kongjie　空姐
Kongquenü　孔雀女
Lei Feng　雷锋
li　礼
lian'ai　恋爱
liangdi fenju　两地分居
Liangdi Shu　两地书
liujingzhibiao　留京指标
Lu Xun　鲁迅
luolita kong　洛丽塔控
Lung Yingtai　龙应台
Ma Yun　马云
mazi　马子
meinü jingji　美女经济
meinü zuojia　美女作家
mendanghudui　门当户对
Meng li hua luo zhi duoshao　梦里花落知多少
My Sassy Girl　我的野蛮女友
nan'gengnüzhi　男耕女织
nan zhuwai, nü zhunei　男主外,女主内
ningzhong　凝重
Niulang　牛郎
nuan nan　暖男
nü hongweibin　女红卫兵
nuohun　裸婚
nü qiangren　女强人
nüxing qizhi　女性气质
Pan Shiyi　潘石屹
piaozi　票子
qiangjian huanxiang　强奸幻想
qiangpo　强迫
qianli gu　潜力股
Qin Guan　秦观
Qinghua University　清华大学
Qingnian Nuquan Xingdong Pai　青年女权行动派
queqiao　鹊桥
Queqiao Xian　鹊桥仙
rang nüren huijia qu　让女人回家去
re'ai　热爱
Renmin University of China　中国人民大学
renxing　任性
sao huang da fei　扫黄打非
shangshan xiaxiang　上山下乡
Shannxi　陕西
Shen Yueyue　沈跃跃

sheng nü 剩女

Shiji Jiayuan 世纪佳缘

shiruo 示弱

shuangxue shuangbi 双学双比

siheyuan 四合院

suzhi 素质

tiantang huayuan 天堂花园

tian zhi jiaozhi 天之骄子

tiaojian bijiao 条件比较

tie guniang 铁姑娘

tinghua 听话

tongqi 同妻

tongxiang 同乡

waidiren 外地人

wailai 外来

Wang Anyi 王安忆

Wang Jinxi 王进喜

wanglian 网恋

wangnianlian 忘年恋

Wang Shi 王实

Weihui 卫慧

Wen Hui Bao 文汇报

wen liang gong jian rang 温良恭俭让

wen-wu 文武

White-Haired Girl, The 白毛女

Wuhan 武汉

wuhao jiating 五好家庭

xiaganggongren 下岗工人

Xi'an 西安

xianneizhu 贤内助

xianqi liangmu 贤妻良母

xiaosan 小三

Xier 喜儿

Xi Jinping 习近平

xinghun (xingshi hunyin) 形婚 (形式婚姻)

xin hao nanren 新好男人

xue jishu 学技术

xue wenhua 学文化

Xu Guangping 许广平

yang 养

yangbanxi 样板戏

yijianzhongqing, congyi'erzhong 一见钟情,从一而终

yinshengyangshuai 阴盛阳衰

yiqing shu 遗情书

yiyeqing 一夜情

200 *Glossary*

yizhu 蚁族
youqian jiushi renxing 有钱就是任性
yuehui 约会
yuehui qiangjian 约会强奸
yuepao 约炮
zaiyiqi 在一起
zaolian 早恋
zhaoyaozhongshang 造谣中伤
Zhang Chaoyang 张朝阳
Zhang Jingsheng 张竞生
Zhinü 织女
zhonghua minzu 中华民族
zhuzhong jiating, zhuzhong jiajiao, zhuzhong jiafeng 注重家庭 注重家教 注重家风
zi bu jiao, fu zhi guo 子不教,父之过
zichanjiejie ziyouhua 资产阶级自由化
ziyou lian'ai 自由恋爱
zou xiang shijie 走向世界

Bibliography

30-Groups. 2011. *A Study on the Predicament of Young Professionals in Hong Kong and Beijing*. Hong Kong: Bauhinia Foundation Research Centre.

Aapola, S., Gonick, M. & Harris, A. 2005. *Young Femininity: Girlhood, Power and Social Change*. New York: Palgrave Macmillan.

ACWF & NBS. 2011. *Report on Major Results of the Third Wave Survey on the Social Status of Women in China*. Beijing: All-China Women's Federation & National Bureau of Statistics of China.

Ai, X. 2004a. Stop phallogocentrism: Review on the case of Huang Jing (Duan jue yang ju chong bai zhi gen: zai lun huang jing yi an). *Feminism in China (Zhong guo nv xing zhu yi)*: 15–25.

Ai, X. 2004b. Striving legal justice for Huang Jing: Our arguments and actions (Wei Huang Jing zheng qu fa lv gong zheng: wo men de guan dian he xing dong). *Feminism in China (Zhong guo nv xing zhu yi)*: 2–14.

Ai, X. 2004c. When did the rape stop? Why? (Qiang jian he shi zhong zhi, wei shen mo zhong zhi?). *Feminism in China (Zhong guo nv xing zhu yi)*: 26–30.

Alarcon, N., Kaplan, C. & Moallem, M. 1999. Introduction: Between woman and nation. In: Kaplan, C., Alarcon, N. & Moallem, M. (eds) *Between Woman and Nation: Nationalisms, Transnational Feminisms, and the State*. Durham, NC and London: Duke University Press.

Alcoff, L. & Gray, L. 1993. Survivor discourse: Transgression or recuperation? *Signs: Journal of Women in Culture and Society*, 18: 260–290.

Andersen, M.L. 2005. Thinking about women: A quarter century's view. *Gender & Society*, 19: 437–455.

Andersen, M.L. & Collins, P.H. 1994. *Race, Class and Gender: An Anthology*. New York: Routledge.

Angeloff, T. & Lieber, M. 2012. Equality, did you say? Chinese feminism after 30 years of reforms. *China Perspectives*, 4: 17–24.

Anthias, F. 2013. Hierarchies of social location, class and intersectionality: Towards a translocational frame. *International Sociology*, 28: 121–138.

Armsworth, M.W. & Stronck, K. 1999. Intergenerational effects of incest on parenting: Skills, abilities, and attitudes. *Journal of Counseling and Development*, 77: 303–314.

Barlow, T.E. 2004. *The Question of Women in Chinese Feminism*. Durham, NC and London: Duke University Press.

202   Bibliography

Bass, E. & Davis, L. 1994. *The Courage to Heal: A Guide for Women Survivors of Child Sexual Abuse: Featuring 'Honoring the Truth, a Response to the Backlash.'* New York: Harper Perennial.

Baumeister, R.F. 2004. Gender and erotic plasticity: Socio-cultural influence on the sex drive. *Sexual and Relationship Therapy*, 19: 133–139.

Beck, U. & Beck-Gernsheim, E. 2014. *Distant Love: Personal Life in the Global Age.* Cambridge: Polity Press.

Beijing Population Development Research Center. 2013. *Report on Beijing Population (Beijing Renkou Fazhan Baogao)*. Beijing: Social Science Literature Publishing House (sheke wenxian chubanshe).

Berger, M.T. & Guidroz, K. 2009. Introduction. In: Berger, M.T. & Guidroz, K. (eds) *The Intersectional Approach: Transforming the Academy through Race, Class, & Gender.* Chapel Hill: The University of North Carolina Press.

Bian, Y. 2002. Chinese social stratification and social mobility. *Annual Reviews of Sociology*, 28: 91–116.

Black, D.A., Heyman, R.E. & Slep, A.M.S. 2001. Risk factors for male-to-female partner sexual abuse. *Aggression and Violent Behavior*, 6: 269–280.

Borochowitz, D.Y. & Eriskovits, Z. 2002. To love violently: Strategies for reconciling love and violence. *Violence against Women*, 8: 476–494.

Brooks-Gunn, J. & Paikoff, R.L. 1993. 'Sex is a gamble, kissing is a game': Adolescent sexuality and health promotion. In: Millstein, S.G., Peterson, A.C. & Nightingale, E.O. (eds) *Promoting the Health of Adolescents*. New York: Oxford University Press.

Brown, C.T. 1993. Woman as trope: Gender and power in Lu Xun's 'soap.' In: Tani, E.B. (ed.) *Gender Politics in Modern China*. Durham, NC and London: Duke University Press.

Brownell, S. & Wasserstrom, J.N. 2002. Introduction: Theorizing femininities and masculinities. In: Brownell, S. & Wasserstrom, J.N. (eds) *Chinese Femininities/Chinese Masculinities*. Berkeley and Los Angeles: University of California Press.

Buitelaar, M.W. 2002. Negotiating the rules of chaste behaviour: Re-interpretations of the symbolic complex of virginity by young women of Moroccan descent in the Netherlands. *Ethnic and Racial Studies*, 25: 462–489.

Buss, D.M. & Shackelford, T.K. 1997. From vigilance to violence: Mate retention tactics in married couples. *Journal of Personality and Social Psychology*, 72: 346–361.

Callaway, H. 1992. Ethnography and experience: Gender implications in fieldworks and texts. In: Okely, J. & Callaway, H. (eds) *Anthropology and Autobiography* (Vol. 29–49). New York: Routledge.

Cao, Y. & Hu, C. 2007. Gender and job mobility in postsocialist China: A longitudinal study of job changes in six coastal cities. *Social Force*, 85: 1535–1560.

Capaldi, D.M. & Crosby, L. 1997. Observed and reported psychological and physical aggression in young, at-risk couples. *Social Development*, 6: 184–206.

Carpenter, L.M. 2001. The ambiguity of 'having sex': The subjective experience of virginity loss in the United States. *The Journal for Sex Research*, 38: 127–139.

Carpenter, L.M. 2002. Gender and the meaning and experience of virginity loss in the contemporary United States. *Gender & Society*, 16: 345–365.

Chan, K.L. 2012. The role of Chinese face in the perpetration of dating partner violence. *Journal of Interpersonal Violence*, 27: 793–811.

Chang, L. 1999. Gender role egalitarian attitudes in Beijing, Hong Kong, Florida, and Michigan. *Journal of Cross-cultural Psychology*, 30(6): 722–741.

Bibliography 203

Chang, Y.L. 2009. Iron girl, better half and fashion girl: Women's images in women's magazines in China. *China Media Report*, 1.

Chavez, V. 2002. Language, gender and violence in qualitative research. *Quarterly of Community Health Education*, 21(1): 3–18.

Chen, A.S. 1999. Lives at the center of the periphery, lives at the periphery of the center: Chinese American masculinities and bargaining with hegemony. *Gender & Society*, 13: 584–607.

Chen, Y. 2014. Uncle Gao Xiaosong and Lolita Xi Youmi. *Women Voice China*, July 4.

Chen, Y. & Yao, Y. 2012. China's economic growth slowdown: Reasons, challenges, and policy suggestions. *Journal of Renmin University in China*, 5: 76–87.

Chi, X., Yu, L. & Winter, S. 2012. Prevalence and correlates of sexual behaviors among university students: A study in Heifei, China. *BMC Public Health*, 12: 972.

Chow, E.N., Zhang, N. & Wang, J. 2004. Promising and contested fields: Women's studies and sociology of women/gender in contemporary China. *Gender & Society*, 18: 161–188.

Chow, E.N. & Zhao, S.M. 1996. The one-child policy and parent-child relationships: A comparison of one-child with multiple-child families in China. *International Journal of Sociology and Social Policy*, 16: 35–62.

Chow, R. 1993. Virtuous transaction: A reading of Three Stories by Lin Shuhua. In: Tani, E.B. (ed.) *Gender Politics in Modern China* (pp. 90–105). Durham, NC and London: Duke University Press.

Chu, G.C. & Ju, Y. 1993. *The Great Wall in Ruins: Communication and Cultural Change in China*. Albany: State University of New York Press.

Chun, L. 1996. Citizenship in China: The gender politics of social transformation. *Social Politics*, Summer/Fall/Fall: 278–291.

Clark, C.D. 2001. Foreign marriage, 'tradition,' and the politics of border crossing. In: Chen, N.N., Clark, C.D., Gottschang, S.Z. & Jeffery, L. (eds) *China Urban: Ethnographies of Contemporary Culture*. Durham, NC and London: Duke University Press.

Collins, P.H. 1990. *Black Feminist Thought: Knowledge, Consciousness, and the Politics of Empowerment*. New York: Routledge.

Collins, P.H. 1998. *Fighting Words: Black Women and the Search for Justice*. Minneapolis: University of Minnesota Press.

Common Language. 2010. *Report on the Situation of Domestic Violence among Lesbians and Female Bisexuals*. Beijing: Common Language.

Connell, R.W. 1993. The big picture: Masculinities in recent world history. *Theory and Society*, 22: 597–623.

Connell, R.W. & Messerschmidt, J.W. 2005. Hegemonic masculinity: Rethinking the concept. *Gender & Society*, 19: 829–859.

Crawford, C.C. 1997. *Is Dating Violence Really Mutual? An Examination of the Occurrence and Severity of Dating Violence and Injuries Sustained from a Resource Theory Perspective*. PhD diss., Rutgers University, New Jersey.

Crenshaw, K. 1993. Mapping the margins: Intersectionality, identity politics, and violence against women of color. *Stanford Law Review*, 43: 1241–1299.

Cui, Z.E. 2010. China's state censorship on films. *East Asian Culture Critique*, 18: 417–423.

Dasgupta, S.D. 2002. A framework for understanding women's use of nonlethal violence in intimate heterosexual relationship. *Violence Against Women*, 8: 1364–1389.

Davis, D.S. & Sensenbrenner, J.S. 2000. Commercializing childhood: Parental purchases for Shanghai's only child. In: Davis, D.S. (ed.) *The Consumer Revolution in Urban China*. Berkeley: University of California Press.

204   Bibliography

Davis, K. 2011. Intersectionality as buzzword: A sociology of science perspective on what makes a feminist theory successful. In: Lutz, H., Teresa, M., Vivar, H. & Supik, L. (eds) *Framing Intersectionality: Debate on a Multi-faceted Concept in Gender Studies*. London: MPG Books Group.

Davis, K. & Evans, M. (eds) 2011. *Transatlantic Conversations: Feminism as Travelling Theory*. Aldershot: Ashgate Publishing Company.

DeKeseredy, W.S. 1989. Woman abuse in dating relationships: The role of peer support. *Dissertation Abstracts International*, 49: 3878.

DeKeseredy, W.S. & Kelly, K. 1995. Sexual abuse in Canadian university and college dating relationships: The contribution of male peer support. *Journal of Family Violence*, 10: 41–53.

DeKeseredy, W.S. & Saunders, D.G. 1997. The meaning and motives for women's use of violence in Canadian college dating relationships. *Sociological Spectrum*, 17: 199–223.

Denov, M.S. 2004. The longer-term effects of child sexual abuse by female perpetrators: A qualitative study of male and female victims. *Journal of Interpersonal Violence*, 19: 1137–1156.

Deutsch, F.M. 2006. Filial piety, patrilineality, and China's one-child policy. *Journal of Family Issues*, 27(3): 366–388.

Deutsch, S. 2000. *Women and the City: Gender, Space, and Power in Boston, 1870–1940*. New York: Oxford University Press.

Dikötter, F. 1992. *The Discourse of Race in Modern China*. London: Hurst & Company.

Dikötter, F. 1995. *Sex, Culture and Modernity in China: Medical Science and the Construction of Sexual Identities in the Early Republican Period*. Honolulu: University of Hawaii Press.

Dirlik, A. & Zhang, X. 2000. Introduction: Postmodernism and China. In: Dirlik, A. & Zhang, X. (eds) *Postmodernism and China* (journal into book). Durham, NC and London: Duke University Press.

Dobash, R.P. & Dobash, R.E. 2004. Women's violence to men in intimate relationships. *British Journal of Criminology*, 44: 324–349.

Du, S. 2002. *Chopsticks Only Work in Pairs: Gender Unity and Gender Equality among the Lahu of Southwest China*. New York: Columbia University Press.

Dunn, J.L. 2005. 'Victims' and 'survivors': Emerging vocabularies of motive for 'battered women who stay.' *Sociological Inquiry*, 75: 1–30.

ECOSOC. 2006. *Addressing Gender-based Violence in Humanitarian Emergencies: Gender-based Violence and the Role of the UN and its Member States*. Segment, H.A. (ed.). New York. www.un.org/docs/ecosoc/meetings/2006/docs/PresentationMr.Michel.pdf.

Edwards, L. 2000. Policing the modern woman in republican China. *Modern China*, 26: 115–147.

Engels, F. 1972. *The Origin of the Family, Private Property, and the State: In the Light of the Researches of Lewis H. Morgan*. New York: International Publishers.

Erel, U., Haritaworn, J., Rodriguez, E.G. & Klesse, C. 2010. On the depoliticisation of intersectionality talk: Conceptualising multiple oppression in critical sexuality studies. In: Taylor, Y., Hines, S. & Casey, M.E. (eds) *Theorizing Intersectionality and Sexuality (Genders and Sexualities in the Social Sciences)*. New York: Palgrave.

Eriksson, M. 2013. Tackling violence in intimacy: Interacting power relations and policy changes. *Current Sociology*, 61: 171–189.

Evans, H. 1995. Defining difference: The 'scientific' construction of sexuality and gender in the People's Republic of China. *Signs*, 20: 357–394.

Bibliography 205

Evans, H. 2008. Sexed bodies, sexualized identities, and limits of gender. *China Information*, 22: 361.

Evans, H. 2010. The gender of communication: Changing expectations of mothers and daughters in urban China. *The China Quarterly*, 204: 980–1000.

Farquhar, J. 2002. *Appetites: Food and Sex in Post-Socialist China*. Durham, NC: Duke University Press.

Farrer, J.C. 1997. 'Opening up': Sex and the market in Shanghai. In: *Sex and the Market in Shanghai*, vii.

Farrer, J.C. 2002. *Opening Up: Youth Sex Culture and Market Reform in Shanghai*. Chicago, IL and London: University of Chicago Press.

Farrer, J. 2006. Sexual citizenship and the politics of sexual story-telling among Chinese youth. In: Jeffreys, E. (ed.) *Sex and Sexuality in China*. London: Routledge.

Fei, X. 1984. *Reproduction Institution (Shengyu zhidu)*. Tianjin: Tianjin People's Press (Tianjin renmin chubanshe).

Ferguson, A. 1997. Two women's studies conferences in China: Reported by an American feminist philosopher. *Asian Journal of Women's Studies*, 3: 161.

Ferree, M.M. 2011. The discursive politics of feminist intersectionality. In: Lutz, H., Vivar, M.T.H. & Supik, L. (eds) *Framing Intersectionality: Debates on a Multi-Faceted Concept in Gender Studies*. Farnham: Ashgate Publishing Limited.

Ferry, M.M. 2003a. Advertising, consumerism and nostalgia for the new woman in contemporary China. *Continuum: Journal of Media & Cultural Studies*, 17: 277–290.

Ferry, M.M. 2003b. Marketing Chinese women writers in the 1990s, or the politics of self-fashions. *Journal of Contemporary China*, 12: 655–675.

Fincher, L.H. 2014. *Leftover Women: The Resurgence of Gender Inequality in China*. London and New York: Zed Books.

Follingstad, D.R., Rutledge, L.L., Polek, D.S. & McNeill Hawkins, K. 1988. Factors associated with patterns of dating violence toward college women. *Journal of Family Violence*, 3: 169–182.

Fong, V.L. 2002. China's one-child policy and the empowerment of urban daughters. *American Anthropologist*, 104: 1098–1109.

Foucault, M. 1976. *The History of Sexuality*. London: Penguin Books Ltd.

Foucault, M. 1977. *Discipline and Punish: The Birth of the Prison*. London: Penguin Books Ltd.

Foucault, M. (ed.) 1997. *Michel Foucault: Ethics – Subjectivity and Truth (Essential Works of Foucault, 1954–1984)*. New York: The New Press.

Fraser, H. 2003. Narrating love and abuse in intimate relationships. *British Journal of Social Work*, 33: 273–290.

Fraser, H. 2005. Women, love, and intimacy 'gone wrong': Fire, wind, and ice. *Affilia*, 20: 10–20.

Freud, S. 1977. *Sigmund Freud on Sexuality*. London: Penguin.

Friedman, S.L. 2006. *Intimate Politics: Marriage, the Market, and State Power in Southeastern China*. Cambridge, MA: Harvard University Press.

Gao, X. & Ma, Y. 2006. 'The silver flower contest': Rural women in 1950s China and the gendered division of labour. *Gender & History*, 18: 594–612.

Gao, Y. and Zhang, X. 2011. Characteristics and analysis of the marriage situation in Beijing, 2004–2009 (Beijing jinnian hunpei zhuangkuang de tezheng ji fenxi, 2004–2009). *Chinese Journal of Population Science* (Zhongguo renkou kexue), 6: 60–71.

Gavey, N. 2005. *Just Sex? The Scaffolding of Rape*. New York: Routledge.

206　*Bibliography*

Giddens, A. 1992. *The Transformation of Intimacy: Sexuality, Love, and Eroticism in Modern Societies.* Stanford, CA: Stanford University Press.

Gil, V.E. & Anderson, A.F. 1999. Case study of rape in contemporary China: A cultural-historical analysis of gender and power differentials. *Journal of Interpersonal Violence,* 14: 1151–1171.

Gilbert, P.R. 2002. Discourses of female violence and societal gender stereotypes. *Violence against Women,* 8: 1271–1300.

Gilfus, M.E. 1999. The price of the ticket: A survivor-centered appraisal of trauma theory. *Violence Against Women,* 5: 1238–1257.

Gomm, R., Hammersley, M. & Foster, P. 2000. Case study and generalization. In Gomm, R., Hammersley, M. & Foster, P. (eds) *Case Study Method: Key Issues, Key Texts* (pp. 98–116). London: Sage.

Gramsci, A. 1998. Hegemony, intellectuals and the state. In: Storey, J. & Hempstead, H. (eds) *Cultural Theory and Popular Culture: A Reader.* Upper Saddle River, NJ: Prentice Hall.

Gray, H.M. & Foshee, V. 1997. Adolescent dating violence: Differences between one-sided and mutually violent profiles. *Journal of Interpersonal Violence,* 12: 126–141.

Greenhalgh, S. 2001. Fresh winds in Beijing: Chinese feminists speak out on the one-child policy and women's lives. *Signs,* 26: 847–886.

Greenhalgh, S. 2008. *Just One Child: Science and Policy in Deng's China.* Berkeley and Los Angeles: University of California Press.

Greenhalgh, S. 2010. *Cultivating Global Citizens: Population in the Rise of China.* Cambridge, MA: Harvard University Press.

Grenz, S. 2005. Intersections of sex and power in research on prostitution: A female researcher interviewing male heterosexual clients. *Signs,* 30: 2091–2114.

Grewal, I. & Kaplan, C. 1994. *Scattered Hegemonies: Postmodernity and Transnational Feminist Practices.* Minneapolis: University of Minnesota Press.

Grewal, I. & Kaplan, C. 2000. Postcolonial studies and transnational feminist practices. *Jouvert,* 5 (Autumn). english.chass.ncsu.edu/jouvert/v5i1/grewal.htm.

Groups, S. 2011. *Rising Sun or Stressed Pillar: Attitudes and Aspirations of Young Professionals in Hong Kong and Beijing.* Hong Kong: Bauhinia Foundation Research Centre (BFRC).

Guo, J. 2003. *Domestic Violence and Legal Assistance.* Beijing: CIP.

Hanser, A. 2005. The gendered rice bowl: The sexual politics of service work in urban China. *Gender & Society,* 19: 581–600.

Hanser, A. 2008. *Service Encounters: Class, Gender, and the Market for Social Distinction in Urban China.* Stanford, CA: Stanford University Press.

Harding, S. & Norberg, K. 2005. New feminist approaches to social science methodologies: An introduction. *Signs,* 30: 1–7.

He, Y. & Zuo, Z. 2004. One ACWF Survey Shows: 30% of Chinese Family Exist Domestic Violence (in Chinese) [online]. *Beijing China Youth Daily.* zqb.cyol.com/content/2004–03/24/content_842543.htm [accessed June 23 2014].

Hengehold, L. 2000. Remapping the event: Institutional discourses and the trauma of rape. *Signs: Journal of Women in Culture and Society,* 26: 189–214.

Hershatter, G. 2007. *Women in China's long Twentieth Century.* Berkeley: University of California Press.

Hershatter, G. 2012. Disquiet in the house of gender. *The Journal of Asian Studies,* 71: 873–894.

Bibliography 207

Hertz, R. 1997. Introduction: Reflexivity and voice. In: Hertz, R. (ed.) *Reflexivity & Voice*. Thousand Oaks, CA: Sage.

Hester, M. 2000. Domestic violence in China. In: Radford, J., Friedberg, M. & Harne, L. (eds) *Women, Violence, and Strategies for Action: Feminist Research, Policy, and Practice*. Buckingham, PA: Open University Press.

Hester, M. 2004. Future trends and development: Violence against women in Europe and East Asia. *Violence Against Women*, 10: 1431–1448.

Heywood, L. & Drake, J. 1997. Introduction. In: Heywood, L. & Drake, J. (eds) *Third Wave Agenda: Being Feminist, Doing Feminist*. Minneapolis and London: University of Minnesota Press.

Hildebrandt, T. 2012. Development and division: The effect of transnational linkages and local politics on LGBT activism in China. *Journal of Contemporary China*, 21: 845–862.

Hird, M.J. & Jackson, S. 2001. Where 'angels' and 'wusses' fear to tread: Sexual coercion in adolescent dating relationships. *Journal of Sociology*, 37: 27–43.

Ho, L.W.W. 2007. The gay space in Chinese cyberspace: Self-censorship, commercialisation and misrepresentation. *Journal of Current Chinese Affairs-China Aktuell*, 36: 45–73.

Hobsbawm, E.J. 1990. *Nation and Nationalism since 1780: Programme, Myth, Reality*. Cambridge: Cambridge University Press.

Holland, J., Ramazanoglu, C., Sharpe, S. & Thomson, R. 2000. Deconstructing virginity – Young people's account of first sex. *Sexual and Relationship Therapy*, 15: 221–231.

Holland, J., Ramazanoglu, C. & Thomson, R. 1996. In the same boat? The gendered (in)experience of first heterosex. In: Richardson, D. (ed.) *Theorising Heterosexuality: Telling it Straight*. Buckingham; Philadelphia, PA: Open University Press.

Holtzman, D. & Kulish, N. 1997. *Nevermore: The Hymen and the Loss of Virginity*. Northvale, NJ: Jason Aronson.

Honig, E. 2002. Maoist mappings of gender: Reassessing the red guards. In: Brownell, S. & Jeffrey, N.W. (eds) *Chinese Femininities/Chinese Masculinities: A Reader*. Berkeley and Los Angeles: University of California Press.

Honig, E. 2003. Socialist sex: The Cultural Revolution revisited. *Modern China*, 29(2): 143–175.

Honig, E. & Hershatter, G. 1988. *Personal Voices: Chinese Women in the 1980's*. Stanford, CA: Stanford University Press.

Hooff, J.V. 2013. *Modern Couples? Continuity and Change in Heterosexual Relationships*. Aldershot: Ashgate Publishing Limited.

Hu, A., Hu, C., Chen, B. & Shen, K. 2014. *The World of Post-1980s Generation*. Shanghai: Fudan Institute of Social Research.

Hu, Y. & Scott, J. 2014. Family and gender values in China: Generational, geographic, and gender differences. *Journal of Family Issues*: 1–27.

Huang, R. 2010. A quantitative study about foreigners in Beijing. *Beijing Social Science*, 2: 53–58.

Hyde, S.T. 2001. Sex tourism practices on the periphery: Eroticizing ethnicity and pathologizing sex on the Lancang. In: Chen, N.N., Clark, C.D., Gottschang, S.Z. & Jeffery, L. (eds) *China Urban: Ethnographies of Contemporary Culture*. Durham, NC and London: Duke University Press.

Illouz, E. 2007. *Cold Intimacies: The Making of Emotional Capitalism*. Cambridge: Polity.

Illouz, E. 2012. *Why Love Hurts: A Sociological Explanation*. Cambridge: Polity Press.

208   Bibliography

Institute of Population Research. 2010. *Report on Accessibility to Reproductive Health among Adolescents in China*. Beijing: Peking University and UNFPA China.

Jacka, T. 2005. Finding a place: Negotiations of modernization and globalization among rural women in Beijing. *Critical Asian Studies*, 37: 51–74.

Jackson, S. 2001. Happily never after: Young women's stories of abuse in heterosexual love relationships. *Feminism and Psychology*, 11: 305–321.

Jackson, S.M. & Cram, F. 2003. Disrupting the sexual double standard: Young women's talk about heterosexuality. *British Journal of Social Psychology*, 42: 113–127.

Jankowiak, W. 1993. *Sex, Death, and Hierarchy in a Chinese City: An Anthropological Account*. New York: Columbia University Press.

Jankowiak, W. 1995. Romantic passion in the People's Republic of China. In: Jankowiak, W. (ed.) *Romantic Passion: A Universal Experience?* New York: Columbia University Press.

Jankowiak, W. 2002. Proper men and proper women: Parental affection in the Chinese family. In: Brownell, S. & Jeffrey, N.W. (eds) *Chinese Femininities/Chinese Masculinities*. Berkeley and Los Angeles: University of California Press.

Jin, Y., Manning, K.E. & Chu, L. 2006. Rethinking the 'iron girls': Gender and labour during the Chinese Cultural Revolution. *Gender & History*, 18: 613–634.

Judd, E.R. 2011. Family strategies: Fluidities of gender, community and mobility in rural west China. In: Evans, H. & Strauss, J.C. (eds) *Gender in Flux: Agency and its Limits in Contemporary China*. Cambridge: Cambridge University Press.

Kaufman, J. 2012. The global women's movement and Chinese women's rights. *Journal of Contemporary China*, 21: 585–602.

Kelly, L. 1996. When does the speaking profit us? Reflections on the challenges of developing feminist perspectives on abuse and violence by women. In: Hester, M., Kelly, L. & Radford, J. (eds) *Women, Violence and Male Power*. Buckingham: Open University Press.

Kelly, L. & Radford, J. 1996. 'Nothing really happened': The invalidation of women's experiences of sexual violence. In: Hester, M., Kelly, L. & Radford, J. (eds) *Women, Violence and Male Power*. Buckingham: Open University Press.

Kipnis, A.B. 2011. *Governing Educational Desire: Culture, Politics, and Schooling in China*. Chicago, IL: The University of Chicago Press.

Kleinman, A. 2011. Introduction: Remaking the moral person in a new China. In: Kleinman, A., Yan, Y., Jing, J., Lee, S., Zhang, E., Pan, T., Wu, F. & Guo, J. (eds) *Deep China – The Moral Life of the Person: What Anthropology and Psychiatry Tell Us About China Today*. Berkeley and Los Angeles: University of California Press.

Knapp, G.A. 2005. Race, class, gender, reclaiming baggage in fast travelling theories. *European Journal of Women's Studies*, 12: 249–265.

Knight, D.S. 2003. Shanghai cosmopolitan: Class, gender, and cultural citizenship in Weihui's Shanghai Babe. *Journal of Contemporary China*, 12: 639–653.

Ko, D. 1994. *Teachers of the Inner Chambers: Women and Culture in Seventeenth-Century China*. Stanford, CA: Stanford University Press.

Ko, D. & Wang, Z. 2006. Introduction: Translating feminism in China. *Gender & History*, 18: 463–471.

Koss, M. 1989. Hidden rape: Sexual aggression and victimization in a national sample of students in higher education. In: Pirog-Good, M.A. & Stets, J.E. (eds) *Violence in Dating Relationships: Emerging Social Issues*. New York: Praeger Publishers.

Kristeva, J. 1986. *About Chinese Women*. New York: Marion Boyars.

Bibliography 209

Kuffel, S.W. & Katz, J. 2002. Preventing physical, psychological, and sexual aggression in college dating relationship. *The Journal of Primary Prevention*, 22: 361–374.

Kurz, D. 1993. Physical assaults by husbands: A major social problem. In: Gelles, R.J. & Loseke, D.R. (eds) *Current Controversies on Family Violence*. Newbury Park, CA: Sage Publications.

Lamb, S. (ed.) 1999. *New Versions of Victims: Feminists Struggle with the Concept*. New York; London: New York University Press.

Laner, M.R. 1983. Courtship abuse and aggression: Contextual aspects. *Sociological Spectrum*, 3: 69–83.

Laqueur, T. 2002. Foreword. In: Brownell, S. & Wasserstrom, J.N. (eds) *Chinese Femininities/Chinese Masculinities*. Berkeley and Los Angeles: University of California Press.

Larson, W. 1999. Never this wild: Sexing the Cultural Revolution. *Modern China*, 25: 423–450.

Larson, W. 2000. Women and the discourse of desire in postrevolutionary China: The awkward postmodernism of Chen Ran. In: Dirlik, A. & Zhang, X. (eds) *Postmodernism and China* (journal into book). Durham, NC and London: Duke University Press.

Lei, Y. 1995. Background and dislocation: Regarding Chinese postcolonialism and postmodernism (Beijing yu cuowei: ye tan zhongguo de houzhimin yu houxiandai). *Reading (Dushu)*: 16–20.

Lempert, L.B. 1994. A narrative analysis of abuse: Connecting the personal, the rhetorical, and the structural. *Journal of Contemporary Ethnography*, 22: 411–441.

Li, C. 2000a. Introduction: Can Confucianism come to terms with feminism? In: Li, C. (ed.) *The Sage and the Second Sex: Confucianism, Ethics, and Gender*. Chicago, IL: Open Court.

Li, C. (ed.) 2000b. *The Sage and the Second Sex: Confucianism, Ethics, and Gender*. Chicago, IL: Open Court.

Li, C. 2013. A biographical and factional analysis of the post-2012 Politburo. *China Leadership Monitor*: 41.

Li, S. 2007. *Imbalanced Sex Ratio at Birth and Comprehensive Intervention in China*. Hyderabad, India: UNFPA China.

Li, S. 2014a. *Chinese Feminism: Twenty Years after 1995 Beijing Conference on Women* [online]. zgcf.oeeee.com/html/201405/13/1026816.html [accessed May 15 2014].

Li, X. 1994a. Economic reform and the awakening of Chinese women's collective consciousness. In: Gilmartin, C.K., Hershatter, G., Rofel, L. & White, T. (eds) *Engendering China: Women, Culture, and the State*. Cambridge, MA: Harvard University Press.

Li, X. 1994b. My path to womanhood. In: Committee on Women's Studies in Asia (ed.) *Changing Lives: Life Stories of Asian Pioneers in Women's Studies*. New York: The Feminist Press at the City University of New York.

Li, X. 2001. From 'modernization' to 'globalization': Where are Chinese women? *Signs*, 26: 1274–1278.

Li, X. 2004. *Academic Questions on Women/Gender*. Jinan: Shandong People Press.

Li, X. & Zhang, X. 1994. Creating a space for women: Women's studies in China in the 1980s. *Signs: Journal of Women in Culture and Society*, 20: 137–151.

Li, Y. 2002a. *Chinese Sexuality and Marriage (Zhongguoren de xingai yu hunyin)*. Beijing: Chinese Friendship Press (Zhongguo youyi chubanshe).

210　*Bibliography*

Li, Y. 2002b. *Love and Sexuality of the Chinese Women* (zhongguoren de qinggan yu xing). Beijing: Zhong guo you yi chu ban she.

Li, Y. 2014b. *Li Yinhe: My Social Observation*. Beijing: Chinese Business Association Press.

Li, Y.M., Chan, D.K.S. & Law, V.W.S. 2012. Gender differences in covert fidelity management among dating individuals in China. *Sex Roles*, 67: 544–558.

LianSi. 2009. *Ant Tribe: A Snapshot of College Graduates Village*. Guilin: Guangxi Normal University Publishing House.

Lin, C. 1996. Citizenship in China: The gender politics of social transformation. *Social Politics*, Summer/Fall: 278–291.

Lin, C. 1997. Finding a language: Feminism and women's movements in contemporary China. In: Scott, J.W., Kaplan, C. & Keates, D. (eds) *Transitions, Environments, Translations: Feminisms in International Politics*. New York and London: Routledge.

Lindholm, C. 1988. Lovers and leaders: A comparison of social and psychological models of romance and charisma. *Social Science Information*.

Liu, B., Jin, Y. & Lin, C. 1998. Women's studies in China. In: Jaggar, A. & Young, I. (eds) *A Companion to Feminist Philosophy*. Oxford: Blackwell.

Liu, J. 2007. *Gender and Work in Urban China: Women Workers of the Unlucky Generation*. London: Routledge.

Liu, L.H. 1993. Invention and intervention: The female tradition in modern Chinese literature. In: Barlow, E.T. (ed.) *Gender Politics in Modern China*. Durham, NC and London: Duke University Press.

Liu, M. 2013. Two gay men seeking two lesbians: An analysis of Xinghun (formality marriage) ads on China's Tianya.cn. *Sexuality & Culture*, 17: 494–511.

Lloyd, S.A. 1991. The darkside of courtship: Violence and sexual exploitation. *Family Relations: Interdisciplinary Journal of Applied Family Studies*, 40: 14–20.

Lloyd, S.A. & Emery, B.C. 2000. *The Dark Side of Courtship: Physical and Sexual Aggression*. Thousand Oaks, CA: Sage Publications.

Lonsway, K.A., Klaw, E.L., Berg, D.R., Waldo, C.R., Kothari, C., Mazurek, C.J., et al. 1998. Beyond 'no means no': Outcomes of an intensive program to train peer facilitators for campus acquaintance rape education. *Journal of Interpersonal Violence*, 13: 73–93.

Louie, K. 2002. *Theorising Chinese Masculinity: Society and Gender in China*. Cambridge: Cambridge University Press.

Lü, D. & Wang, X. 2012. Born in 1980s: Comparative study of the predicament of young professionals in Beijing and Hong Kong. *Journal of Beijing Normal University*, 6: 78–88.

Lü, P. & Zhu, B. 2011. *Report on Anti-Domestic Violence Action in China*. Beijing: Chinese Sociology Press.

Lu, S.H. 1997. Art, culture, and cultural criticism in post-new China. *New Literary History*, 28: 111–133.

Lu, X. 1989. Reassessing the farmers' problems: Changes of Chinese peasants in the past decade. *Journal of Sociology Studies*, 6: 1–14.

Lubell, A.K.N. & Peterson, C. 1998. Female incest survivors: Relationships with mothers and female friends. *Journal of Interpersonal Violence*, 13: 193–216.

Ma, C., Shi, J., Li, Y., Wang, Z. & Tang, C. 2011. The new trends of changing family forms in urban China. *Sociology Studies*, 2: 182–216.

Bibliography 211

MacCannell, D. & MacCannell, J.F. 1993. Violence, power and pleasure: A revisionist reading of Foucault from the victim perspective. In: Ramazanoglu, C. (ed.) *Up Against Foucault: Exploration of Some Tensions between Foucault and Feminism.* London and New York: Routledge.

MacKinnon, C.A. 2013. Intersectionality as method: A note. *Signs: Journal of Women in Culture and Society,* 38: 1019–1030.

Makepeace, J.M. 1981. Courtship violence among college students. *Family Relations,* 32: 97–102.

Mann, S. 1997. *Precious Records: Women in China's Long Eighteenth Century.* Stanford, CA: Stanford University Press.

Mann, S.A. & Huffman, D.J. 2005. The decentering of second wave feminism and the rise of the third wave. *Science & Society,* 69: 56–91.

The Maple Women's Psychological Counseling Center. 2001. *Cases by Women's Hotline on Domestic Violence Research Report.* Beijing: Domestic Violence in China: Research, Intervention and Prevention Sub-program.

Mardorossian, C.M. 2002. Toward a new feminist theory of rape. *Signs: Journal of Women in Culture and Society,* 27: 743–775.

May, S. 2011. Bridging divides and breaking homes: Young women's lifecycle labour mobility as a family managerial strategy. In: Evans, H. & Strauss, J.C. (eds) *Gender in Flux: Agency and its Limits in Contemporary China.* Cambridge: Cambridge University Press.

May, V.M. 2014. 'Speaking into the void?' Intersectionality critiques and epistemic backlash. *Hypatia,* 29: 94–112.

McHugh, M.C., Nichols, A.L. & Ford, A. 2005. A postmodern approach to women's use of violence: Developing multiple and complex conceptualization. *Psychology of Women Quarterly,* 29: 323–336.

Meng, Y. 1993. Female images and national myth. In: Barlow, T.E. (ed.) *Gender Politics in Modern China.* Durham, NC and London: Duke University Press.

Meng, Y. & Dai, J. 2004. *Emerging from the Horizon of History: Modern Chinese Women's Literature (Fu chu li shi di biao: xian dai fu n?wen xue yan jiu).* Beijing: Zhongguo ren min da xue chu ban she.

Milwertz, C. 2003. Activism against domestic violence in the People's Republic of China. *Violence Against Women,* 9: 630–654.

Milwertz, C. & Bu, W. 2005. *Popular Feminist Organizing in the People's Republic of China: Communicating Oppositional Gender Equality Knowledge.* Hong Kong: Hong Kong University & French Centre for Research on Contemporary China Conference: Emerging Social Movement in China.

Milwertz, C. & Bu, W. 2009. Non-governmental organising for gender equality in China – Joining a global empancipatory epistemic community. *The International Journal of Human Rights,* 11: 131–149.

Min, D. 2005. Awakening again: Travelling feminism in China in the 1980s. *Women's Studies International Forum,* 28: 274–288.

Ming, D. 1997. From asexuality to gender difference in modern China. In: Yeo, E.J. (ed.) *Mary Wollstonecraft and 200 Years of Feminisms.* London and New York: Rivers Oram Press.

Mohanty, C.T. 2002. 'Under Western eyes' revisited: Feminist solidarity through anticapitalist struggles. *Signs: Journal of Women in Culture and Society,* 28: 499–535.

Mohanty, C.T. 2003. *Feminism Without Borders: Decolonizing Theory, Practicing Solidarity.* Durham, NC and London: Duke University Press.

212 Bibliography

Molidor, C. & Tolman, R.M. 1998. Gender and contextual factors in adolescent dating violence. *Violence Against Women*, 4: 180–194.

Monson, C.M. & Langhinrichsen Rohling, J. 2002. Sexual and nonsexual dating violence perpetration: Testing an integrated perpetrator typology. *Violence and Victims*, 17: 403–428.

Moore, S.G., Dahl, D.W., Gorn, G.J., Weinberg, C.B., Park, J. & Jiang, Y. 2008. Condom embarrassment: Coping and consequences for condom use in three countries. *AIDS Care*, 20: 553–559.

Moskowitz, M.L. 2008. Multiple virginity and other contested realities in Taipei culture. *Sexualities*, 11: 327–352.

Naples, N.A. 2003. Deconstructing and locating survivor discourse: Dynamics of narrative, empowerment, and resistance for survivors of childhood sexual abuse. *Signs: Journal of Women in Culture and Society*, 28: 1151–1185.

Nash, J.C. 2013. Practicing love: Black feminism, love, politics, and post-intersectionality. *Meridian: Feminism, Race and Transnationalism*, 11: 1–24.

Ng, J. 1993. *The Experience of Modernity: Chinese Autobiography of the Early Twentieth Century*. Ann Arbor: The University of Michigan Press.

Ngai, P. 2004. Engendering Chinese modernity: The sexual politics of Dagongmei in a dormitory labour regime. *Asian Studies Review*, 28: 151–165.

Ngai, P. 2005. *Made in China: Women Factory Workers in a Global Workplace*. Durham, NC and London: Duke University Press.

O'Keefe, M. 1997. Predictors of dating violence among high school students. *Journal of Interpersonal Violence*, 12: 546–568.

Osburg, J. 2013. *Anxious Wealth: Money and Morality among China's New Rich*. Stanford, CA: Stanford University Press.

Osnos, E. 2014. *Age of Ambition: Chasing Fortune, Truth and Faith in the New China*. New York: Farrer, Straus & Giroux.

O'Toole, L.L., Schiffman, J.R. & Edwards, M.L.K. 2007. *Gender Violence: Interdisciplinary Perspectives*. New York: New York University Press.

Ottens, A.J. & Hotelling, K. 2001. *Sexual Violence on Campus: Policies, Programs, and Perspectives*. New York: Springer Publishers.

Pan, S. 2006. Transformations in the primary life cycle: The origins and nature of China's sexual revolution. In: Jeffreys, E. (ed.) *Sex and Sexuality in China*. London: Routledge.

Pan, S. & Huang, Y. 2013. *The Change of Sexuality: Sex Lives of Chinese People in 21st Century* (Xing zhi Bian: 21 Shiji Zhongguoren de Xingshenghuo). Beijing: China Renmin University Publishing House.

Pan, S. & Yang, R. 2004. *Sexuality of Chinese College Students: A Ten-year Longitude Nationwide Random Study* (in Chinese). Beijing: Social Science Documentation Publishing House.

Parish, W.L., Laumann, E.O. & Mojola, S.A. 2007. Sexual behavior in China. *Population and Development Review*, 33: 729–756.

Parish, W.L., Wang, T., Laumann, E.O., Pan, S. & Luo, Y. 2004. Intimate partner violence in China: National prevalence, risk factors and associated health problems. *International Family Planning Perspectives*, 30: 174–181.

Parker, R. & Aggleton, P. (eds) 2007. *Culture, Society and Sexuality: A Reader*. New York: Routledge.

Bibliography 213

Pei, Y. 2013. *Sex and City: Sexuality of Shanghai Young Women Born in the 1970s* (*Yuwang dushi: shanghai qilinghou nvxing yanjiu*). Shanghai: Shanghai Renmin Publishing House.

Pei, Y. & Ho, S.Y. 2006. Iron girls, strong women, beautiful women writers and super girls: A discourse analysis of the gender performance of women in contemporary China. *Lilith: A Feminist History Journal*, 15: 61–73.

Pei, Y. & Ho, S.Y. 2009. Gender, self and pleasure: Young women's discourse on masturbation in contemporary Shanghai. *Culture, Health & Sexuality*, 11: 515–528.

Pickowicz, P.G. 1991. The theme of spiritual pollution in Chinese films of the 1930s. *Modern China*, 17: 38–75.

Pimentel, E.E. 2006. Gender ideology, household behavior, and backlash in urban China. *Journal of Family Issues*, 27: 341–365.

Plummer, K. 2003. *Intimate Citizenship: Private Decisions and Public Dialogues*. Montreal: McGill-Queen's University Press.

Prins, B. 2006. Narrative accounts of origins: A blind spot in the intersectional approach? *European Journal of Women's Studies*, 13: 277–290.

Pun, N. 2003. Subsumption or consumption? The phantom of consumer revolution in 'globalizing' China. *Cultural Anthropology*, 18: 469–492.

Rachman, A.W. 2000. Ferenczi's 'confusion of tongues' theory and the analysis of the incest trauma. *Psychoanalytic Social Work*, 7: 27–53.

Rai, S.M. 1999. Gender in China. In: Houndmills, B. (ed.) *China in the 1990s*. London: Macmillan Press.

Rein, S. 2012. *The End of Cheap China: Economic and Cultural Trends that will Disrupt the World*. Hoboken, NJ: John Wiley & Sons, Inc.

Reinharz, S. 1992. *Feminist Methods in Social Research*. New York: Oxford University Press.

Rhatigan, D.L., Moore, T.M. & Street, A.E. 2005. Reflection on partner violence: 20 years of research and beyond. *Journal of Interpersonal Violence*, 20: 82–88.

Rofel, L. 1999. *Other Modernities: Gendered Yearnings in China after Socialism*. Berkeley and Los Angeles: University of California Press.

Rofel, L. 2007. *Desiring China: Experiments in Neoliberalism, Sexuality, and Public Culture*. Durham, NC: Duke University Press.

Rose, N. 1992. Governing the enterprising self. In: Heelas, P. & Morris, P. (eds) *The Values of the Enterprise Culture: The Moral Debate*. London: Routledge.

Rose, N. 2007. *The Politics of Life Itself: Biomedicine, Power, and Subjectivity in the Twenty-First Century*. Princeton, NJ: Princeton University Press.

Russell, B.L. & Oswald, D.L. 2002. Sexual coercion and victimization of college men: The role of love styles. *Journal of Interpersonal Violence*, 17: 273–285.

Ryan, K.M. 1998. The relationship between courtship violence and sexual aggression in college students. *Journal of Family Violence*, 13: 377–394.

Saich, T. 2011. *Governance and Politics of China* (third edition). New York: Palgrave Macmillan.

Sarantakos, S. 2004. Deconstructing self-defense in wife-to-husband violence. *The Journal of Men's Studies*, 12: 277–296.

Saunders, D.G. 2002. Are physical assaults by wives and girlfriends a major social problem? A review of the literature. *Violence Against Women*, 8: 1424–1448.

Schaffer, K. & Song, X. 2007. Unruly spaces: Gender, women's writing and indigenous feminism in China. *Journal of Gender Studies*, 16: 17–30.

214   Bibliography

Schein, L. 2001. Urbanity, cosmopolitanism, consumption. In: Chen, N.N., Clark, C.D., Gottschang, S.Z. & Jeffery, L. (eds) *China Urban: Ethnographies of Contemporary Culture*. Durham, NC: Duke University Press.

Schlegel, A. 1991. Status, property, and the value of virginity. *American Ethnologist*, 18: 719–734.

Schwartz, M.D. & DeKeseredy, W.S. 2000. Aggregation bias and woman abuse: Variations by male peer support, region, language and school type. *Journal of Interpersonal Violence*, 15: 555–565.

Shen, A.C.T., Chiu, M.Y.L. & Gao, J. 2012. Predictors of dating violence among Chinese adolescents: The role of gender-role beliefs and justification of violence. *Journal of Interpersonal Violence*, 27: 1066–1089.

Shoads, R.A. & Gu, D.Y. 2012. A gendered point of view on the challenges of women academics in the People's Republic of China. *Higher Education*, 63: 733–750.

Shook, N.J., Gerrity, D.A., Jurich, J. & Segrist, A.E. 2000. Courtship violence among college students: A comparison of verbally and physically abusive couples. *Journal of Family Violence*, 15: 1–22.

Shu, X. 2005. Market transition and gender segregation in urban China. *Social Science Quarterly*, 86.

Shu, X., Zhu, Y. & Zhang, Z. 2007. Global economy and gender inequalities: The case of the urban Chinese labor market. *Social Science Quarterly*, 88: 1307–1332.

Sigley, G. 2006. Sex, politics and the policing of virtue in the People's Republic of China. In: Jeffreys, E. (ed.) *Sex and Sexuality in China*. London: Routledge.

Spakowski, N. 1994. Women's studies with Chinese characteristics? On the origins, issues, and theories of contemporary feminist research in China. *Jindai zhongguo funushi yanjiu*, 2: 297–322.

Spakowski, N. 2011. 'Gender' trouble: Feminism in China under the impact of Western theory and the spatialization of identity. *Positions*, 19: 31–54.

Spivak, G.C. 1996. *The Spivak Reader: Selected Works of Gayatri Chakravorty Spivak*. New York: Routledge.

Sprecher, S., Barbee, A. & Schwartz, P. 1995. 'Was it good for you, too?': Gender differences in first sexual intercourse experiences. *The Journal of Sex Research*, 32: 3–22.

Squire, C. 1998. Women and men talk about aggression: An analysis of narrative genre. In: Henwood, K., Griffin, C. & Phoenix, A. (eds) *Standpoints and Differences: Essays in the Practice of Feminist Psychology*. London: Sage.

Stets, J.E. 1991. Psychological aggression in dating relationships: The role of interpersonal control. *Journal of Family Violence*, 6: 97–114.

Stets, J.E. & Straus, M.A. 1989. The marriage license as a hitting license: A comparison of assaults in dating, cohabiting, and married couples. *Journal of Family Violence*, 4: 161–180.

Stith, S.M. & Straus, M.A. (eds) 1995. *Understanding Partner Violence: Prevalence, Causes, Consequence and Solutions*. Minneapolis: National Council on Family Relations.

Straus, M.A. 1997. Physical assaults by women partners: A major social problem. In: Walsh, M.R. (ed.) *Women, Men, and Gender: Ongoing Debates*. Hackensack, NJ: Northeastern Graphic Services.

Straus, M.A. 2004. Prevalence of violence against dating partners by male and female university students worldwide. *Violence Against Women*, 10: 790–811.

Bibliography   215

Straus, M.A. & Hamby, S.L. 1997. Measuring physical and psychological maltreatment of children with the conflict tactics scales. In: Kantor, G.K. & Jasinski, J.L. (ed.) *Out of Darkness: Contemporary Perspectives on Family Violence.* Thousand Oaks, CA: Sage Publications.

Straus, M.A., Hamby, S.L., Boney, M.S. & Sugarman, D.B. 1996. The revised Conflict Tactics Scales (CTS2): Development and preliminary psychometric data. *Journal of Family Issues,* 17(3): 283–316.

Sugarman, D.B. & Hotaling, G.T. 1989. Dating violence: Prevalence, context, and risk markers. In: Pirog-Good, M.A. & Stets, J.E. (eds) *Violence in Dating Relationships: Emerging Social Issues.* New York: Praeger Publishers.

Sun, P. 2012. *Who is Going to Marry My Daughter? Shanghai Blind Date Corner and 'Grey Date.'* Beijing: China Social Science Publishing House.

Sun, W. & Guo, Y. 2013. *Unequal China: The Political Economy and Cultural Politics of Inequality.* Abingdon and New York: Routledge.

Sun, Y. 2010. *Saving Boys.* Beijing: Writers Publishing House.

Tan, S. 1993. Social transformation and women's employment in China. In: *Chinese Women and Development.* Tianjin: Tianjin Normal University Press.

Tan, S. 1995. Women's studies and I. In: Wong, Y.L. (ed.) *Reflections & Resonance: Stories of Chinese Women Involved in the International Preparatory Activities for the 1995 NGO Forum on Women.* Beijing: Ford Foundation International Club.

Tang, C. 2005. Sexual harassment in China. In: Tan, L. & Liu, B. (eds) *Review on the Chinese Women's Studies in Recent 10 Years.* Beijing: Social Science Academic Press.

Tang, C.S.K., Wong, D. & Cheung, F.M.C. 2002. Social construction of women as legitimate victims of violence in Chinese societies. *Violence Against Women,* 8: 968–996.

Tao, J. 1996. Women's studies in China. *Women's Studies Quarterly,* 1&2: 351–363.

Taormina, R.J. & Ho, I.K.M. 2012. Intimate relationship in China: Predictors across genders for dating. *Journal of Relationships Research,* 3: 24–43.

Tjaden, P. & Thoennes, N. 2000. *Full Report of the Prevalence, Incidence, and Consequences of Violence Against Women.* US Department of Justice, Office of Justice Programs, National Institute of Justice.

Tong, X. & Su, Y. 2010. Gender segregation in the process of college student job seeking: A survey of higher education as a prelabor market factor. *Chinese Education and Society,* 43: 90–107.

Trent, K. & South, S.J. 2012. Mate availability and women's sexual experiences in China. *Journal of Marriage and Family,* 74: 201–213.

Tsui, M. & Rich, L. 2002. The only child and educational opportunity for girls in urban China. *Gender & Society,* 16: 74–92.

UNFPA. 2012. *Sex Imbalance at Birth: Current Trends, Consequences, and Policy Implications.* Bangkok, Thailand: UNFPA Asia and the Pacific Regional Office.

Walby, S. 2007. Complexity theory, systems theory, and multiple intersecting social inequalities. *Philosophy of the Social Sciences,* 37: 449–470.

Walker, L.E. 1979. *The Battered Woman.* New York: Harper & Row.

Walker, L.E. 2000. *The Battered Woman Syndrome.* New York: Springer.

Wang, Q. & Zhou, Q. 2010. China's divorce and remarriage rates: Trends and regional disparities. *Journal of Divorce & Remarriage,* 51: 257–267.

Wang, X. 1999. Why are Beijing women beaten by their husbands? A case analysis of family violence in Beijing. *Violence Against Women,* 5: 1493–1504.

Wang, X. 2004. Youth dating violence in China (Qingchun zai lian'ai baoli zhong zhi xi). *China Youth Daily* (*Zhongguo qingnian bao*), 8, June.

216   Bibliography

Wang, X. 2009. *Intimate Partner Violence: A Survey based on 1015 College Students.* Tianjin: Tianjin Renmin Publishing House.

Wang, X., Fang, G. & Li, H. 2013a. *Gender-based Violence and Masculinities Study: Chinese Quantitative Research Report.* Beijing: UNFPA China.

Wang, X. & Ho, S.Y. 2007a. My Sassy Girl: A qualitative study of women's aggression in dating relationships in Beijing. *Journal of Interpersonal Violence*, 22: 623–638.

Wang, X. & Ho, S.Y. 2007b. Violence and desire in Beijing: A young Chinese woman's strategies of resistance in father-daughter incest and dating relationships. *Violence Against Women: An International and Interdisciplinary Journal*, 13: 1319–1338.

Wang, X. & Ho, S.Y. 2011. 'Female virginity complex' untied: Young Beijing women's experience of virginity loss and sexual coercion. *Smith College Studies in Social Work*, 81: 184–200.

Wang, X. & Nehring, D. 2014. Individualization as an ambition: Mapping the dating landscape in Beijing. *Modern China*, 40: 578–604.

Wang, X., Qiao, D., Yang, L. & Nehring, D. 2013b. *Hard Struggles in Times of Change: A Qualitative Study on Masculinities and Gender-based Violence in Contemporary China.* UNFPA China Office.

Wang, X. & Wang, Y. 2012. Critical review and prospect on sexuality education research in the new millennium. *Youth Study*, 12: 48–57.

Wang, Z. 1998. Research on women in contemporary China. In: Hershatter, G., Honig, E., Mann, S. & Rofel, L. (eds) *Guide to Women's Studies in China*. Berkeley, CA: Institute of East Asian Studies, University of California.

Wang, Z. 2005. 'State feminism'? Gender and socialist state formation in Maoist China. *Feminist Studies*, 31: 519–551.

Wang, Z. & Zhang, Y. 2010. Global concepts, local practices: Chinese feminism since the Fourth UN Conference on Women. *Feminist Studies*, 36: 40–70.

Weber, I. 2002. Shanghai baby: Negotiating youth self-identity in urban China. *Social Identities*, 8: 347–368.

Weeks, J. 2000. *Making Sexual History.* Oxford: Blackwell.

Wesoky, S.R. 2002. *Chinese Feminism Faces Globalization.* New York: Routledge.

Wesoky, S.R. 2007. Rural women knowing all: Globalization and rural women's organizing in China. *International Feminist Journal of Politics*, 9: 339 358.

West, C. & Zimmerman, D.H. 1987. Doing gender. *Gender & Society*, 1: 125–151.

White, J.W. & Kowalski, R.M. 1994. Deconstructing the myth of the non-aggressive woman: A feminist analysis. *Psychology of Women Quarterly*, 18: 487–508.

White, J.W., Smith, P.H., Koss, M.P. & Figueredo, A.J. 2000. Intimate partner aggression – What have we learned? Comment on Archer. *Psychological Bulletin*, 126: 690–696.

Whyte, M.K. & Parish, W.L. 1984. *Urban Life in Contemporary China.* Chicago, IL: University of Chicago Press.

Wilkinson, S. 1998. Focus groups in feminist research: Power, interaction, and the co-construction of meaning. *Women's Studies International Forum*, 21: 111–125.

Woo, M.Y.K. 1994. Chinese women workers: The delicate balance between protection and equality. In: Gilmartin, C.K., Hershatter, G., Rofel, L. & White, T. (eds) *Engendering China: Women, Culture, and the State*. Cambridge, MA: Harvard University Press.

Worcester, N. 2002. Women's use of violence: Complexities and challenges of taking the issue seriously. *Violence Against Women*, 8: 1390–1415.

Bibliography 217

Woronov, T.E. 2004. In the eye of the chicken: Hierarchy and marginality among Beijing's migrant schoolchildren. *Ethnography*, 5: 289–313.

Wu, F. 2011. Suicide, a modern problem in China. In: Kleinman, A. (ed.) *Deep China – The Moral Life of the Person: What Anthropology and Psychiatry Tell Us About China Today*. Berkeley and Los Angeles: University of California Press.

Wu, W. 2005. Sassy women: More violent, more beautiful. *Trends Health*, 1: 168.

Wu, X. 2010. 'Working well' or 'married well': The identification crisis and subjectivity construction of urban women in the marketization. In: Meng, X. (ed.) *The Living Status and Social Emotion of Chinese Women*. China Social Science Publishing House.

Xiao, M. 2015. China's feminist awakening. *International New York Times*.

Xiao, Z. 1989. Virginity and premarital sex in contemporary China. *Feminist Studies*, 15: 279–288.

Xin, T. & Yihui, S. 2010. Gender segregation in the process of college student job seeking: A survey of higher education as a prelabor market factor. *Chinese Education and Society*, 43: 90–107.

Xu, F. 2009. Chinese feminism encounter international feminism: Identity, power and knowledge production. *International Feminist Journal of Politics*, 11: 196–215.

Xu, G. & Feiner, S. 2007. Meinu Jingji/China's beauty economy: Buying looks, shifting value, and changing place. *Feminist Economics*, 13: 307–323.

Xu, X. 1997. The prevalence and determination of wife abuse in urban China. *Journal of Comparative Family Studies*, 28: 280–303.

Xu, X., Campbell, J.C. & Zhu, F.-C. 2001. Intimate partner violence against Chinese women: The past, present, and future. *Trauma, Violence, & Abuse*, 2: 296–315.

Xu, Y., Bentley, R.J. & Kavanagh, A.M. 2011. Gender equity and contraceptive use in China: An ecological analysis. *Women & Health*, 51: 739–758.

Yan, H. 2003. Spectralization of the rural: Reinterpreting the labor mobility of rural young women in post-Mao China. *American Ethnologist*, 30: 578–596.

Yan, Y. 2003. *Private Life Under Socialism: Love, Intimacy, and Family Change in a Chinese Village, 1949–1999*. Stanford, CA: Stanford University Press.

Yan, Y. 2009. *The Individualization of Chinese Society*. Oxford: Berg.

Yan, Y. 2010. The Chinese path to individualization. *British Journal of Sociology*, 61: 489–512.

Yan, Y. 2011. The changing moral landscape. In: *Deep China – The Moral Life of the Person: What Anthropology and Psychiatry Tell Us About China Today*. Berkeley; Los Angeles: University of California Press.

Young, M. 1989. Chicken Little in China: Women after the Cultural Revolution. In: Kruks, S., Rapp, R. & Young, M. (eds) *Promissory Notes: Women in the Transition to Socialism*. New York: Monthly Review Press.

Yu, Y., Xiao, S. & Liu, K.Q. 2013. Dating violence among gay men in China. *Journal of Interpersonal Violence*, 28: 2491–2504.

Yu, J. & Xie, Y. 2011–12. The varying display of 'gender display': A comparative study of Mainland China and Taiwan. *Chinese Sociological Review*, 44: 5–30.

Zhan, S. 2011. What determines migrant workers' life chances in contemporary China? Hukou, social exclusion, and the market. *Modern China*, 37: 243–285.

Zhang, E.Y. 2005. Rethinking sexual repression in Maoist China: Ideology, structure and the ownership of the body. *Body & Society*, 11: 1–25.

Zhang, E.Y. 2011. China's sexual revolution. In: Kleinman, A. (ed.) *The Moral Life of the Person: What Anthropology and Psychiatry Tell us about China Today*. Berkeley and Los Angeles: University of California Press.

218   Bibliography

Zhang, J. 1988. *The Ark (Fang zhou)*. Beijing: Beijing October Arts Publishing House (Beijing shiyue wenyi chubanshe).

Zhang, L. 2001. Contesting crime, order, and migrant spaces in Beijing. In: Chen, N.N., Clark, C.D., Gottschang, S.Z. & Jeffery, L. (eds) *China Urban: Ethnographies of Contemporary Culture*. Durham, NC and London: Duke University Press.

Zhang, L. 2009. Chinese women protesting domestic violence: The Beijing conference, international donor agencies, and the making of a Chinese women's NGO. *Meridians: Feminism, Race, Transnationalism*, 9: 66–99.

Zhang, L. 2012. *Social Ecology of Domestic Violence: A Case Study of Wife Murdering*. CFP: Beijing Normal University.

Zhang, N., Parish, W.L., Huang, Y. & Pan, S. 2010. Sexual infidelity in China: Prevalence and gender-specific correlates. *Archives of Sexual Behavior*, 41: 861–873.

Zhang, N., Parish, W.L., Huang, Y. & Pan, S. 2012. Sexual infidelity in China: Prevalence and gender-specific correlates. *Archives of Sexual Behavior*, 41: 861–873.

Zhang, Y., Hannum, E. & Wang, M. 2008. Gender-based employment and income difference in urban China: Considering the contribution of marriage and parenthood. *Social Force*, 86: 1529–1560.

Zhang, Z. 1999. The world map of haunting dreams: Reading post-1989 Chinese women's diaspora writings. In: Yang, M. (ed.) *Spaces of their Own: Women's Public Sphere in Transnational China*. Minneapolis and London: University of Minnesota Press.

Zhang, Z. 2000. Mediating time: The rice bowl of youth in fin de siècle urban China. *Public Culture*, 12(1): 93–113.

Zheng, T. 2009. *Red Lights: The Lives of Sex Workers in Postsocialist China*. Minneapolis; London: University of Minnesota Press.

Zhong, X. 2000. *Masculinity Besieged?: Issues of Modernity and Male Subjectivity in Chinese Literature of the Late Twentieth Century*. Durham, NC: Duke University Press.

Zhong, X. 2006. Who is a feminist? Understanding the ambivalence towards Shanghai Baby: 'Body writing' and feminism in post-women's liberation China. *Gender & History*, 18: 635–660.

Zhong, X. & Ho, S.Y. 2014. Negotiating intimate relationship: The expectations of family relations and filial piety among only child parents. *Open Times*.

Zhou, J. 2003. Keys to women's liberation in communist China: An historical overview. *Journal of International Women's Studies*, 5: 67–77.

Zhou, X. 2004. *The State and Life Chances in Urban China: Redistribution and Stratification, 1949–1994*. New York: Cambridge University Press.

Zhou, Y.R. 2012. Changing behaviours and continuing silence: Sex in the post-immigration lives of Mainland Chinese immigrants in Canada. *Culture, Health & Sexuality*, 14: 87–100.

Zuo, J. 2003. From revolutionary comrades to gendered partners: Marital construction of breadwinning in post-Mao urban China. *Journal of Family Issues*, 24: 314–337.

Zuo, J. 2013. Women's liberation and gender obligation equality in urban China: Work/family experiences of married individuals in the 1950s. *Science & Society*, 77: 98–125.

Index

Ai, Xiaoming 5, 21, 140
Abortion 7, 148–50, 166, 192
Abusive men (husbands, boyfriend) and abused women (wives, girlfriend) 6, 135, 173
ACWF 8, 22, 34, 30–1, 47
Agency 5, 7–8, 12, 16, 23, 35, 37, 42–4, 48, 160, 170, 173, 175, 180, 193
Ah, Shanghainese Men 111
APEC blue 7
arranged marriage 16, 58, 176
Anti-Domestic Violence Network 5, 21, 24
Anti-Domestic Violence Law 24, 141

Backlash 8–9, 134–35
battered women's syndrome 23
Beijinger 12, 54–91, 161,176, 182; and Non-Beijinger 64; new Beijinger 54, 58, 70–9, 81, 90–1, 160, 176, 181–2
Beijing conference (The Fourth World Conference on Women in 1995 in Beijing) 17, 19, 40
Beijing Smog 7
beauty economics 35
bourgeois 107, 123, 130, 156; and bourgeois lifestyle 69, 77, 103; bourgeoisie women images 35–6; bourgeois liberalization 157

chastity 16, 31, 75, 122, 144–47, 156–57, 168
Chow, Rey 102, 144, 183
cold war 115, 174
college students 25–7, 54, 58, 60–4, 82, 94, 98, 105, 142, 148, 151–59, 176, 185
Confucianism 12, 46, 48, 52, 134, 137, 183; and Confucian thought16; Confucian ideas 15, 36, 39, 44–8, 51–2, 75–6, 102, 122, 156–57, 181, 183

contraception 149–52
cosmopolitanism 4, 35, 37, 183; and cosmopolis (cosmopolitan Beijing) 4, 11, 123
cohabitation 5, 19, 28, 68, 110, 141, 186
courtship 5, 10, 13, 28, 86, 103, 146, 175–7
cheating 87, 89, 113–4, 117, 121, 151, 153, 177;
China Communist Party (CCP) 4, 8, 32, 111, 123, 130, 157
Chinese intersectionality 5, 12, 15–6, 48–51, 172, 179–80
Chinese masculinity: literacy masculinity 112; talented scholar/beautiful woman 112; wen-wu 112; wen masculinity 112
civil society 18
CTS (Conflict Tactics Scales) 26
cultural hybridity 4–5, 16, 51
cyber-stalking 114–5, 174
cycle of violence 41, 109–10, 117, 173

date rape1, 3, 5, 20, 138–41; and attempted date rape 1, 138; acquaintance rape 33, 156; 'women's fantasy of being raped' 153
dating: dating experience 44, 80, 95, 97, 152, 172, 176, 184, 186–87, 192–94; dating culture 7, 11, 37, 51, 154, 187; dating (love) geography: 12, 54, 58–60, 82–3, 85, 90–2;
dating hegemony 55–6, 91; dating hierarchy 59, 68, 90–2, 176, 182; dating landscape 12, 54, 59, 90, 92, 175
daughter of the party 33
desire:42, 48, 55, 63, 66, 68, 72, 73, 76, 77–8, 81, 84, 90–2, 102, 112, 123, 126, 127, 130, 135, 143, 145, 148–49, 153, 155–57, 160–66, 169–71, 175, 177,

220   *Index*

179, 182–3; and women's desire 149, 155–7, 160–64; desiring self 48, 67, 75, 78, 92, 176, 180
Dikötter, Frank 10
DINK (dual earner, dual income, no kids) 10
divorce (divorce rate) 10, 17, 22, 24, 32, 86, 109–10, 139, 157, 159, 160–62, 166, 173
divided self 48, 75, 180
doing gender (sexuality) 12, 27, 79, 94
domestic violence 3, 5, 16–29, 39–40, 47, 109, 119–21, 141, 172–73, 189
Dong, Shanshan 24
'don't ask, don't tell' 11, 155, 167; and 'no advocacy, no opposition' 155
double burden 33, 52, 57, 132–34

eating bitterness 75–6, 79, 91, 177
eating spring rice (the rice bowl of youth) 68, 70
emotional blackmail 115–17, 148, 174
enterprising self 48, 75, 180
Evans, Harriet 10.
extra-marital affairs 11, 56, 157, 187

Face 60, 64, 108, 141, 150, 164
Female virginity complex 11, 139, 145, 150, 153, 160, 170, 174, 179
feminist scholarship 15, 44, 52, 96, 135, 172
feminist activism 21
femininity 4, 13, 25, 35–6, 68, 93, 94, 98, 100–3, 108, 111–2, 128, 134–6, 143, 152, 179, 182
formative marriage 11
Foucault, Michel 38, 48, 84, 157
Four Modernizations 30
floating population 79–82

Gavey, Nicola 42
girl power 10, 103, 136
Gender: gender awareness (raising) 3, 168; gender-based violence 3, 15–25, 29, 39–42, 44, 46, 48, 97, 153, 172–73, 189; gender equality 4, 8, 25, 29, 31–4, 51–2, 76, 111, 118, 124–5, 128, 130, 132–6, 139, 150, 165, 168, 171, 173–4, 178–80, 183–4; gender discrimination 3, 22, 28; gender role 9, 95, 127–28, 130–3, 136, 173, 178, 183–84; gender studies 9, 15–16, 18, 37, 50; gender stereotypes 22, 136; gender main-streaming 18; gender norms 23, 25, 33,

133, 135, 168; gender performance 124, 136
GGGR (Global Gender Gap Report) 8, 14
glass ceiling 8–9, 81, 131
globalization 4, 16, 30, 38, 43, 46, 48, 50–1, 68, 77, 81–3, 85, 90, 92, 113, 155, 164, 172, 175

Harmonious society 46–7;
Harmonious family 47
hegemony 4–5, 9, 45, 50, 55, 92, 175; and dating hegemony 5, 12, 55–6, 9; gender hegemony 5, 12–3, 135; sexual hegemony 5, 12–3, 171, 175; scattered hegemonies 55
hegemonic masculinities 111–12; and real men 111; 'the sick men of East Asia' 111; success as 'defining quality of masculinity' 113; save boys 131
Hershatter, Gail 10, 18, 164
heterosexual relationship 5, 154
hook-up date 5
hold up half the sky 8, 102
Homophobic hate crimes 20
homosexual relationship 11, 20, 21
Hua, Mulan 31, 52
Huang, Jing 3, 140
Husband leads and wife follows 9
Hukou 54–91
Hukou system 54, 55, 58, 60, 64, 70–2, 82, 89, 91, 176, 180, 182; Beijing *hukou* 54, 58, 60, 62–3, 72, 77, 82, 89, 161; *hukou* quota for entering Beijing 61–3, 82, 90, 182; *hukou*-holders 62, 72, 79, 81; *Beijing* citizenship 63

indigenization 45; indigenous studies 39, 44–8; also see women's studies with Chinese characteristics 45, 47
in-depth interviews 126, 184–85, 187
individualization 50, 74, 86, 123, 179
infidelity 80, 89–90, 109, 113–5, 117–8, 121, 124, 135, 174
international dating 50, 83, 85–6, 92, 177, 180; also see transnational dating 59, 90, 180, 189
intersectional self 5, 8, 12, 48, 54, 152, 172, 180
intersectionality 5, 12, 15–16, 42–4, 48–51, 60, 91, 94–5, 136, 172, 179–80; race-class-gender matrix 43; constructive intersectionality 43; interactive intersectionality 43

Index 221

intimacy (sexual intimacy) 5, 7, 11, 28, 43, 48, 83, 95, 99, 103, 105, 125, 136, 171, 178, 190,
intimate partner violence 19–20, 23, 34, 40, 96, 125, 141, 173, 184
'If You are the One' 12, 154
iron girls 33, 36, 102

Kaufman, Joan 17
Kang-Liang reform 31, 112, 146, 197
Kang, Youwei 32, 146
Kenlao 126
Kleinman, Arthur 48, 63, 75, 180

Lamb, Sharon 42
Learned helplessness 23, 41
Leftover women 11, 29, 37, 118, 169, 176
Let women go home 9, 31, 133–4
LGBT 3, 5, 11, 18, 20–1, 27, 157, 167–69, 177
Li, Xiaojiang 29–30, 45, 133–4
Li, Yinhe 69, 165
Liang, Qichao 32, 75, 146
long-distance relationship 59, 83, 86–91, 106, 175, 177, 193–95; long-distance dating 86, 88, 90, 177, 187, 194
love: confluent love 162, 179; Distant Love 85; global chaos of love 85; ideal love 75–6, 78–9, 82, 91, 122–23, 175; pure relationship 162, 179, 193; purity of love 92, 156; true love 75–6, 90, 160; love at dusk 61
love and violence (co-existed love and violence) 5–7, 97, 121, 124, 153
loyal and faithful from beginning till death 57, 75, 91, 122,
Lu, Xun 86–7, 146
Lung, Yingtai 111

Maoist China 4, 8, 34, 36
Marriage Law 19, 24
masculinity and gender-based violence 25, 153
mate selection 5, 10, 29, 50, 58, 64, 100, 103, 126, 127, 176, 181; and mate selection agency 58; match-making TV programs 58 (also see 'If You are the One' 12, 154)
May Fourth Movement 10, 14, 16, 35, 47, 122, 134
middle class 53, 63, 70, 77, 85, 92, 126, 180
Min, Dongchao 16

modernization (four modernization) 4, 30–2, 37, 68, 81–2, 155, 164, 166, 172, 181
modern men 81, 104–05, 179
modern women/girl 16, 31, 35, 129–30, 163,168, 174
modernity7, 10, 12, 16, 30–2, 37, 55, 63, 77, 113, 123, 135, 156, 164–65, 181, 183
money 10, 64–7, 69,72; anxiety of money 110; looking only at money 64; lack of money 76, 113, 176; money and gift 76
monogamous relationships 55, 162
mutual violence 6, 95–6, 119, 139, 151–52, 170, 174; and 'reciprocal' violence 96, 152; gender-asymmetric modes of mutual violence 139, 151–3, 170, 174
multi-level and multi-sectoral approach 24
Muzi Mei 163, 167

Nabokov, Valdimir 69
naked marriage (*nuohun*) 63
neo-liberal market 9, 54, 70, 91; and neo-liberal capitalism 66; global capitalism 37–8, 77
new women 35, 163
NGO 11, 17–18, 21–2, 24, 55, 124, 173

one-child policy 3, 9, 22, 32, 124, 134, 136, 164–66, 180, 187

Pan, Suiming 140–1, 148, 154–5, 158–9, 165–68
parental influence 71, 124–7; and 'parents are all hurtful and harmful' 127; filial piety 125–27
patriarchy 34, 51, 101–03, 113, 144, 146, 168, 171, 178; and patriarchal system 36, 96, 130, 133, 175
peacock girl and phoenix boy 70–3
performance art 3, 13, 21–2
physical assault 5, 13, 20, 26, 52, 95, 152, 173–74, 187; and physical abuse 25, 74, 108–9, 139–40; physical violence 20, 26, 27, 74, 89, 95, 109, 110, 115, 117, 135, 138, 140, 152, 173, 174
post-socialist China 4–5, 47–8, 51, 55, 68, 90, 171, 178
power struggles 12, 54–5, 85, 91, 113, 152, 174–75, 188
premarital sex 10–11, 142–45, 154, 157, 159, 166, 169, 175

222 Index

psychological aggression 5, 13–14, 20, 26–7, 52, 95, 113, 187, 193; and psychological violence 12, 20, 27, 95, 118, 124, 135, 139, 151, 174, 187, 193
Pun, Ngai 38, 77

Qualitative research 26–7, 190

red guards 34, 101–3
reflexivity 190–1
Renxing 98–9, 137
Rofel, Lisa 10, 32, 48, 51, 67, 78, 92, 101, 113, 132, 135, 157, 176, 180
romantic love (Romance) 4, 6, 10, 22, 58, 67, 75–6, 80, 83, 90, 118, 121–23, 156, 162, 164–65, 176, 195; 'being loyal and faithful to the one you love from beginning till death' 75, 91, 122; 'falling in love at first sight' 56, 75, 122; 'happily ever after' 76, 122, 162, 175; 'one and only' love 121–23, 162, 175; romantic love and free dating 10, 122, 156
Rose, Nicholas 48, 67, 180
rural-urban gap 4

sassy girl 12, 94–137, 173, 177–8, 181, 184, 188
school Bullying 3, 20–1
semi-feudalism and semi-colonialism 16, 47, 112, 123
severe violence 6, 20, 95, 108, 110, 173
sex education 11, 13, 154–56, 189; and family sex education 155
sex ratio 8, 14, 83, 104, 131; and male to female sex ratio at birth 104
sexual coercion1, 5, 13–14, 20, 27, 42, 52, 95, 138–71, 178–9, 187–8
sexual double standard 12, 136, 146–47, 149, 153, 164, 168–69, 171, 179, 182
sexual harassment 3, 13, 20–2, 27
sexual revolution 12–13, 138–9, 164–71; and 'primary life cycle' 166, 168; 'sex for pleasure' 165; separation of sex from reproduction 166; transformation of sexuality 13, 165, 171, 178
Sexism 3, 29, 41, 51, 118, 178
slave of the apartment (*fangnu*) 63
social division of labor 132; and men work outside, women work inside 9, 132; men plow and women weave 132
social stratification 59, 62, 71
social transformation 13, 171, 178
spectrum of violence 6, 20

spiritual pollution 157, 167; and censorship of sexual issues 167; sweeping the erotic and cracking the illegal campaign 167
state and market 15, 37–9, 44, 50–1, 73, 82, 91
state discourse 10, 15, 35, 38, 47, 50, 55, 66, 72–3, 79, 82, 97, 102, 117, 130, 136–37, 156–57, 164–65, 181–82
Subjectivity 7–8, 12, 16, 37–8, 42, 48, 55, 58, 85, 90–2, 122–23, 130, 137–39, 156, 163–64, 171, 175, 181
suzhi 30
Survivor 19, 23, 42, 140

Tamara, Jacka 81
tender boy 12, 94–137, 173, 178; and *nuan nan* 105
tie guniang 33, 36
tongqi 126, 169
tongxiang 80–1
tradition and modern 10, 38, 164, 181, 183
transnational dating 59, 90, 180, 189

upward mobility 4, 55, 82, 90–2, 169, 175–76, 181–83
Uncle-Lolita complex 67–70

verbal aggression (violence) 13, 52, 113, 187
victim: make use of the role of 'victims' 119–21; victimization 27–8, 41–2; victim-blaming 96, 141; victimized women image 37, 42
violence against women 3–4, 12, 15, 19, 23, 28–9, 35, 41–2, 45–8, 51–2, 135, 153–54, 183, 191
The Vagina Monologues 22, 41
virginity loss 138–71; and first sex 11, 143, 148–49, 170, 174, 180; timing regarding sex 158; 'gatekeepers' 142; 'uncomfortable', 'unpleasant', and 'unwanted' sex 144–8; unexpected pain 149; contraceptive use 149–50
virtuous transaction 102–03, 136, 144, 183
virtuous wife and good mother (*xianqi liangmu*) 36, 100, 136; good insider helper (*xianneizhu*) 128; 'work well' or 'marry well' 130

Waidiren 12, 54–6, 58–60, 63–4, 70–2, 76, 79, 82–3, 90–1, 176, 182
Wang, Anyi 35, 163

Index 223

Wang, Zheng 34, 39
Wu, Xiaoying 130
Weihui 163, 167
wen-wu 112
western feminism 15, 39–42, 44–7
willfulness (*renxing*) 99–100, 106–8, 137,
   180
women's aggression 13, 94–137, 138, 152;
   the lion roars 101–02, 178; 'non-
   aggressive women' 96; Red Guards 34,
   101–03
Women date up and men date down: 56,
   71, 105, 129, 162
women's empowerment 33
women's images 34–9, 51
women's problems 29–30, 34
women's liberation 16, 30–3, 40, 134
women's rights 2–3, 9, 17, 22, 134

women's studies 15–17, 21, 28, 37, 44–45,
   47, 51, 134, 160, 172;
White-Haired Girl, The 33, 52,
   156
wife-battering (wife-beating) 19

Xier 33, 52, 156
Xu, Guangping 86, 199

Yan, Yunxiang 103, 127
youth autonomy 10, 103
youth hotline 2, 188
young feminist activist 3–4

zaolian 155
Zhang, Jingsheng 156
Zhong, Xueping 111
Zuo, Jiping 33

eBooks
from Taylor & Francis
Helping you to choose the right eBooks for your Library

Add to your library's digital collection today with Taylor & Francis eBooks. We have over 50,000 eBooks in the Humanities, Social Sciences, Behavioural Sciences, Built Environment and Law, from leading imprints, including Routledge, Focal Press and Psychology Press.

Choose from a range of subject packages or create your own!

Benefits for you
- Free MARC records
- COUNTER-compliant usage statistics
- Flexible purchase and pricing options
- 70% approx of our eBooks are now DRM-free.

Benefits for your user
- Off-site, anytime access via Athens or referring URL
- Print or copy pages or chapters
- Full content search
- Bookmark, highlight and annotate text
- Access to thousands of pages of quality research at the click of a button.

Free Trials Available

We offer free trials to qualifying academic, corporate and government customers.

eCollections
Choose from 20 different subject eCollections, including:
- Asian Studies
- Economics
- Health Studies
- Law
- Middle East Studies

eFocus
We have 16 cutting-edge interdisciplinary collections, including:
- Development Studies
- The Environment
- Islam
- Korea
- Urban Studies

For more information, pricing enquiries or to order a free trial, please contact your local sales team:
UK/Rest of World: **online.sales@tandf.co.uk**
USA/Canada/Latin America: **e-reference@taylorandfrancis.com**
East/Southeast Asia: **martin.jack@tandf.com.sg**
India: **journalsales@tandfindia.com**

www.tandfebooks.com